❖ The Fortune Teller's Kiss

American Lives ❧ *Series editor:* Tobias Wolff

The Fortune Teller's Kiss

Brenda Serotte

University of Nebraska Press

Lincoln and London

Source acknowledgments for previously published
material appear on p. xi.

Library of Congress Cataloging-in-Publication Data
Serotte, Brenda.
The fortune teller's kiss / Brenda Serotte.
   p.   cm.—(American lives)
ISBN-13: 978-0-8032-4326-2 (cloth: alk. paper)
ISBN-10: 0-8032-4326-x (cloth: alk. paper)
ISBN-13: 978-0-8032-4353-8 (paper: alk. paper)
1. Serotte, Brenda—Childhood and youth. 2. Jews—
New York (State)—New York—Biography.
3. Sephardim—New York (State)—New York—
Biography. 4. Poliomyelitis—Patients—New York
(State)—New York—Biography. 5. Jews, Turkish—
New York (State)—New York—Anecdotes. 6. Bronx
(New York, N.Y.)—Biography. 7. New York (N.Y.)—
Biography. I. Title. II. Series.
F128.9.J5S434   2006
974.7'1'004924—dc22
                              2005014035

Set in Quadraat by Bob Reitz. Designed by A. Shahan.

For my mother and father, fighting and dancing in *Gan Eden*. *Opa!*

My first loyalty is not to history or bearing witness. It is to the stories that arise out of my life. ❧ KAZUO ISHIGURO

Contents

Illustrations

Following page 96

Acknowledgments

Many thanks to the Money for Women / Barbara Deming Memorial Fund, whose grant enabled me to visit the old neighborhood a few more times.

I'm also grateful to the editors of the following journals who published excerpts of this book in various forms:

Hopscotch: A Cultural Review, Duke University Press (January 2000), under the title "Turkish Days: Snapshots of a Sephardic Girl's Life in the Bronx"; The Raven Chronicles (Fall 2000), "Turkish Coffee"; Rosebud 20 (May 2001), "Frogs & Snakes"; and Fourth Genre (Spring 2003), "Contagious."

Without the encouragement and support of my friends, my family, and the talented writers and teachers who cared about my story and emboldened me every step of the way, this book would have stopped when the weight of memory became almost too much to carry. But there are those who knew I could do it: My bro, Charlie, always; Ross and Dana; my dear friend and good reader Dr. Alice Griffin; and my Florida and New York primos y primas, who fed me Sephardi dinners and listened to the early drafts. Besos!

Rosalie Siegel, my agent, believed in the memoir at a time when I really needed that; Mike Steinberg, you've been such a help; and thanks to Mimi Schwartz and, of course, Scotia MacRae.

I'm indebted to the writers and teachers in summer workshops, coast to coast, with whom I've worked, starting with Phillip Lopate, the first one who laughed out loud at the story, and Roger Weingarten as well, for two constructive summers in Vermont.

To my polio survivor buddies in Palm Beach County, especially Phyllis and Jody, I say: *Salud!* We are Action Heroes, are we not?

Liz G., thanks for announcing: "I'll read it!" Miss you.

And always, my loving thanks to Jeff, an Ashkenazic find, for every single thing—none of the above possible without you.

The photos in this book come from the author's personal collection unless noted otherwise.

Some of the names of family and friends have been changed to protect their anonymity.

 The Fortune Teller's Kiss

1 ❖ Turks

Aunt Kadún had been kidnapped at age thirteen by a Turkish sultan and placed in his harem. It happened in Çanakkele on the Dardanelles, the region once known as Troy, sometime during the revolution of 1908. My family treated the incident as one of their bigger secrets, tantalizing in its lack of details. The bare facts were repeated through gossip, to a very few, and always in Ladino, our offbeat Spanish dialect. I heard that she had been very pretty (like you! they told me) and that the same could happen to me if I wasn't a good girl or if I didn't finish my entire meal. And these meals were large.

Dire warnings were always followed by this incantation: "Whoever wishes you harm, may harm come to them!"

Then: "Garlic and cloves! Keep the Evil Eye away! The sooner the better!"

Then a big belly laugh, and they'd all kiss me. The first phrase was enough to repel evil, as long as you said it right away. Considering how many thousands of times in a week I heard these words, it seems I must have been in constant mortal danger.

Most Turks wore something to ward off the Evil Eye: a bead, a real-looking blue eye, a tiny hand, or a small sack of garlic mixed with cloves that was pinned to the underclothing. Beautiful children were the number one targets of the Evil Eye, and for that reason they were never to be excessively praised or complimented. Beauty was a curse; combined with talent, it invited disaster.

If someone told me how wonderful, how cute, or how talented I was, they had to repeat, "Whoever wishes you harm . . . ," right away to keep the Evil Eye at bay. For good measure it was good to shout, "Ugly! Ugly!" at me. For the first four years of my life I was confused: Was I ugly or not? Couldn't they make up their minds? Then, when I was around six, I figured out the part about charm reversal. Even today, I am affected by the frequent warnings not to laugh a lot or become overly happy with anything because laughter always turns into tears.

Whatever charm one wore or carried, it was important to have something that would knife through the surrounding dark spirit forces. The fortune teller herself made the one I wore. It was a small heart made of soft red cotton, covered on one side with hand-sewn tiny blue beads, and stuffed full of cloves, the good luck herb. I wore this pinned to my undershirt, and, even though it was uncomfortably bulky, I never took it off—at least, I don't think I did. All it takes is one lapse to be cursed. For added protection I also wore a blue, very real-looking eye on a gold chain that my father said came from Izmir. The eye looked so authentic it scared the younger children in our building, some of whom cried every time they saw it. It also made their older brothers and sisters more suspicious of me and my family.

I was four years old, sitting at the kitchen table with my mother and her two sisters, Tante Allegre and Tante Sultana, eating halvah spread thin on a chunk of French bread, when I first heard Aunt Kadún's story. Usually, it was rehashed over Turkish coffee on late afternoons in winter. One version went like this: The sultan and his servant followed her from the market. They kept close behind as she made her way down the winding streets to the docks, past the old Ottoman clock tower. She finally stopped to rest, and one of them grabbed her dress, from behind, which caused her to trip and fall. Then they picked her up and carried her off to the harem. At that point in the story Tante Allegre would envelop me in her large, flabby arms, give me a thousand loud kisses so fierce they sucked the skin off my cheek, and declare, "Star of your aunt's harem!"

Another version had it that, as Kadún was being accosted by a Greek, a Muslim Turk came along, beat up the scoundrel, and carried her off to his harem. The whispered, most intriguing version was that the sultan "took her," right there on the docks. Mother didn't like her sisters talking about such things in front of me because she knew I understood Ladino, although from early on I learned to maintain a blank face that showed no reaction so they wouldn't hold back. When they spoke of this or other tragic events in the lives of Turks, it was always in matter-of-fact tones. And then they ate.

Along with too much *fritada*, spinach pie, and gelatin candies called "Turkish Delights," I ate up their stories about how our family once lived in Spain and their tales from Turkey. I liked hanging around my tantes; they always had a juicy secret to share.

Happily, Aunt Kadún was "kidnapped back" into the family at some point. She could just as easily have been banished from the village or marked as unmarriageable, but her father, a loving and accepting man, welcomed her home as if nothing terrible had occurred. In fact, he declared her pure enough to marry a Jew, which she did, twice in her lifetime, and she lived well into her eighties on Long Island.

But her star was cursed, Tante Allegre once remarked. Tante Kadún's only son, Nathan, a gifted pianist, was drafted, then killed, in Germany during the Second World War.

The youngest of the three sisters' children, I was much teased. On a bad day they told me I was destined to be the fourth wife in the harem, the one least in demand. On a good day they said maybe I'd be the first wife, the one who selected all the others. In fact, Kadún means "first wife." No wonder it was such a popular name among Sephardim. So were Oro (gold), Diamante (diamond), Sultana (Arab queen), and my favorite, Zimbúl (jasmine). A woman had to be beautiful inside and out, even her name, as well as talented and obedient. They said I was talented and beautiful, but it was no secret that I was disobedient. I got into trouble daily, breaking glasses, refusing to eat, sneaking out of the apartment in my pajamas.

When I was three, there was the dumbwaiter incident. I decided one day that my grandmother's new black shoes weren't clean enough, so I washed them by dipping them in the toilet bowl and flushing. Mother was so incensed that—despite Nona's pleading with her not to—she bullied my dad into holding me upside down in the dumbwaiter shaft and shaking me like a bag of laundry. I can still feel the blood rushing to my head and hear my heart pound, thinking he was going to drop me down into the roaring basement furnace where our super burned the garbage. Years later I asked her how she could do such a thing. "Oh, that," she said. "We lived on the ground floor. You wouldn't have had far to fall."

Ostensibly named in honor of my father's mother, Behora, meaning "firstborn," I also had an American name inspired by Brenda Frazier, the 1940s society deb whose escapades my mother avidly followed in the gossip columns.

To appease my maternal grandmother, Nona Benvenuta, my mother said I was named for her; both grandmothers having a B name helped soothe ruffled feelings. The Sephardic tradition of naming children after living relatives began in Spain hundreds of years ago, when Jews were forced to adopt certain Christian customs. To the Ashkenazi, whose children were named only after deceased relatives, the custom was ghoulish.

I was the center of attention, at least for five years until my brother came along, and I reveled in the praise of my "gorgeous" hair, my "rich" singing voice, and my "keen" intelligence ("Whoever wishes me harm . . ."). Thanks to Tante Allegre, who considered me a family jewel, I never wanted for tender affection. My mother hated kissing and hugging anyone, even my father, but my aunt's loving attitude toward me and her hands-on attention throughout the years saved me. Even when I was ill and thin, unrecognizable even to myself, she continued to tell me I was beautiful.

Allegre was the matriarch of the three sisters, Sultana was the middle one, and my mother, Rosika, was the youngest. She called herself a freak because of her height—she was five foot ten—and her red hair. The neighbors knew them as Alice, Suzy, and Rose; the rest of the family referred to them as "the Council." They were inseparable. Each day they strolled the Grand Concourse three abreast, the statuesque redhead in the middle, flanked by her shorter, darker older sisters, all three clutching identical black purses.

They shopped at Matarasso's Turkish Grocery on Sheridan Avenue and searched for clothing bargains across the Concourse, down Jerome Avenue. Often they joined the Yids at the fish market to yell at the fish man, whom nobody trusted. In the afternoons they gathered in our apartment to gossip and drink Turkish coffee, the bitter brew whose grounds could reveal your fortune.

In Turkey, they claimed, the sultan's mother ran not only the harems but the entire country. This was true in our family, too. The men were demanding, temperamental, and bossy, but the women ran the households. Their husbands respected and feared one important thing: Many Turkish women knew how to fix the sick.

Carried with them from Spain to the Balkans in the fifteenth century were a mélange of medicines developed over the ages, combining a belief in spirits, folklore, and the Evil Eye so strong that none dared question it. Even our European Ashkenazi neighbors, who had their own superstitions, respected these special healing talents. Tante Allegre and my father's mother, Nona Behora Downtown, or Behora the Fortune Teller, as the grandchildren called her, were both gifted in that area. It was said that, if Grandma had been alive when I contracted my "cursed illness," she would have fixed me right up. Either that, or I would have died of fright from the ritual itself.

There were tales for mealtimes and tales for bedtimes. I devoured them all, and sometimes they devoured me. My aunts marveled at how unafraid I was of most things, but often, as a preventive for a story they were about to tell, I was forced to take the medicine for a big fright: I had to swallow a heaping teaspoon of dry sugar, followed by a glass of warm water, or drink three teaspoons of sugar dissolved in warm water. Either way, I gagged. And for good measure, after I choked down the nauseating sugar water, they'd bathe my face with the rest of it.

Luckily, I never had to experience the extreme cure: mumya, as in "mummy." Mumya was actually the dried remains of the bones of a dead person found ages ago in the Sinai desert, a cure that Sephardic women had used for centuries. In modern times, however, the mumya with the most healing qualities came from the dried foreskin of a baby boy's circumcision, pulverized to a fine powder.

This remedy was the best; it cured anything when stirred into sugar water. Mumya was hard to find, and only a few Sephardic women in the network—the healers and the sorceresses—knew where to get it. Of course, Behora, being a well-known and multitalented clairvoyant, knew. It was fact that she had saved, using that and other remedies, mortally ill people from sure death. She would venture all the way to the dark continent of Brooklyn to purchase the powder from an old woman they called "La Vieja"(the old one), who lived way out in Coney Island.

Despite all the precautions I was subjected to, shortly before my eighth birthday I came down with polio. It was the fall of 1954 (almost immediately thereafter the polio vaccine would be perfected) on a Monday night. The evening before, I had performed the "Dance of the Seventh Veil" for company. Later I had a hard time even walking down the foyer to my bedroom.

The next night Mother had "the girls" over for the weekly mah-jongg game. I was at the card table, straightening the "wall" of ivory tiles for their next game, when I sank to the carpet as if someone had pulled a string on top of my head. One day I was a wild child, running and free; the next, an invalid surrounded by weeping women, who said: "Sickness was first a guest of the house, then it became the master of the house."

It was apparent to all that somebody at that Sunday night party had been jealous of my talents and had "eyed" me with either a blue or green eye. My mother and my aunts went crazy for months afterward trying to figure out who it was. All light-eyed persons we'd come into contact with in recent weeks were suspect, including the kosher butcher's green-eyed sister, who sometimes helped out in the store.

But Grandma Behora used to say that a person's true fate was foretold at birth. She'd even ridicule her own fortune-telling powers, insisting that she merely interpreted a person's life changes, which had been preordained. Mother said Behora liked to say that to ward off curses. Before my parents were married, Grandma "read" my mother's Turkish coffee grounds, which foretold that the firstborn child would be very sick. Mother never forgave her: "The words came out of the mouth of a witch, who didn't want me to marry her son at all because he was her favorite boy and the only boy out of four who gave her money from his own family's pocket!"

My mother was an odd mixture of twentieth-century modern woman and old-world Sephardic daughter. On the one hand, she claimed she was too educated to worry about superstitious Turkish nonsense. On the other, though, I knew the prediction about my getting sick haunted her.

My Turkish-born tantes and the old women on my father's side of the family had no such doubts. For simple but offbeat cures they didn't have to travel to Coney Island; they had them right at home. There was even one for girls like me who refused to go to bed—because I didn't want to miss a word of the adults' stories, and the best ones came out late at night. This "cure" came in the form of a bedtime story, "The Woman with Seven Breasts."

"When the woman with seven breasts gets here, she'll give you her milk, so you will fall asleep fast," began Tante Allegre. This was meant to be soothing, but it had the reverse effect on me: "She is not! I'm not going!" I yelled. "I don't believe you!"

"It's true!" Tante kept insisting, with so much conviction I almost bought it. Of course, she added, if I chose to go to bed myself, then they could save the goddess a trip. One of the tantes would distract me, while another one flung the seven cotton balls up to the ceiling in various places, where they stuck like glue.

"Look at the breasts!" they cried. "She's here!" Then one aunt prepared my bed, ready to overpower me and throw me in it, and the other gyrated or rocked back and forth, thanking the goddess for showing up. Even though I didn't believe a word of it, I would occasionally have a bad dream about a large woman crashing down on top of me in my bed—anyone with seven breasts had to be fat!

In August 1492, the same time Christopher Columbus sailed to America, Jews were ordered to convert to Christianity or leave Spain, where they had lived since the tenth century. Those who refused to convert were burned at the stake in *autos-da-fé*, "acts of faith" ceremonies carried on during the Inquisition. Those who did convert were called "conversos." Others, called "marranos," tried to beat the system by practicing Judaism and sacred rituals in secrecy, but they were often discovered, imprisoned and tortured, then paraded through the streets wearing yellow vestments and burned. Christianity was a touchy subject at home.

When I asked, innocently enough, if any of us were Catholic, I'd get a look to kill. No explanations.

The first contingent of Spanish Jews sailed from Cádiz to North Africa in July 1492. Soon hundreds of Jews from Seville, Toledo, Córdoba, Granada, and Zaragosa made their way down the Guadaquivir River to the port in Valencia and on to Italy, where they stayed for either a hundred years or ten, nobody knows for sure. Mother was sure that our family took this route because our Ladino was peppered with so much Italian. Our ancestors then went to Turkey and Rhodes. Others went overland to Morocco and Fez. "We were luckier," she said. "The Jews who made it to Morocco were butchered almost immediately, even though they were *conversos.*"

Eventually, most who survived made it to the Balkan countries and into the welcoming arms of the Turkish sultans. They found their way to Greece, Bulgaria, Armenia, and to the islands of Rhodes, Chios, and Cyprus; to the Dardanelles and to cities such as Salonika, Monastir, Izmir, Erdine, and Bulgaria, where they remained, mostly happily, for the next four centuries. They paid a heavy poll tax for the pleasure of Turkish citizenship, but, because they were Turkish subjects protected by an ancient pact, they were allowed to keep their Jewish faith, their Spanish customs, and, most important, their ancient Spanish language: Ladino.

Although Mother preferred to believe that we had descended from Spanish nobility, we definitely were not, either by birth or by marriage, the Sephardim known as the Grandees. They were the wealthy, regal Jews of colonial times who settled in Charleston, South Carolina, and Savannah, Georgia, as early as 1702. Most likely, we were descendants of Andalusian flamenco dancers and guitar-playing *zinganos,* the gypsy Jews of Muslim Spain.

Mother's hair was a natural fiery red. The Irish teachers used to send her home from school with nasty notes telling my grandmother to "stop putting henna in the child's hair." She was the only redhead in the family until I was born, and my hair was more auburn than orange. Considering how swarthy my father's side of the family was, our ancestry was most likely a bouillabaisse of Moors, Berbers, North Africans, and Arabs. One of Dad's cousins, Vera, was called "La Negra," meaning "bad girl" in Ladino and implying that she was dark-skinned.

Our history confused me from the beginning. I was never quite sure whether we were Spanish, Jewish, or Turkish, and our oddball Espanyol didn't help. I'd ask various grownups at least once a week whether or not we were really Jewish and, if so, why didn't we come from Russia, Hungary, or Poland, like my friends' grandparents, aunts, and uncles. Why was it, exactly, that we didn't speak Yiddish? Didn't they understand I had to defend myself in the streets? Our block and the surrounding radius were entirely made up of Ashkenazi families, plus a few Irish and Italians.

In reply to my questions, Mother would snap: "Not that again! We're more Jewish than all your Yid friends will ever be! We're the highest; we're Sephardi!"

They'd talk about how the Catholics took over Spain and kicked us out. One of my father's cousins, Zimbúl, a hefty woman with a man's mustache, still held the key to her ancestral house in Córdoba, which her family had left four hundred years before. This amazed me. "That's called symbolic," Mother said, "for when we return to our homeland."

"So, we're really Spanish, and we're going back to Spain one day?"

"Of course not!"

"But you said!"

"I did not!"

My aunts were no help. "Are we Spanish, Tante?"

"Si!"

"And Jewish, too?"

"Si!"

"But not really Turkish, right?"

"Si! Of course we're Turkish! Shut up already, crazy girl!"

We lived at 1410 Grand Concourse between 170th and 171st streets, across from the Luxor Movie Theater, where I spent whole Saturdays with my friends watching double features. The theater manager, a bulky blond Irishman, thought my dad was a cop, so he let us in free. Up the block from the Luxor, above a curtain and drapery store, was the Sephardic Social Club, where the old Turks drank Turkish coffee and played a card game they called "dangerous dice."

Tante Allegre and Uncle Victor lived on the next block, at 1440 Grand Concourse, and Sultana and Ovadiah lived a few buildings up, on the corner, in 1460. My dad's brothers were nearby on Townsend and Washington avenues. The West Bronx had become a Sephardic hub by the mid-1950s, with several thousand Turks and Greeks spread around from north to west, all speaking Ladino with varying dialectal differences. We didn't quite blend in with the Ashkenazim, who never trusted us.

My friends of European ancestry were generally aghast at what we ate, and vice versa. Ellen's Grandma Molly made something called "borscht." Ellen convinced me once to taste it. I promptly gagged and almost threw up on her kitchen linoleum. I repaid the favor when she came to my house by uncovering a pot of Mother's specialty, simmering cow brains in tomato sauce. Ellen screamed and ran out.

When the High Holy Days came, hundreds of families came from all over the Bronx and Manhattan, even those who had moved to Queens, and gathered at the one Sephardic synagogue, located in the middle of the hill on 169th Street between the Concourse and Walton Avenue. The Ashkenazim, "white Jews," my mother called them, went to the synagogue at the top of the hill to worship.

The trees were always a golden color and really pretty by Rosh Hashanah time, as we walked slowly to our synagogues in a big group—my friends and I, plus classmates we picked up along the way. There we parted; I went to my shul, with maybe one or two other girls at most. At the break we'd meet again.

Everything about the two religious services was different. Our Sephardic Rabbi Murciano chanted the prayers in a Middle Eastern, Arabic-sounding way. The songs from the Sabbath service were unique, and many were sung in Ladino. Of course, we thought ours was a much more beautiful service than theirs. Even the layout of our shul was different: the podium, where the rabbi read, sat smack in the middle of the floor with all the men huddled around it; the Ashkenazi synagogues had it placed in front, near the Torah. Like most of the girls I hung out with, I did not read or understand a word of Hebrew.

If you lived in the Art Deco beige and red-brick prewar buildings that lined the Concourse, you lived an open life. Everyone knew your business, and you knew theirs. Residents didn't lock their doors; you just knocked twice and walked in if you were a friend or relative or even if you were the insurance man who came once a month to collect your premium. No door in our house was allowed to be shut, not even the bathroom door—not that we could shut them, they were so warped. Our bathroom was opposite the front door. One time, stately Uncle Ishuah actually walked in on Mother as she sat on the toilet, and after that I was allowed to partially close that particular door only.

I had no privacy at all. If I tried to go off by myself for any length of time, the grownups were all over me: "Where's la chika? What are you doing? Come in here, Little Devil." The only person I knew with less privacy was my best friend, Ellen, who lived in the same apartment directly below us, because she shared a bedroom with her two younger sisters. She taught me how to make siblings miserable. I was not above locking Charlie, my younger brother, in the closet and telling him he was taking a trip to outer space.

Most of us were marginally poor: candy store owners, factory workers, shoe salesmen, and the occasional professional, such as accountant or teacher. That didn't count Dr. Hirschfeld, whose medical practice was in the building, and Dr. Steinberg, the dentist, who lived and worked up the block in the "fancy" building known as the Astor Court. It had an inner courtyard with grass and flowers, so it was considered a step up from the stoop buildings.

It was just a few years after the end of World War II. I knew nothing of my refugee neighbors' unfathomable torment in concentration camps. For the first few years of my life nothing evil existed, although Mother did always say that we were the "lucky Jews" because only an ocean separated us from death. Everyone felt content and lucky to be living decently in the Bronx, even if they faced an alley or the back of another building. It was prestigious to be living on the Grand Concourse then.

At six o'clock sharp every night our super, Mrs. Smith—we called her Smitty—sent the dumbwaiter up to collect the garbage. This was the number one way to learn about your neighbors, by listening to snatches of their conversations up and down the line. But the moment we opened the door, the stench of everyone's accumulated garbage rose up the shaft along with the raucous dinnertime arguments. Soon neighbors up and down the shaft would be yelling at each other to "SHAD UP!" until Yiddish erupted from someone's grandmother, which of course nobody in our house understood, and that put an end to the fracas.

Both Sultana's and Allegre's husbands were short; Uncle Ovadiah was meek and silent, unusual for a Turk, and Uncle Victor, a waiter at Levine's Kosher Deli on 171st Street, was cranky. Sometimes he crossed over from cranky to mean, like the time he ripped Tante's new dress right off her back and then tore it in half because she had failed to ask his permission before buying it.

"Can't he see he's no pasha, just another ordinary schmo with an ordinary job?" demanded my mother. "They think they're Turkish kings!"

Allegre, whom I called "Tante Alice," was my favorite—very loving, unlike my mother, whom I could never please. Tante would not give a child a letter to mail "in case the kid got hit by a car crossing to the mailbox." Her daughter, my cousin Doris, who was ten years older than I, loved watching hockey games on TV, and she never got into trouble. One year, when my mother had emergency gall bladder surgery, I stayed in Tante Alice's house for two happy weeks. "Maybe she'll never come home!" I remarked.

Tante told me that God would punish me unless I apologized out loud for saying such a thing. "Say only good from your mouth!" she admonished. The Turks deeply believed that whatever a person said out loud might actually happen.

Cleanliness was Allegre's middle name, and her pots and pans, in fact the entire house, twinkled. But no matter what I spilled or dirtied, she never got mad. She was also the best Turkish cook in the family. Mother refused to acknowledge that her older sister's cooking was better than hers, and often this led to a food fight. From time to time Tante Alice would cook a Turkish breakfast: a three-egg, feta cheese omelet, which was customarily eaten right from the iron skillet. "She ate the whole thing," Tante would tell Mother.

"Impossible!" Mother would insist. "She hates eggs!" (I didn't like the way my mother cooked them.)

"Yes, it's true!"

"I don't believe it!"

Silence. They wouldn't speak to each other for days. Finally, Mother had to walk over to Allegre's building on the next block and apologize, never the other way around. You had to show respect to the family elders.

I remember being reprimanded by Tante Alice once only, when I was five, on the day my newborn brother, Charlie, was brought home from the hospital. Taken by the sudden urge to crawl into his crib and see what it felt like to be a baby, I did so—shoes, clothes, and all. When my aunt discovered me, curled up sucking my thumb, with my dirty street shoes resting on the immaculate crib sheet she had just washed and ironed, she yanked me out by my braids and gave me a good hard slap on my backside. Her anger stunned me. Of course, I hated my new brother from that day on.

Tante Sultana, "Suzy," was the middle sister, twelve years Mother's senior. Mother got along much better with her. Whereas Allegre was fastidiously clean, Sultana was sloppy. Neither she nor my mother cared about housecleaning: Tante Suzy thought her house looked great as it was; Mother resented housework and felt it was beneath her: "Can you see Brenda Frazier cleaning a toilet?" she'd ask.

When she cooked dinner, even if she was frying fish, my mother wore a dress, high heels, and jewelry. She owned one apron but rarely put it on. She liked to converse, even with strangers, and she could do stand-up comedy for a crowd of guests. She never sat down without a book. She didn't knit, crochet, or sew hems either. For that we hired an old, ugly Turkish spinster named Stella, reputed to be a witch who could put curses on people.

There was another Stella, also a spinster but very pretty: short and trim, with dark hair and soft brown eyes. Her well-known secret was that her betrothed had gone crazy a week before their wedding day and had been committed to Bronx State Hospital for the insane. Soon this would be her own fate as well. "The nut-hatch guys came for her," Dad said matter-of-factly, when I asked where they took her. For that he got a withering look from Mother and a jab with her right elbow.

"She just couldn't get over it," Mother said, quickly adding, "Whoever wishes you harm . . . ," to ward off any possibility that I would be a spinster.

Nothing Tante Suzy cooked tasted good to me, except her mustachudos. These were delectable, anise-flavored, chewy little walnut balls, made with cinnamon and orange rind and then rolled in powdered sugar. She was famous in the Sephardic community for this confection. Making it was an arduous business involving chopping, grinding, slicing, cutting, whipping, and a complicated two-step baking process.

After the mustachudos had cooled, my aunt would line empty Barton's candy boxes with wax paper and place the balls into straight rows, like little soldiers. Each full box was then "safely" tucked away in my aunt's underwear drawer, which I then raided. Sometimes, out of guilt, I left one or two in the box for Uncle Ovadiah then placed the nearly empty box below a full one, which went back underneath the girdles.

When the theft was discovered, Tante Suzy would come looking for me, calling me names as she chugged up the two flights of stairs to our house. My mother and Tante Allegre would laugh their heads off. I was bad, they agreed, but it was her own fault; she should have hidden the *mustachudos* elsewhere for once!

Uncle Ovadiah was cowed by Tante Sultana, who was loud, bossy, and liked to give him orders. She was enough excitement to last this man a lifetime. My father enjoyed teasing my aunt: "Your husband is a mute!" She'd sigh, agreeing. Mute as he was, my uncle, from wherever in the house he happened to be and for no special reason, would suddenly yell out my aunt's name: "SULTANA!" Then she, on cue, would scream back: "OVADIAH!" And that was it; that's all they had to say at periodic intervals during the day.

One thing did rouse my uncle, though, and that was hearing his favorite Turkish dance number, "Oglan, Oglan," from the *All Points East* album. Uncle Ovadiah loved that song so much that the minute he heard the recording he would snap his fingers and begin dancing around the room. What a relief to hear him yell, "OPA! OPA!" That's how we knew he was still breathing.

Ovadiah worked at the American Paper Plate factory in Brooklyn. His job was to lug gigantic bales of paper from one side of the plant to the other and then inventory the shipments. He was so frail—a pale, bald wisp of a man, really—that no one could figure out how he did it. One day he collapsed from the strain, sustaining a mild heart attack. When he returned to the factory, they assigned another worker to help him drag the paper bales across the floor. After that Ovadiah did nothing else but go to work. For the rest of his life when he came home, he sat like a fixture by the front window, which faced the Grand Concourse.

In Turkey long ago many men had four wives. Some of my uncles thought that that was still a good idea, even in the Bronx. Mother said the men considered themselves to be descendants of the great sultan, Suleiman the Magnificent. They also believed they came from Spanish nobility and had to be the progeny of Moses Maimonides, a famous philosopher, or of Isaac Abravanel, the wealthy Spanish Jew who helped finance Columbus's voyage. And in biblical days, certainly, they were the esteemed elders of the holy desert tribes of ancient Judea, never the ordinary pagans who worshipped the golden calf. In other words, the Sephardim felt they were the best, better than all other European or Ashkenazi Jews.

While other kids giggled and made fun of my family's Ladino, one of my relatives, usually my dad, would curse them in Turkish. These epithets were of the vilest nature and repeated with a perfectly straight face and friendly smile.

"Welcome, wicked, spiteful, low-class bastard!" he would say in Turkish, "How pretty you look today!" in English. A favorite parting shot was, "To damnation with you and your whole family!" in Turkish; "Bye now, come again!" in English; then, "Go to hell, scoundrel-pimp!" in Turkish. My friend Ellen was smarter than most and suspected she was being made fun of. When we had a fight, she threw my father's own words back at me, calling me a "niggin-yanna-banana-goose-a" or a "muscle-bashy," among other things.

And so it went. I had to make myself a pest in order to gather some information about our Spanish heritage to sling back at my tormentors. But it sure was tough getting my relatives to talk about anything except exotic sultans, harems, and belly dancers.

At twenty-eight my maternal grandfather, Rabbi Nissim Sedacca, had been matched with Benvenuta Pesso, then only fourteen. The child and the man traveled by boat from town to town, wherever he could get work. She had eleven children in all, four of whom survived.

War, poverty, and the frequency of blood libels, coupled with accusations of ritual murder of Christian babies leveled against them, prompted a mass exodus of Turkish Jews from the Balkans after 1908. That was when an uprising known as the Revolution of the Young Turks, led by Mustafa Kemal, also called Attatürk, "the father of Turkey," deposed the last sultan, Abdul Hamid, kicked out the Greeks, and changed Turkish society forever.

Whatever nobility the Jews had enjoyed in Muslim Spain was almost nonexistent in Turkey. They were fruit vendors, match sellers, water carriers, and porters. Some were beggars; others became notorious international smugglers of arms and munitions. There were a few esteemed rabbis, like my grandfather, who were trained in the Yeshiva seminary in Rhodes.

It became so unsafe for Allegre and Sultana, my aunts, in their hometown of Çanakkele that the rabbi, being somewhat progressive, enrolled them in a Greek convent school housed in a monastery on the island of Chios. There they were given free food and clothing from Protestant missionaries who financed these schools and were permitted to leave the class when catechism was taught. "But it was there, in that convent," my mother said, "that they developed all their superstitions. It was all they ever talked about."

Every day they took the ferry to the convent, where Greek nuns met them at the locked gates. Inside were tremendous wall paintings, tapestries, and frescoes of angels and saints. Allegre described a horizontal fresco depicting a gigantic fish in the process of devouring a bunch of men whom the nuns described as "Turkish sinners."

A horrible cholera epidemic lasted for years and suffocated the Dardanelles region. It was a miracle, with how poorly they ate, Mother said, that they didn't get sick: "My parents lived on bread and leeks. Period." Then came a series of natural disasters of almost biblical proportion: great fires in towns and cities, two or three earthquakes, and drought. Turkey and Italy were involved in a fierce war, too, which went on and on and further devastated the population. The fate of Sephardic communities in the Balkans was dismal. The Spanish Jews were about to disappear—maybe this time for good. Our family made it out. Others weren't so lucky. During World War II almost all of these Sephardim who chose to stay in the land that welcomed them hundreds of years back, with their unique cultures, dialects, and heritage, were annihilated by the Nazis in a coordinated massacre of thousands in the cities of Salonika and Rhodes.

My mother's family sailed for New York on the *Kaiser Franz Josef I*, from Patras, Greece, in the Dardanelles on May 16, 1914. Rabbi Sedacca was fifty-one and old in appearance even then. He was accompanied by Benvenuta, then thirty-seven, and Allegre and Sultana, eleven and eight. Their son, my Uncle Jaime, had left Çanakkele two years before. When upheaval and strife rocked the towns along the Dardanelles, he fled to Montevideo, Uruguay, to avoid conscription into the Turkish army, which by then had become compulsory. He was only sixteen, and it broke Nona's heart, but Jaime wasn't about to fight the Balkan Wars for Turkey. At the same time, but not on the same ship, nine draft-dodging uncles on my father's side also came over.

Turkish Jews had a tough time in America. Not only were they at odds with Ashkenazi Jews, but they couldn't even get along with each other. "The Turks from Çanakkele were the highest class, no question," Mother said. "But those from Monastir, Rhodes, Izmir, also considered themselves the highest. And then the ones from Istanbul practically claimed Topkapi Palace as their own!" The insults accumulated to the point where some groups on the Lower East Side refused to recognize others. Their attitudes were astounding.

In the Great Hall on Ellis Island fights were frequent among Oriental Jews. Many wore elaborate clothing or turbans as a sign of their superiority. They could barely understand each other's Ladino, and certainly nobody knew English or Yiddish. Jewish representatives from aid organizations passed our people by. When the boats docked, the immigrants who weren't wearing Western clothing were in trouble. This was their first experience with discrimination from Ashkenazim, who did not believe that the dark, Arab-attired Sephardim could possibly be Jews.

According to my mother, some were shipped back, even with children. Luckily, that didn't happen to Rabbi Sedacca's family, although they did have trouble when they arrived. Like thousands of other confused, exhausted passengers, Grandma and Grandpa remained silent because they understood nothing. No one showed up to greet them or translate for them. Either someone didn't remember to come, or they didn't get the letters sent from Turkey. My grandparents remained at Ellis Island for three days before a communication, through the Jewish agency HIAS, located a cousin who knew another Turk from Rhodes who knew and vouched for the rabbi.

They settled on Rivington Street on the Lower East Side of Manhattan, like millions of other poor immigrants. My paternal grandparents lived nearby on Suffolk Street. The rabbi attracted a small congregation and, according to Mother, became the first licensed Sephardic rabbi in

New York at that time. She spoke of her father with reverence. When they were able, they moved uptown, to Madison Avenue and 116th Street in Harlem, which soon became a Sephardic hub. That's where Mother spent most of her childhood. My aunts, fifteen and twelve years my mother's senior, were of marriageable age by then, so they had little time for her. Being the youngest daughter, she was the one designated to live with and care for Nona Benvenuta, especially after the rabbi died.

"It wasn't what you'd call a normal American life," she told me. "When I came home from school, guess who greeted me? Six Turkish women, sitting around in a circle, sewing. And guess what they were sewing? Their shrouds!"

The rabbi had the gift of poetry, and Mother felt she had inherited it: "You have it, too," she once told me. It was the only time she ever acknowledged my writing. Rabbis never earned enough to eat, either in Turkey or America, so my grandfather's talent for poetic composition served him well. He was a fixture at Mt. Hebron Cemetery in Queens, where he performed prayer readings for the dead and immortalized them in stone with his epitaphs. These memorials, all written in Judeo-Spanish with Hebrew characters, were flowery and emotional: "Stand here and read my tombstone carefully . . . my life went down the drain," read one.

My mother, born when Benvenuta was forty-five, was considered the mistake. "Your Nona tried hard to lose me. It was a big shame for the rabbi's wife to be pregnant so old," my mother recalled. "I came anyway."

For three years Nona hid her youngest child in the house, but then the old rabbi said it was enough, He adored his chika, or little one, and he took her everywhere. "My father was so respected," said my mother, "the room hushed when he walked in."

One wedding turned out to be traumatic. After my grandpa performed the ceremony, he oversaw an old Turkish custom in which the bride was required to jump over a tub of water containing a live fish. If she cleared it, the couple's union would be blessed and fruitful. At this particular wedding there was a little boy who was mute. After the bride had successfully jumped the tub, a healer named La Tia grabbed the wriggling fish and, while two other women held the boy down, stuffed it into the boy's mouth. The fish bit the boy's tongue. "Now, he'll speak!"

Tia proclaimed. My mother swooned. That story explained to me why Mother drew endless pictures of fish—fish doodled on napkins, on odd scraps of paper, on the edges of the newspaper. Even on fogged windows.

No one could agree about how my grandfather died. Mother was certain he slipped on a banana peel, broke his hip, and went into a coma. One relative thought he was mugged on the Brooklyn Bridge at dawn. Another insisted he died at the cemetery where he hung out much of the day. Another believed he collapsed on the train going home from the cemetery.

It was left to my mother, the only one who spoke "good English," to identify her father at the morgue. They handed her his amber worry beads, the rabbi's only legacy, which she wore as a necklace. Once, when she was running to catch a train, the string snapped and the ancient beads scattered everywhere along the subway tracks. Without a second thought, Mother jumped down off the platform to gather them up, one by one, while people screamed at her to get away from the rails.

My father's father, Chelebón Lévy, and his eight brothers were originally from Çorlu, which Mother referred to as "the lower depths"—actually, it was in the mountain region. His wife, my grandmother Behora, the gifted fortune teller and medicine woman, came from Celebria, a suburb of Istanbul; however, many believed, or else they got the story wrong, that she actually came from Izmir, where many clairvoyants practiced.

"Her profession was a good segue to her sons' thievery," Mother sniffed, referring to my father's two brothers, Albert and Kelly, whom she disliked. But she also intimated that it wasn't beneath my father to obtain items that "fell off a truck." I imagined my dad and my uncles standing on the side of the road near Mosholu Parkway, plucking like flowers the nice sweaters, bathing suits, and pocketbooks they brought home to us. I wondered why the owners of those rickety trucks didn't fix them.

There were obvious differences between my mother and father. She was educated, a high school graduate, a reader; he had completed eighth grade before being sent off to "reform school." Her father had been a rabbi, while his family came from "mountain-trash Turks of

Istanbul, who needed only sabers and horses to complete the picture."

My parents fought a lot, and they fought hard; when things got physical, doors slammed, dishes were smashed against the dumbwaiter, pictures were knocked askew. Sometimes the telephone wire was yanked out of the wall after one of them noticed that the receiver had been knocked off its hook, and Mrs. Bloom, our neighbor, was listening in on the party line.

They argued over bills that couldn't be paid, the business successes of my father's brothers, bookies who demanded payment, his gambling on the horses. It seemed as if every time my father played he missed making millions by just one number.

Minor, shorter fights, although no less intense, broke out about my father's frankness. An "honest" observation, such as, "Boy, Betty, how'd you get so fat?" would be rewarded with a not-so-discreet elbow jab or a kick with her heel under the table. When they got home, she'd say, "No tact! No finesse!"

He would mock her: "*Feen*-niss, I don't got, huh?" And off they'd go another round.

When I got older I suspected my father was a good liar—maybe even a terrific liar—certainly, he was a great denier of many things. Gossip had it that he was a runaround with women. All I knew was that I lived for the sight of him the moment he strode in the door at night and scooped me up in his arms—"C'mere, *Werka!*"

A Sunday fight at our house might begin with a comment from my mother, "Face it, Vic, you just don't have the head for business that your brother Al does." I got scared when my father's black eyes flashed blacker and he scowled. He never touched my mother, but it often looked as if he might. He'd stomp into their bedroom, take down the battered brown valise, throw some clothes into it, and tie it up with rope. By the time he had finished packing, Mother had finished instigating. She'd lean against the refrigerator, dragging deeply on her Philip Morris.

I would get teary-eyed and beg him not to leave. If the phone was intact, I would call Uncle Al because only he could calm my father down. If my father didn't end up spending the night at the Turkish baths, he would sit in the living room nursing a cup of reheated coffee listening to melancholy Turkish songs sung by tormented, wailing men. I'd wait until he closed his eyes, fully into the music, then struggle to lug the old valise down the hall as fast as I could, just to get it out of sight.

When my father would come home from the Turkish baths after one of their big fights, my mother would try to conceal her relief by pretending to study the newspaper, but I could tell from what she said under her breath that she was happy to see him.

Because of the fights, I knew Uncle Al's number by heart from the time I was five. When I was recovering in the hospital, and out of quarantine, Uncle Al and Aunt Vicky came to visit me. They were the only ones on my father's side who did come; everybody else was too scared. They brought my cousins, Sandra, Alan, and Larry, who waited across the street in the first snow of November. Uncle Al actually pushed my bed near the window, and, upon his signal, all three kids waved frantically, with all six hands, toward the window they guessed was mine.

This gesture, small though it was, brought me back to everyday life. When I had entered the hospital, half-dead, it was September and very hot. I never forgot how my cousins were dressed that day and how surprised I was to see them in their buttoned-up winter coats, wearing hats and gloves.

People said that Uncle Al bore a resemblance to the mobster Al Capone. He had that kind of wide moon-face, always a big grin, and he wore his hat at a jaunty angle. Mother called him "smooth." Aunt Vicky was dark-skinned and beautiful. She was only sixteen when they married. My mother was fiercely jealous of her and referred to her as "the janitor's daughter" because Vicky's father had been the superintendent of a building on Washington Avenue. "The janitor's daughter bought white carpeting, I heard," Mother would tell her sisters. Or, "The janitor's daughter is serving prosciutto, excuse me!"

All my parents' differences dissolved when they went out dancing. When they dressed up, they looked like movie stars. My mother often wore a blue satin cocktail dress with billowy skirts and a "sweetheart" neckline and black suede high heels strapped across the ankle. Sometimes she'd let me spray her, and myself, with her perfume, Jealousy. They would come home late, especially if they went to the Egyptian Gardens nightclub on Eighth Avenue, which always had a belly dancer. When they stayed in, they'd put on Xavier Cougat and mambo in the living room.

My father was tall and dark, and everybody thought he was exceptionally handsome. He wore his black hair, which matched his black eyes, slicked back, and he always had a thick mustache. When I got older, I understood what "flashing eyes" meant. Women turned around to look at him when he walked by, and Mother never failed to notice it: "See that one? Too bad she didn't fall into the sewer just now when she tripped!"

In 1943, the year my parents married, my father looked very much like Clark Gable. Many people did a doubletake when they saw him in uniform. Once, at a USO function, he had the nerve to ask the actress Lana Turner to dance. According to my mother, "She turned him down flat." When Dad told the story, he'd demonstrate the wild lindy hop he and Turner had danced, with the entire army base watching.

My parents met and married on the same day. Some neighborhood Turk had given Mother his army address, and she felt obliged to write to him because he was Sephardic. My father had, by then, broken three engagements with Sephardic women. My mother was twenty-eight and worked in an office but was considered old, practically a spinster. "They didn't understand," she said, referring to her Turkish, old-world family, "I loved being single. They made me get married."

Mother worked at Alfred A. Knopf, with a coworker friend named Bob Jordan, whom she palled around with, even after she got married and my father was overseas. "Bob didn't go for women," she said. "He was the perfect date." He took mother dancing and dining at fancy clubs like 21, El Morocco, and the Copacabana.

"I could have lived that life forever," she said, because she got to know Pat and Blanche Knopf personally, and a couple of times they took her to lunch at the Oak Room of the Plaza: "I got to order whatever I wanted, plus drinks!" Mother spoke of her executive secretarial job at Knopf throughout her life; it seemed as if it was the best time she ever had. It was also the last time she'd work for twenty years. One of the authors she met was Harold Robbins. "He came in all the time; he called me Rosie."

Robbins's *A Stone for Danny Fisher* was my mother's favorite novel and one she quoted from often, telling anyone who listened: "Show appreciation for those you love now; don't wait until it's carved in stone!"

She beamed when people called her smart. She knew more words than anyone else, big words, like *cabriolet* and *expedient*.

My dad, on the other hand, was a poor reader. Growing up, we'd laugh like crazy whenever he read the newspaper out loud. He even mispronounced simple words: "The hurry-cane reached havoke in the South, Rosie—"

My parents corresponded for six months before they met, sending pictures and letters back and forth from wherever my dad was stationed. I found these letters one rainy afternoon when I was about fifteen and shamelessly read them all. They were tucked away behind a stack of yellowing Turkish towels, forgotten for years. In the letters my parents called each other "Precious," "Doll-baby," and "My Heart." They signed them, "Eternally Forever" or "Always, Your Darling Lover." Somebody must have helped my father write his letters because the words were all spelled correctly. But Mother's were shocking in the depth of feeling they expressed. She talked about her love for him "being equal to the brightness of the moon / the rainbow hue of sky."

"It was his picture I fell in love with," my mother insisted. "Even Bob Jordan wanted to marry Victor when he saw it."

Then, just like my father, he tricked her. He was training in Presque Isle, Maine, to become a voice radio operator who would guide air force planes to land in blinding snowstorms. Right before he shipped out to Goose Bay, Labrador, the godforsaken place near Newfoundland where he'd spend the next eight months of World War II, he had a buddy send Mother an urgent telegram saying Victor had been injured and that she should come up to Maine to see him right away.

Her sisters bid her farewell: "We should see you a bride!" they said, in the customary blessing. Her widowed mother, Benvenuta, said, "Daughter, *Kaminos de leche y miel!*" May your path be lined with milk and honey!

When she arrived in Maine, Mom discovered that Dad's injury was minor. He had caught his pinkie in the door of a jeep, and it was wrapped in a big white bandage. Nonetheless, they found a justice of the peace that very night and got married. My father even had a wedding band for her. Somebody had told him about a farmer nearby who had some jewelry to sell. My father offered the farmer all the money he had for it, which was two dollars. At this point in the story, Mother would say, "And I should have known my *destino* right then."

In the neighborhood they called Dad "the Arab," "the Turk," or, believe it or not, "the Armenian." Nobody dared call him a Greek. My job was to run to buy him his daily two packs of Lucky Strikes at Jaffee's, which was across 170th Street and up the block from the Luxor Movie Theater. My dad had just a few friends, but the ones he did have were colorful. There was a huge, swarthy Sephardi, a "black Turk" by the name of Sam Abravaya. They called him "Fat-Sam-the-Turk." He was an entertainment promoter who searched for a successful "colored" singing group for as long as we knew him, so he could cash in.

There was the day he visited us, panting, mopping his sweaty fat head, and breathlessly told my dad that he had found three beautiful, talented black girls who he believed "had the goods" to become singing stars. "I'd think about it, Sammy," Dad said. "You know, I kinda liked those three blonde girls from the East Bronx. Maybe you should go with them?" In the end Fat-Sam-the-Turk turned down the trio. It didn't take long for them to become famous as The Supremes.

Then there was "Harry Mekanik," who, strangely, didn't fix a thing; "Jerome Centa," who didn't live in the center of Jerome or any other avenue; and the strangest friend of all, the mysterious "Murray-the-Shylock."

One day Dad and I were at the movies, and we ran into Murray, smoking a big fat cigar in the lobby. The two of them got into a serious, low-voiced conversation right away. After twenty boring minutes I tugged at my father's coat and asked: "Daddy, what's a shy lock?" My father dragged me home by my arm, which surprisingly did not come out of its socket, and I didn't get to see the second feature.

Mother said that my father was a frustrated cop: "He should have been one—or part of the Mob. Too bad he made neither." He failed the police physical because of a blind right eye from a cataract and two stumps in place of the forefinger and middle finger on his right hand. He said these were war injuries. He enjoyed pointing his two stumps at my friends' eyes, at which they'd squeal and run away.

His physical drawbacks never deterred my dad from pretending to be a cop. On a Sunday morning he'd stroll down to Mt. Eden Avenue and visit Friedhoffer's Bake Shop across from Lebanon Hospital. He'd greet the workers behind the counter warmly, as if he were part owner of the place, and often the chief baker himself came out to shake my father's hand and say hello.

The story went that my father had once foiled a robbery in the shop by chasing the would-be thief down the block with a knife he had grabbed from behind the counter. So the baker was only too happy to fill an order, gratis. My dad would point to what he wanted, and the girls would fill up bags and boxes with rolls, bagels, bialys, and assorted Danish, "for the wife and kids." The bags would be marked "Special for Sgt. Vic Foster, 13th Precinct."

On weeknights, though, after a day at the factory, Dad didn't speak to anyone right away, not even me. He would throw his coat and hat carelessly over a chair, despite the fact that he was very particular about his hats; I wasn't allowed to try them on or push the brim out of shape. He'd wash up and go straight to bed for a nap, after which he'd be fine—until, of course, a fight started at the dinner table: "Dr. Hirschfeld is reading *Anna Karenina* in his spare time; my husband is studying the Aqueduct Racing Form. Such is my life!"

Dad worked as a buffer–metal polisher at the Everlast Lamp Factory in lower Manhattan, shining bronze, brass, and copper lamps and fixtures, plus delicate gold filigree, leaf-shaped ashtrays. We had about twenty such ashtrays in our house, and I managed to hide one away for myself in my drawer. They were so pretty before the tons of cigarettes that everyone smoked stained them gray in the center. At least, my mother would say, he was in a good union, Local 3 of the Electrical Workers Union, and would get a pension. He worked there for seventeen years and quit to work for his brother, Uncle Al, a choice that ended badly, with the brothers not speaking. So Dad never did get that pension.

Dad was the only father in our building—maybe even in the Bronx— who dressed as a bank executive to work in a factory. Always particular about his clothes, he owned no sports shirts or casual wear at all; one of his nicknames was "White-Shirt Vic," and he liked lots of starch. Nor did he have sneakers, workboots, boat shoes, or moccasins. Dad spit-polished his shoes; he wore either a black mohair or dark blue gabardine or a gray sharkskin two-piece suit, and he had three soft cashmere topcoats in black, dark brown, and light beige. He never left the house without his black or gray felt fedora either. When he got to the factory, he changed into overalls. Nobody else I knew looked, acted, or dressed like my father. My friend Ellen's dad, Herman, a baseball fanatic who was called "Honey" by his wife, often wore a baseball cap, polo shirt, and shorts.

Because of Dad's attire and his purposeful stride through the lobby when he arrived home at night, despite his exhaustion, some of our neighbors were fooled into thinking we were secretly rich. He liked it that way. When Mother mentioned that Mrs. Bloom had tried to find out what bank he worked in, it delighted him: "I should dress in a baseball uniform, maybe? Like Honey?"

"No, but maybe you should carry a machine gun like Elliot Ness once in a while, so they'd get the real picture!"

He was a Turk all the way. He liked his Turkish meals served on time and just right, like the rest of them. He went to the baths with the others every week. His loud fights with Mother and the public arguing with his brothers scared me. I learned of his sensitive side only when I got sick. He'd point his stump finger at me, wink, and whisper, "I'm on your side!" This never proved more true than when I lay inert in isolation, with one leg in this world and one in the other. When I got better, but before I could walk again, he'd lift me up and carry me in his massive arms, higher than the top of the Ferris wheel at Rockaway Playland, and I would feel like a queen instead of a tiny, crippled kid.

We even owned a special hat. It was called a scholar's turban, and it was supposed to make the wearer smart. This lavish, purple wrap-around had a green feather sticking up through the top and a diamond clip in its center. It had been with us as long as I could remember, but nobody knew who brought it over from the Dardanelles. The day I became paralyzed, Uncle Ovadiah and my father took turns wearing it. Through a gauzy fever haze I saw each one enter my room with the turban on, trying, I think, to get me to stand up. Till the minute the ambulance came, everyone believed I was faking.

For sure, no other kid's father went to the Turkish baths or danced to Middle Eastern music in their living room with other men. My friends' storage closets contained catcher's mitts, baseball gloves and bats, spaldeen balls, and fishing rods. Ours were stuffed with tapestry bed-spreads from Istanbul that were heavy as carpets, which my dad said gave him a hernia lifting; gold long-handled pots used for Turkish cof-fee; and piles of white bath towels "borrowed" from the baths.

When my dad came home, he would, more than likely, find the Coun-cil sitting around storytelling and munching on something disgust-ing, like the creamy salmon-colored fish roe they spread on Saltines. The women liked singing melancholy love ballads popular in medieval Spain and handed down orally from generation to generation. In fact, everything they did was oral: eating, yelling, singing, mimicking, and storytelling. They sang exotic lyrics that spoke of "drunken louses" in love with "beautiful dark-eyed shepherdesses." Some songs contained a mix of Ladino, Greek, Arabic, French, and Italian lyrics. Music played in our house at all times. I loved the festive Turkish afternoons when vis-itors from Istanbul or other parts, and my uncles, too, wore red fezzes and sat cross-legged on our rug, smoking a hookah. Always, upon en-tering our house, the guest stepped in with the right foot first, for luck, and then bellowed the familiar greeting, HABIBI! To which my father bellowed back the welcome, BUYROUM!

Then they rolled up their sleeves and used our round living room table — amazingly called a "drum table" — for bongos. Sometimes a vis-itor brought along a real dumbek or played an hourglass-shaped drum called a darbuka or brought an oud to accompany the record. Every house had castanets, and most of us owned a pair of zills, which belly dancers put on their fingers. When we were desperate for an instrument, we played the kucharas, two spoons held back-to-back with a finger in-between and slapped against the palm of the hand.

Aunt Sultana had a deep baritone, almost like a man's, but even when the lyrics to the song were joyous, she wound up crying. As soon as one started crying, another picked it up, then the whole room joined in. Afterward, I knew, would come the eating—with piles of food and sweets to make us feel better.

They may have been sentimental for Espanya in song, but it was for Turkey that they retained a deep, nostalgic longing. All of them prac-ticed being Americans but remained Turkish to the bone, more than my friends' grandparents were Polish or German. To Turkey they felt a great allegiance, even though we had barely any relatives left there.

An uncle once told me that, because of the generosity and fairness of the sultans centuries ago, Turkey would always be considered their home: "Nunka avla mal de Türkiye." One must never speak ill of the good name of Turkey.

Mas vale fortuna en tierra ke bonacha en
la mar. Good luck on the ground is
worth more than sailing on a clear sea.

LADINO PROVERB

2 ❖ Fortuna

When my father was a very young child, acutely ill with spinal meningitis, his own mother saved his life. To cure him she performed a "secret ceremony" that involved heating a lump of lead in a special bowl, uttering holy prayers known only to her, and enclosing the nearly dead boy under a sheeted tent.

"She melted the *kourshoum*, lead, in a bronze bowl," my father said. "The lead hissed and popped; pieces shot up to the ceiling. The whole place filled with smoke."

His fever raged for three days, but Nona refused to call an ambulance. Like many immigrants, the elders in my family were terrified of the "hospital men" who regularly came roaring down Suffolk, Orchard, Ludlow, or Rivington streets to take sick children away. Many times their mothers never saw them again.

According to other family members who remembered this, the ritual could be performed only on the day of the new moon, according to the lunar calendar. When they told the story, my aunts argued about how many healers were actually present. Some said four women, some said only two plus Behora. Tantes Sultana and Allegre didn't do these kinds of rituals, which were in the realm of healers and medicine women of a certain higher caliber. My paternal grandmother, obviously, was the real thing, and when she held sessions like these, superstitious neighbors who got wind of what was going on fled the building.

Even with her magic, my father got worse. On the fourth day of his enclosure ritual, Nona resorted to a drastic measure: she changed her son's name. Born Samuel, she changed my father's name to Victor, recited the Evil Eye incantation for a "new" boy, and Dad miraculously recovered. Most people had no idea he had once been Samuel.

Behora's mother and grandmother had also been healers in Celebria, near Istanbul, where she was born—if that's really where she came from. It could have been Izmir; in her case history was fuzzy. I learned to not expect accurate details because stories changed every day. We do know that the province was filled with clairvoyants, and no one doubted her gifts.

Instinct told me that she was different from other grandmas. She scared me more than a little, not like Mother scared me, with unexpected bouts of rage, but in a subtle way. Like when you turn to talk to someone who's vanished. There was something simple about my friends' grandmas that Nona Behora wasn't.

To visit her apartment was a treat I looked forward to. She had curios and trinkets from Turkey: spangled head coverings many Turkish women wore, called *yemeni*, hookah pipes, long- and short-handled gold Turkish coffee pots, a battered, hand-carved oud that had belonged to my grandfather, and an opaque "wishing" ball, her version of a crystal ball. I was allowed to touch and look at everything but was extremely careful when I did. At Nona Behora's I caused no mischief.

Although she practiced all manner of fortune-telling, Nona's main business was reading, with astounding accuracy, the black-patterned mud, or grounds, left over from a cup of Turkish coffee. In this she saw your past, your future, and your soul and also if your soul had been cursed. In that case she was an expert at "soul retrieval"; you'd have to pay more, naturally, but she could lift the curse and remove the ink, dark as coffee grounds, that was staining your essence.

If you held out your hand, she'd read your palm and tell you something intimate about yourself that she couldn't possibly have known. She read tarot cards, which she kept in an old shoebox, triangle-wrapped in a black cloth, and she read runes, hieroglyphic alphabet stones engraved with cryptic symbols, which she wore pinned to her slip in a blue felt bag. They jiggled as she moved.

She used her healing gifts combined with mumya powder to solve mysterious maladies of the skin or a bad case of measles. It was rumored that she actually reversed measles-induced blindness once in an eight-year-old girl. This embittered Mother, the fact that her brúsha, witch mother-in-law, had died before she could heal my illness: "She would have done magic on you before you ever saw the inside of a hospital. I know it." It made me long all the more for my grandma.

On Sundays Mother slept late. Dad liked to spirit me out of the house early to go downtown. I barely had time to stuff an arm in my coat before being whirled, dervish-like, down the stairs. He'd adjust the brim of his hat in the lobby's gilt-framed mirror, and we were off. Usually, it was still dark out; even the garbage trucks hadn't yet rumbled down the block. He walked fast, faster than anyone, even his brothers, and no one matched his stride. I struggled to keep up, my little hand snug and warm inside his huge one, skipping along with the wind gusts that carried the swirling leaves and scraps of paper.

My father was a champion walker. Everybody walked in those days — few people we knew owned cars — but Dad really walked. He was always putting on his hat, grabbing his coat, and "going for cigarettes" or "getting the paper" or "getting some air" or "going out to see what's going on." The truth was, he just couldn't stay in one place. Mother said that was why we never moved to the suburbs like "normal" people.

"How would your father have played his numbers or fixed his horses if there were no corner candy stores?"

When I got tired of dragging along, he'd lift me onto his shoulders like he did at the Macy's Thanksgiving Day Parade. I never had to beg him. Silent and majestic in the half-dawn, the Grand Concourse emptied of cars and people was a more interesting street at that time of morning. Across the wide boulevard yellow, white, and red brick art deco buildings, some built with mock facades to look like the Empire State Building, lit up as soon as sunlight spilled over their arched windows and geometric-patterned roofs. Dad pointed them out to me: "Look at that!" I thought it wondrous, too. For a long time I believed that the sun fell from the sky onto the buildings of the Grand Concourse before it touched any other street in the city.

We boarded the practically empty D train at 170th Street and changed at 42nd Street for the forty-minute ride to Delancy. Dad read the paper, and I always had a book, just recently discovering how to read. It never seemed like a long trip. Magically, it was full morning when we emerged from underground. But we never immediately went to Grandma's; first, we strolled all around the Lower East Side. We explored whichever stores were open on Delancy, Grand, Houston, and Orchard. All the Jewish-owned businesses opened Sundays, and although we rarely bought anything, Dad would point to things in the windows and say, "I'm gonna buy you this . . . and this—" and that was enough.

Near Grandma's building, at the corner of Suffolk Street, I knew what was coming. He liked to tell me the truck story, how, during the war, he maneuvered an amazingly skillful turn down that very same narrow block, driving a U.S. Army transport truck full of ammunition. My father was to drive one of a caravan of trucks to Florida from the army base at Fort Dix, New Jersey, when he was struck by this incredible longing to see his mother. Impulsively, he turned the truck around after crossing the George Washington Bridge, detoured to Suffolk Street, and went to his mother's for breakfast.

The stunt naturally earned him an AWOL. When he finally caught up to the transport in Georgia, his excuse to the sergeant was the truth: "I had to have Mama's breakfast. I needed it!" I was convinced that my father could charm the whole U.S. Army and every officer in it.

I would conjure up the details of those Sundays for many months, even for years to come, particularly in hospitals or when I was forced to endure painful procedures on my legs. Often nurses left me alone to cry; you had to be brave, they told us, or else "How will you get well?" So I'd close my eyes and fantasize that I was sitting on top of my father's shoulders as he walked downtown to Nona's. That turned off the hysteria that starts in the groin and climbs slowly up to your neck and makes a lump there. I discovered a hidden roadway far enough inside me that I escaped to, and there, often, I smelled lamb cooking, or fresh-baked boyos, the Sephardic version of challah bread.

The first time I willed myself inside one of those Sundays was during the two weeks I spent in isolation. They said I was very brave, but what child has the choice? Throughout my months, years, of hospital visits, I never met one cowardly child. We were all "brave." Bravery is easy when you haven't figured out how sick you really are nor the enormity of that sickness in relation to the rest of your life.

Healers of different ethnicities existed all over the city in the 1950s, but few were authentic diviners: "Your grandmother was notorious, the real thing," Mother said, "and much in demand. How do you think she survived?" Nona was widowed at forty-seven. Grandpa Chelebón, "Charles," whom all the brothers' sons on my dad's side were named after, died long before I was born. He had worked in a Christmas lights factory along with his eight brothers, and there was talk about branching out, adding colored lights as ornaments. But it wasn't to be. On the night of my grandparents' twenty-fifth wedding anniversary, while the family assembled in Nona's apartment for a party, my grandfather had a massive heart attack at the factory, and they found him the next morning, buried under a pile of tiny lights and tangled wires.

"My father *knew* Christmas lights would one day be a big business in this country," Dad said, sighing. It was the family curse: all nine uncles would *almost* get rich, *almost* invent something useful.

Suddenly alone and penniless, his young widow had no choice but to practice her art. Thus, Nona Behora became a famous Lower East Side fortune teller. Lines formed on her stoop day after day, queuing up into the narrow, smelly stairwell. The stairs were steep, hard for me to climb as a little girl, and I marveled at how she did it on those lumpy, swollen legs. It was amazing, in fact, that she even fit in the narrow stairwell, she was so huge.

Nona Behora was obese, fatter than any other person I'd ever seen then and even now. She was six times bigger than my friends' grandmothers, and so she hated having her picture taken. Every picture of her shows her clutching a big black pocketbook to her belly in a vain attempt to hide her ruptured stomach. It was the size of her babies that caused her belly to rupture in three places, they said, and that was what eventually killed her. Of course, they told me a lie about her death. The crazy story I got was that "she caught a *really* bad cold, and it didn't get better." Thereafter, whenever I caught one, I was sure I'd die.

All her boys were hefty at birth, but the last one, my uncle Albert, weighed a gigantic sixteen pounds. Some family members said fourteen, but no matter. Mother said the hospital took a mother-and-baby picture and sent it to one of the daily newspapers. My fears alternated between catching a really bad cold and giving birth to a monster baby.

She had a lovely face, though. Atop that wide neck and misshapen body sat a doll's head with chiseled features, smooth and unblemished. Her olive skin and silky black hair was a replica of the graceful flamenco dancer whose face we had on a postcard from Spain. Nona never complained, that I remember, but her obese body must have suffered. At her death, a cousin swore, she weighed four hundred pounds and was too huge to be carried down the narrow stairwell. Carpenters were called to remove the large front window frame in order to get her out.

"They hoisted her down, poor thing, while the whole block watched."

Nona's regular customers would wait as long as it took for one of her famous readings, often long enough to finish the Mirror, Daily News, Jewish Daily Forward, or La Vara, a Sephardic newspaper in print until the late 1940s that was written entirely in Ladino with Hebrew characters. She charged three bucks for a reading—two if you were short of cash.

All the Turks read cups or pretended to. In Middle Eastern homes it was a mark of hospitality to serve Turkish coffee the minute company arrived. You were not a benedám, a decent human being, if you didn't and were talked about as having the "manners of a horse." To be asked: "Kieres un kavesiko?" Would you care for a little Turkish coffee? was a formality. You never refused, and you never asked for a second cup, or you'd lose face and not be invited back. Either the host or a girl of marriageable age brought out the tray with the good demitasse cups, glasses of water, Jordan almonds, Turkish Delights candies, or a rare delicious treat: a white-jelly fondant called sharope.

Behora always had a large crowd and neighborhood women to assist her, and once in a while this helping neighbor got into trouble. Grandma had a hard rule about how the libríks, those tall gold coffee pots, should be washed. In order to preserve the coffee's special flavor, you were to wash them in cold water only. An incident occurred when the woman tried to do it her own way, by scrubbing the pot with steel wool and then soaking it in hot water. She was ejected from the apartment.

"Out the window, Nona?" I asked, excited. I knew well their obsession with throwing things out of windows. She laughed.

"Yes, mi kookoovaya!" She called me her "little owl" because she thought I was very smart.

Of the many stories concerning my Grandma Behora, this out-of-the-window stuff, which my dad inherited, was among the strangest. I never figured it out. Echelo por la ventana: throw it out the window, became a catchphrase for anything that displeased them. An in-law legend in the family had to do with the time Nona met her son Kelly's betrothed. The girl's parents came with a cake, but apparently they failed to make a favorable impression on my grandmother. There was an argument; the future in-laws walked out in a huff, Behora marched to the window, and, just as they passed underneath it, she dumped the remainder of the chocolate cake out the window.

"My brother and his novia, bride, nearly stepped in it!" my dad howled. "It just missed her shoes!"

The Recipe for Destiny began with three heaping teaspoons of the fine, pulverized grind to each small cup of water. I've seen my uncles come to fisticuffs over this recipe, whether or not to use equal amounts of sugar to coffee before boiling. All agreed that it had to be boiled three times — taken off and then put back on the flame. Why three? "It just has to be," Dad said. Individual cups were then heated with boiling water, and some of the coffee foam was spooned into each one before filling.

It was bitter tasting, even watered down and sugared, but you got used to it. Guests either loved kave Turko or pretended to, scared not to drink it. After the proper amount of time and conversation, the remaining liquid in your cup was swished around, the cup turned upside down, and your hands placed crisscross on top of it, so that the cup could leech your "spirit," one of the first steps in retrieving a damaged soul. Then, when the fortune teller was ready, she announced: "Kaves d'alegria!" a prayer for "happy news."

Then, with the seriousness of a doctor's examination, Nona diagnosed your fate.

I learned some useful information by listening, stuff I'd one day use at parties to become, what else, the center of attention: Numbers were always about time. A large number meant years in a person's life;

smaller numbers meant days or hours. Palm trees signified good luck, but other trees, like oaks or maples, meant prepare for a catastrophe. Airplanes—Grandma always made out their wings, no one else ever saw them—meant travel, of course, as did boats, but a boat usually foretold a romantic end. Also, boats could mean a desire to escape something. These shapes Grandma easily discerned: "See Chika?" She'd point, showing me here and here and there, and I'd pretend to see what she saw.

Every so often, money made a cameo appearance. Those times guests became ecstatic. Round shapes were coins, small moneys; rectangles were the larger, dollar amounts. Grandma usually saw rectangles, not coins. Or, in the middle of a reading, she'd see a bizarre picture. Once she saw a horse's head in my father's cup. "How apropos!" Mother said, rolling her eyes. And she almost always saw a boat in his cup, declaring out loud that her son had a desire to escape his life:

"Ah . . . Victor, Victor . . . he wants to travel . . . he'll leave on a long journey." It infuriated Mother.

"It's all crap! His mother reads whatever she damn well pleases in those cups!" But even Mother admitted that, if she was one thing, Grandma was smart. She kept her mouth shut and didn't ask questions; she let people give her the questions they wanted answered, so that they blabbed all their own information. "All the professionals work that way," Mother said.

For large family readings on weekends, my grandmother sometimes ventured out of her own neighborhood. A visit to the Bronx was rare, but occasionally she did it. Those times, I'm sad to say, I was ashamed of her because of her size and tried not to acknowledge her as my relative. If I spotted her dark head emerging from the 170th Street subway stop, I ran into the building before she saw me. I always seemed to be outside when she came. Once she saw me, I had to walk to her and help her carry her things, and endure snickers and giggles from all the kids. I baked in shame as her elephantine figure approached.

Some kids were mean enough to point; they laughed as she trudged snail-like up the Concourse. This in itself was a remarkable feat, given her size and condition. I was so torn. One part of me wanted to run to her, open my arms as wide as possible, like I did when I entered her house, and hug her. The other side of me wished she had stayed home.

She seemed out of place on the wide, sunny street, dressed, even on the warmest days, in that tremendous black overcoat. I didn't always understand that it was meant to cover up her body. She dragged two loaded shopping bags, one in each hand, so heavy with foodstuffs and clothing that they scraped the sidewalk.

"Look at the fatso!" kids shouted. Some told me, "Your grandma's *fat and ugly! She looks like a man!*" That was because of the faint but noticeable mustache on her upper lip. No matter that the bags were filled with gifts for me and my brother—flannel pajamas, shirts, blouses, and the sweet delicacies we loved that were found only on the Lower East Side—I still cringed.

If I didn't make it into the lobby before she saw me, where I could hide, I was forced to watch her climb. I held my breath as she struggled up the outer stoop of four steep steps, often teeter-tottering backward. The shopping bags had a seesaw effect; they pulled her one hand forward, while the other side fell back. But it prevented a fall. Then she climbed the inner stoop, which was a longer flight of marble steps—all this without ever holding the banister—and, finally, she made it into the lobby. We lived in the rear of the building, so her journey wasn't through; now she had to make it across the lobby and up two more flights of stairs to our apartment. My mother would be waiting at the door most times with a glass of water.

When all the uncles and their wives and kids got together, someone was bound to play a joke on the fortune teller. When she got up to go to the bathroom, they switched coffee cups. When Nona came back she continued the reading, amazingly making sense, predicting something fitting to the person, even if his cup had been switched. It was uncanny.

"Nobody fooled Mama," Dad said. "Nobody."

For twenty dollars, which was a lot of money for most folks, Nona performed a believable table séance, where she communicated with *los muertos*, dead loved ones. Even hearing about it gave me nightmares. This communication involved some preparation. The drapes were pulled shut, so that it was dark even on the sunniest day. She'd put on a dreamy Turkish record of slow, instrumental oud music, and one of her card-playing Sephardi cohorts was paid a couple of dollars to thump the wall in the adjoining room from time to time, for further atmosphere. The same person would also watch that the record didn't skip.

"Trouble always happened," Dad said. Dead people's relatives started out excited but soon became agitated and frightened. "It was more than they bargained for." Some screamed; some wept uncontrollably. In general it caused a commotion, and neighbors called the cops. Grandma got arrested, for the fifth or sixth time, for "engaging in gypsy practices." A couple of hours later one of her sons bailed her out, and in a few days she was back in business, with many of the same Irish cops who had arrested her as new clients.

I asked her once if she could truly speak to the dead and if she had ever talked to her husband, Grandpa Chelebón, about me. She winked, smiling mysteriously: "He knows you, sí."

"What did he say about me?"

"He knows you don't like your brother. He said it's okay!"

It was a relief to know that Grandpa in heaven forgave me for hating the baby. I was under the childish impression that no one knew I wished he'd never been born. Everyone adored the baby. It was a brand-new experience for me; up until five I was the *kadún* of the harem for a long while, and then there was a sultan-in-training usurping me. When no one was around, I uncovered my brother in his crib and stared at his naked pink body, wondering why, when I thought him so ugly, they thought him so special. I was beginning to get an idea of how important it was to be a *boy*.

A few times I had the privilege of watching my grandmother work. I was six when she died, so I had her three more years and knew her much better than I knew my mother's mother, Benvenuta. I felt a bond with Nona Behora, and it's a good thing I paid attention to her words because soon, for my own survival, I would employ the same, innate perception skills when I needed to "read" people. Her intelligence concerning human nature was vast. Although Mother called her a "professional," which really meant she was a fake, I believe she knew quite a lot.

For one thing she could tell what was going on with people on the inside. She read faces and body language, while allowing for discretion, and could turn on a dime if she thought a prediction she was about to give might upset a client, especially to the point of nonpayment. Then she'd switch it and make up different "good" news.

"Remember," she told me, "tell good news." Even Mother concurred that only amateurs told the bad stuff. "Your grandmother knows better.

Or else they blame the clairvoyant for all their troubles." I wondered why my mother didn't realize that she, too, blamed Nona for all her troubles.

No poker-faced player could have better concealed visions of illness or marital strife than my grandmother. After the client left, she'd tell me the real story about them. When she read, if she raised just one eyebrow or if her mouth twisted to one side, the future was dim. Similarly, if she pursed lips, it meant that she was figuring out what to say, stalling for time. When she bit her lower lip, real trouble: usually health. Money problems? She'd nod once. I got to know the code after a few times, and later, in the hospital, I became an expert in figuring out the doctors.

When they made their rounds, they put on certain faces. Almost never did they tell the truth, certainly not to kids. When they examined me they gave themselves away by biting or pursing their lips or by lifting an eyebrow. I got to know how a tilted head at a certain angle meant they were surprised by something—not necessarily bad. That's when I knew I wasn't going to die, too. When doctors conferred with parents, their faces and their coloring changed entirely, especially when delivering bad news. They'd step back, turn pale, and bite their lip.

Kind nurses blinked a lot. The mean ones didn't look at me at all, kept their heads rigid, had perennially furrowed brows, and their lips were always "skinny." The meaner the nurse, the taller and straighter they held themselves. Good nurses always slumped a bit. This is what Nona taught me.

I had no doubt that Nona was brilliant. She spoke Arabic, Turkish, French, and Spanish fluently but could neither read nor write English, though she spoke it well enough to attract a few Irish-American and Italian customers. Yiddish she steadfastly refused to learn, but she understood enough to know when her Ashkenazi clients talked behind her back. Those times they'd get a reading they wished they hadn't.

"She had a way about her that, when she read, the whole room got quiet," Mother said. In any language she could restore your health or curse you mightily and was equally fond of doing both. There were many family stories concerning her uncanny powers and just as many about her fractured relationships with people in and outside the family: "If my mother cursed a person, gave them a maldisyón," my father said, "it meant doom." And when she could think of nothing to say, she was so good at making things up. One thing she told everybody was that soon they'd receive a letter, an *important* letter. Why? "Because *everyone* gets a letter!"

Mothers would bring her their daughters' bras to study. The bra clung to the body and was therefore a good indicator of a girl's sexual appeal; that's how you knew when she'd marry. Eyes closed, Nona felt the fabric, "listened" to what it told her. Here, too, she acted professionally. She had to be careful of what she said at all times, as it was against Jewish law to stop a wedding ceremony, even if she predicted that the guy was no good. This was touchy, and often she had to keep it to herself. Worse than that kind of trouble was spinsterhood, God forbid. Yet even that had a remedy.

Like many fortune tellers, Grandma doubled as a marriage broker. For a few dollars more she'd tactfully offer her services in the hunt for a suitable man. Tack another dollar on, and she'd read the mother's cup, too, to discern whether or not in-law trouble was in store. Her readings were never boring.

It happened on one of these special Sundays that Behora told my fate. That day we let ourselves in as quietly as possible when we saw she was "in session," deep into reading someone's cup. When she was like that, Dad said, we had to be invisible. Across from her sat the client, a small woman, scrunched down into her chair, who seemed to shrivel up even smaller as the reading continued. I spied on them from Nona's half-open bedroom door.

At one point, close to the end of the reading, the woman wiped her eyes with a tissue, obviously moved by something Grandma had told her. A second after that she laughed, attesting to Nona's brilliant skill for turning things around. Finally, the reading was over. I watched as the lady counted out some dollars and left them on the table. Nona's custom was to not touch money until after the client departed. "Thank you! Thank you!" she said, sounding grateful, and left. I knew my grandmother would be in a very good mood, as the session had ended well. She knew, of course, I had been spying.

"Welcome namesake!" she called out, without turning around. This was my usual greeting, plus a crushing, smothering hug. Her belly was grotesquely lopsided from that unrepaired hernia, the knob of which pushed into my ribs when she held me close. Then she would put me at arm's distance and study my face. She loved it that I looked like her, had her eyes and nose, but I think she wished my hair wasn't red like Mother's. I wondered, and was a little scared about it, if one day I would become as hugely fat as she was. According to my father, I certainly would, but he said it laughing, and I know he loved teasing me.

She was not overly affectionate or demonstrative toward me, certainly not like Tante Alice, and she rarely smiled because she had poor teeth, but for me she managed a turned-up corner of her mouth, a half-smile. It's a habit I copy to this day. That day she was happier than usual to see us. She wasn't one to talk or interact with kids—in fact, you hardly heard her voice unless she was reading fortunes—but I knew she loved me by other things she did, like taking my head in her hands and moving it from side to side. She did that, then she patted the chair next to her.

My love of books amused her, especially that I couldn't yet read them. The books I had were all well-worn, hard-covered classic editions passed down from older cousins, which I looked forward to one day reading. I loved even the *feel* of a book, of turning it over, opening it, smelling the binding. I would spend hours trying to decipher a single sentence.

That day Nona examined the Nancy Drew mystery I carried and, gratefully, put it down. Once or twice in the past she had done the window thing: taken a book I left on the table, opened it as if to see if she approved of the subject matter, though she couldn't read any better than I, then tossed it. It seemed weird, but she didn't do it angrily. Normally, I would have *screamed*; with Nona Behora, though, I didn't dare. There was something about her that I instinctively didn't want to disturb. *Glenda of Oz* went this way, as did a picture book of exotic tropical fish, which I managed to retrieve from the gutter on our way home.

She asked me that day if I wanted a little cup of Turkish coffee. I didn't but said yes anyway. It seemed that she wanted to read my fortune right away, although she usually served the coffee after breakfast. My father carried in a demitasse cup filled with just a bit of milk, to which she added some coffee. Mother really disapproved of this habit of reading children's cups—she said because they needed to *live* their lives, not have it told to them. Then she'd bite her forefinger and repeat the prayer for protection.

I drank the little cup as fast as I could without choking, turned it upside down, waited a couple of minutes, and then sat back as she read my grounds.

Nona envisioned two things happening to me but told me of only one: that I was going to get lost, probably in the summertime. What she didn't tell me but told my father was that I was going to get sick with an illness I might die from. The premonition, or whatever it was, devastated my father then and my mother later. It changed everything in all our lives for all time, primarily because many Turks believed that she was powerful enough to have stopped it. This was the second time Nona foresaw that her son's firstborn child would be sick.

She studied my cup for so long that morning that I became impatient. "What does it say, Grandma? What does it *say*?" All I could see was mud. She squinted, concentrating harder. It was always fun to have your fortune told — so far. Many times she had told her grandchildren whether or not they'd be getting a new dress for a party or a doll for Chanukah. But that day I sensed her tension and unease, and it transferred to me and made me a little scared. When she finally looked up, she stared past me at a fixed point in the distance. I turned around to look, too; of course, nothing was there. During all this Dad had been looking out the window, smoking, lost in thought. He didn't see his mother place her right hand on top of my head and lift my chin until I found her eyes.

"De tu kaza no te mankes!" May you never be missing from your home! she said.

At that moment my father turned to stare at us. I didn't recognize the look on his face. What she had given me was a standard Ladino blessing for children, one I'd heard many times before. They'd say it if you went to the hospital to get your tonsils out or if you were going on a trip. This insured that you'd come home. It was Nona's tone that made the difference. She spoke so low I could barely hear her, and she started to breathe heavily, too.

The apartment became so quiet for those few seconds that I clearly heard the tick-tocking of the table clock from the next room. Then she leaned forward and tenderly kissed my forehead.

"Don't worry, *Chika*," she said, in her choppy English, "they find you fast!"

It wasn't these strange, out-of-character actions I feared as much as my father's openmouthed face. He took a step toward us then stopped. Finally, the moment ended, she slapped her knees, said "*Venga!*" Come! and we followed her to the table.

I couldn't wait to run into what passed for a kitchen to see what goodies she had prepared for us that morning. The misshapen, "holy" bronze bowl used for the lead-popping ceremonies was stored underneath the sink, where no grandchild dared touch it. Amazing to me was the fact that her kitchen also contained a bathtub and a toilet bowl. It was so narrow a space that a couple of times a year her dress caught fire on the burners, and we'd get a frantic call in the Bronx to come quick, she had scorched her stomach again.

Out of that unbelievably cramped, claustrophobic space came the most wonderful meals, and out of her mouth the best stories. These tales were different than the ones Tantes Sultana and Allegre told. Nona Downtown, as we grandchildren called her, told Turkish ghost stories from the old country, stories about curses that had come true for evil people and predictions that *endivinas* had made that came to pass.

If any of her grandchildren became too wide-eyed or fearful, even better. She seemed to love scaring us; she'd show us an empty cup and ask, "See? See what's in there?" Of course, we were too scared to look. This made her laugh and slap her thighs. All of them, on both sides of the family, were fond of scaring and teasing kids, especially before meals.

Her breakfasts were legendary; Nona Downtown began the day with a feast. My other grandma had been too sickly to ever prepare a meal, let alone a lavish Turkish one, and Mother hated to cook. Even her sisters didn't cook like Nona. She had risen extra early that day to get things ready. The table had been set with a fine, white, flower-embroidered linen cloth from Istanbul. Three plates of oblong, phyllo dough pastries called *borekas*, filled either with cheese or spinach, were already waiting. Next she brought out the large bread rings, the *boyos*, and there was enough for fifteen.

She had cooked us *yaprakes*, stuffed grape leaves, that morning, with hard-boiled brown eggs, from an ancient Sephardic recipe, where the eggs cook in a slow oven for many hours before being braised with onionskins and coffee grounds to give them their brown color. As always, there was a wide assortment of favorite cheeses: feta; goat; the delicious, yellowy *kashkaval*; and a sharp "white cheese" that I refused to taste. My one problem: How would I fit in dessert?

Oh, the sweets! I taste them still. I managed to eat to Downtown Nona's satisfaction—you wouldn't *dare* not to—and I always had room for the best part, her homemade, hard cookie *biscochos*, marble halvah, delectable airy-white meringue balls, miniature Greek baklavas, and the remarkable *mustachudos*—not as delicious as Tante Sultana's walnut balls but remarkable nonetheless. And, of course, Turkish Delights gelatin candy, sesame-crunch candies, and chocolate-covered jelly bars. By the time we were up to the *pepitas*, roasted sunflower seeds that Dad and his brothers ate by the pound, I was pretty nauseous. So Nona packed up everything in case I got hungry on the subway home.

Food hasn't tasted as good since. It may have been too much at one time, but I learned to love food too well—after a two-year hiatus for illness, when I refused to eat at all. Our entire clan loved to eat those famous breakfasts with the master. How could my young cousins and I know that one day we'd all have the infamous "Nona hips"? You simply *had* to eat—and praise the food as well.

"Look at the size of this pastry!" my father said. "What perfect eggs! Where did you find them so big? The chicken must have weighed twenty pounds, Mama! *Ke pransa!* What a banquet! Mama, you're my life, my star!"

My father and grandmother shared a special camaraderie of secrets and private jokes. He could always make her laugh by mimicking a relative's walk or odd speech, and she'd slap her big leg and roar. But her moods were mercurial; without changing facial expressions, she'd go from belly laughter to fist pounding, suddenly yelling out a curse for a customer who might have tried to cheat her or a cousin who had possibly offended her: "Low-luck fiend!" she'd shout in Turkish, making me jump. Then the mask lifted, and she was herself, laughing and eating.

Her shifting moods, according to my mother, were the very thing that caused our own bad luck. "She got carried away one day and forgot that she was cursing her own son!" I don't know if Mother truly believed that her mother-in-law was that evil, but I know that I was torn between believing my mother and siding with my dad. I favored Dad, of course, but, still, there was something strange about this huge, dark person . . . I saw Mother's point.

A formal procession was made of serving each dish. Like most Turkish women, Nona deferred to her sons, waiting on them, catering to their needs, and not allowing them to help. I carried what I could, but it was Grandma who brought the heavy *platas* laden with goodies from the kitchen to the front room, making at least ten trips. When the table was crammed full so that not another spoon fit, she finally plopped down into the nearest chair, cursing her bad legs for their slowness, gasping in pain. That's how I remember seeing her the last two or three times we visited—in agony.

We buried ourselves in the work of eating for a long while. Then, as if prearranged, the moment came when both of them dropped their forks, leapt up from their seats—as fast as someone her size could leap—and flew into each other's arms, kissing and hugging. Sometimes she cried or my dad cried; often they both did. I thought that no one could love a mother the way my father loved his. My terrible secret was that I often felt that I didn't love my mother at all. She yelled at me for no good reason or when I spilled something, and I overheard her telling people that I had a "bad disposition." When I asked Dad what that meant, he said he didn't know. "Don't pay attention," he said.

"Why?"

"Because Y is a crooked letter."

Nona Downtown knew my secret, I'm sure. She'd pat my braids and examine my scalp when I came, as if she'd seen Mother yanking my hair from its roots that morning as she brushed it. I hated her for that, of course, but not as much as I did for being obsessed with my one-year-old brother. Her whole *face* changed when she picked him up out of his crib. She stopped scowling. It wasn't just me; Dad was jealous of Charlie, too. When *she* stopped scowling, *he* scowled, and it was always when Mother was feeding, holding, playing with, or talking to the baby.

"Oh, you're both such babies!" she liked to say. "Worse than this little guy, aren't they?" Then she'd coo and cluck and say disgustingly loving things to my brother. But I knew I was right. She never took *my* face in her hands and made sounds like that. "But you're not a baby anymore!" she'd say. After mentioning that I hated my mother a couple of times and getting slapped by Sultana for saying it, I kept my mouth shut.

Nona and my father had a fierce attachment like that, too. They dwelled in a theater of gluttony and raw emotion. I tried to find a place to fit into and couldn't, even though my dad made me feel special. When I was in Tante Allegre's house, I came close—until her own family came home.

When Grandma lay on her deathbed, a woman named Tia Awahdeesh came to see her. Years ago this lady had been elected by the Turkish community to mediate the dispute between Nona and the superstitious parents of girls her sons wanted to date. They were afraid to let their daughters go out with the boys because of their mother's reputation for cursing those she didn't like—which was just about anyone they dated.

"They had to find a very strong woman to face down your grandmother," Mother said. "One like Tia Awahdeesh, who herself had borne only sons."

Apparently, this Tia Awahdeesh lady did her job because all four of Behora's sons eventually married. People came in throngs, curious to see a legend. By then she, too, was respectfully referred to as "honored Aunt" and was given the title Tia Behoroocha. Privately, though, many still called her the Turkish Witch or the Suffolk Street Sorceress or Spanish Gypsy and, certainly, *La Gorda*: The Fat One.

Some came to give *bezemano*, the practice of kissing the hand of an esteemed elder; some to ask forgiveness for any wrongs they might have knowingly or unknowingly committed. "Most came," Mother said, "so she'd put in a good word for them on the other side."

I don't know at which point I knew that Nona did not read from a script that she had scotch-taped to the bottom of each flowered porcelain cup. I thought this originally because, for everyone, she told variations on the same fortune theme. But I came to know that people's lives weren't all that different. Unattractive women had a harder time finding a man to marry; beautiful women had "many men interested in you" but were often unhappy as well. And everyone got letters. Some people would know sadness early, some later on. Occasionally, there was a terrible prediction and great grief, but, usually, a lucky happenstance, not to worry, was right around life's corner.

The clients created their own futures as they sat through their readings. When Grandma shouted, "Oh, my God!" it didn't necessarily mean that she had seen something awful; invariably, though, the person would jump up or cry out: "I knew it! I *knew* it!" What did they know? They had chosen to believe that a fortune teller knew something, when, in fact, she had foretold nothing. Nothing at all. Even I recognized that this was silly but was careful not to laugh, especially when Grandma winked at me.

Her séances and late-night sessions unearthed the darker side of fortune-telling. I couldn't fathom paying money to be frightened, nor did I understand why anyone would want to contact a ghost or a dead spirit. Yet even the terrified believers returned again and again. I put it together when I got older. It all had to do with Possibility, the hope that a clairvoyant, by saying something, could change something, alter your life significantly or even just a little.

No matter what Mother said about her being "crooked" and "vindictive," words I loved hearing and saying almost as much as *spinster* and its Ladino counterpart, *soltéra*, I was fiercely attached to my exotic, Janus-faced grandmother. Half of us believed in her powers, the other half in her moneymaking skills.

The last time I saw her was the day she told me I'd get lost. As we were about to leave, she whispered to Dad, "Take good care of her!" And he promised he would. He tried, too. But no one stops Fate. Because my father was a man who could never keep his mouth shut, he blabbed about the vision to my mother, who became so incensed with the prediction I would get lost that she smacked me for it in advance and then berated Dad.

"You dope! *Azno!* Donkey's ass! Son of a *witch!*"

She was frightened and furious at the same time. They fought bitterly until he finally slammed out, probably to the Turkish baths. Right away, Mother interpreted Nona's prediction as a curse, and, sadly, she allowed a fortune teller's vision to govern the rest of her life. She chose to believe that the very person who had foreseen it, if only she hadn't said it, could have diverted her *mazál preto*, black luck.

When we left 117 Suffolk Street that day, I looked up as I always did to wave good-bye. Nona was seated by the large front window mechanically shuffling cards, and from where I stood she looked very much the gypsy, her yellow-and-red spangled *yemeni* wrapped around her head. The wooden fortune teller behind glass at the boardwalk penny arcade was dressed almost identically. I always wondered who wrote those fortunes, the ones that fell out of the slot.

I kept looking at her long after she stopped waving to me. She was already lost in thought, probably thinking of an entertaining little *konsejika*, a story, to tell a client. I believed in stories, had already come to the point of needing to hear them.

3 ✤ Lost

In the summer of 1954, a year-and-a-half after my fortune-telling grandmother predicted it, I got lost in Rockaway Beach and spent most of the
day with a family of gypsies. I didn't care that they were gypsies—I was
happy someone found me—and it was the first time all summer that
I felt wanted. My contentedness was momentary, but at the time I was
positive that I'd found a new, loving family.

My sole occupation that summer, up until the day I got lost, had been
torturing my two-year-old brother by doing whatever was in my power
to make him cry. I'd pull out his pacifier, hide his toys, trip him as he
waddled happily along, and bop him on the head in the fraction of a
second it took for Mother to turn hers. He claimed deep emotional scars
in later life; I challenged his memory. His shrieks delighted me, though
I got slapped plenty for the pleasure.

We shared rooms with Aunt Sultana and Uncle Ovadiah, which
meant that for two months I had two mothers. I didn't love Sultana the
way I loved Allegre, to whom I was reigning hanúm. With Tante Allegre I
ruled the harem; with Sultana I ruined it. Uncle Ovadiah, who introduced
himself as "Irving," was okay but perpetually quiet, except for early
mornings when he woke me, calling, "SULTANA!" and she screamed

back, "OVADIAH!" But, just like in their Bronx apartment, once they acknowledged each other's presence, they had nothing more to say.

Everyone was in love with my brother Charlie, the little Turkish pasha, who had turned two in April. Chubby and with a "sunny disposition," Mother liked to tell people who stopped us when she wheeled the carriage: "having one good one and one with a *bad* disposition is enough for me!" By then I knew what the word meant.

Each day after breakfast my aunt and uncle took Charlie by the hand and went searching in and out of the beach blocks for the Dugan Bakery truck, so that "Duggie the baker" could personally hand the baby his donut. I was not invited on these excursions, nor did Aunt Sultana refrain from preserving my feelings. Emotionally ignorant is putting it mildly; she said whatever she felt like saying whenever she felt like saying it, even singing an old Ladino song with lyrics like *Hija Mala*, the Wicked Daughter, in that loud baritone. Or she'd get up close to my face and shout "Bre!" This, I mistakenly thought, was short for Brenda. It was actually a Ladino idiom for "You, brat!"

Tante came after me more than once that summer with her *boreka* dough rolling pin. This was reason for me to spit at her and run away. First, I practiced being wicked; gradually, the role became me. There was not a dinner that I didn't knock over a glass of something, either accidentally-on-purpose or for real. By day I threw screaming fits, and by night I refused to stay in bed, overcome with wanderlust. The balmy beach atmosphere called to me.

One night, as they all sat talking and drinking coffee, I crept past them in my pajamas and stole downstairs. They found me sitting face forward on the boardwalk railing by the ocean, watching the fireworks. Every Wednesday night at ten, two men in a small boat traveled a couple of miles out into the ocean and shot spectacular fireworks into the night sky for the boardwalk crowd to enjoy.

Sultana gasped when she saw I was *deskalsa*, without shoes, which was forbidden, even on carpeting. Chills, they believed, started at the soles of the feet and worked their way up the body. Lucky for me, another fast rule was: Never hit a child before *sueños*, dreams, took her, or she'd have nightmares for the rest of her life. There was no rule about pulling a kid's hair to get her off a railing.

That was the last time I had the pleasure of running away. I was to become docile, too, though not by my own design. As if I alone had a premonition of what was in store for me, I began a daily ritual of energetic tantrums. When they tried ignoring them, I screamed and kicked until I was hoarse and we were all exhausted. I acted much more like a two-year-old than my brother. In fact, when they told the baby no, he actually listened. The more jealous I got the less patience Mother had for me in general, and the madder she got the more disturbances I created.

With all their superstitions, prayers of "protection," and supposed insights from reading Turkish coffee grounds, not one of them had an inkling about the catastrophe our family was about to suffer. Had my indifferent mother or scolding aunt suspected a cyclone was blowing our way, I'm sure they would have joined me on that railing to watch purple starbursts, yellow spaghetti streamers, and silver-flowered sunbursts explode among the stars.

The Rockaway peninsula, a barrier beach on the southern shore of Long Island, bordered by Jamaica Bay and the Atlantic Ocean, was a summer oasis for middle-class Bronx and Brooklyn families who fled the sweltering city. The more money you had, the closer to the ocean you lived; some even had bungalows adjacent to the boardwalk. The more affluent usually stayed at Long Beach or Atlantic Beach, and the poorest, like us, were happy to rent in a rooming house, even a few blocks from the beach.

To save money, we waited until the Fourth of July weekend was over, when most families had already been at their summer places for over a week. That way Mother was able to haggle a better price for us for our apartment, and we took whatever was left. The problem was, we didn't actually have the place at the time we arrived, starving, fighting, and hot.

My mother and father were incapable of any team endeavor without histrionics. They'd get up on a particular morning, fight as usual, then decide on a moment's notice it was time to go, and Dad packed up the entire house in two hours, every dish, pot, and towel. He hauled two cartons at a time down the two flights of stairs—three, if you count the stoop—wedged them like a gigantic, awkward-fitting puzzle into the back seat of the car, then raced back upstairs three at a time to hoist another load, all while Mother harangued him.

She criticized his packing, the way he scribbled identifying markers on the cartons, how he put clothing into the cartons, the order in which he packed the items, and the arrangement of cartons in the back seat. From a kitchen chair, inert but bitching, she directed the operation. She was basically useless, unable to lift a finger to help or pack a single dish, while Dad did the job of three stevedores.

When he finished, rivers of sweat poured down his face and soaked his T-shirt. His eyes took on that glazed-over scary look my brother and I got to know well. He grabbed a fast drink of water, motioned with his thumb for Mother to move us out, and we headed for the stairs, running, as if the apartment were on fire. He cleared two spots in the stuffed back seat and fit me and my brother into them. My dad was beyond words at that point, just a seething, breathing, sweaty bundle of nervous energy, a volcano about to erupt. He turned the key in the ignition, and most times the car fired up. Thus began our journey.

About half an hour out of the Bronx, I vomited. I knew I would, and they knew I would. This was inevitable whenever I took a car trip. They'd quiz me over and over before we left: "You're not feeling sick, today, right? Tell us if you have to throw up *right away*. Tell us *now!*" I promised, but of course I didn't have to, not then, not until the heat and tumult mixed with the smoke from my father's endless Lucky Strikes got to me.

So we stopped, took care of the mess, and piled in again. Next the car broke down. This, too, was a sure bet. Mother, who had been quiet for a while, started in again as he limped the "crappy heap of scrap metal," as she called it, toward the side of the road. He did drive too fast. A perpetual speeder, when cops stopped us they were shocked at the violations on his license.

Typically, our summer cars were junky. Dad would buy a car at the end of June, patch it together with the help of his non-mechanic friend, Harry Mekanik, and then sell it in September. Ellen's father owned a 1950 black Studebaker forever, while we had a Buick, an Oldsmobile, or a Chevy but never the same make twice. Some of the cars made it through the summer pretty well; others were lemons from day one. And each summer my mother said something like,

"Think you can find an *older* car in worse condition next time?"

"It should happen to my brothers!"

"But it won't, will it? They drive *good* cars."

"Si, hijos de perro!" Yes, those sons of *dogs!*

A couple of scary times, when he couldn't take it anymore, he leaned across the passenger side while driving, left hand on the wheel, and tried to open her door. She definitely shut up then, and I was impressed how remarkably calm Mother could be when she wanted to. Her door actually sprang open once, but she managed to yank it shut right away. Still, unbelievably, Mother had to get in one last word, not quite under her breath.

"Boor!"

"What, Rose? *Otra vez!* Say it again!"

"Nothing."

Then I vomited for the second time.

Sometimes the highway patrol stopped us. Those cops really scared me because they were more serious looking and seemed taller than ordinary cops, and they wore those long boots, even in summer. Often Mother told the cop a fast joke—"have you heard the one about the pregnant woman . . ."—and he'd laugh in spite of himself. Other times they were stolid, unbending. If they made my father get out of the car, we were in trouble. Once we got fined a hundred dollars, plus lectured about speeding with children in the car. Then, when Dad stomped out his cigarette on the side of the road as if it were a giant roach, we got a fine for littering. Mother cursed that cop and his entire generational line forever.

Things settled down after a while, my father drove mute the rest of the way, and even Mother said little. As soon as we arrived, she went into action finding us rooms, and when at last we found a place, my father emptied the car as quickly as he had filled it in the Bronx then disappeared for the night.

Living arrangements in Rockaway were tight the summer of my gypsy experience. We were far back from the boardwalk, maybe two city blocks, in a large turn-of-the-century Tudor-style frame house with a wraparound porch. The house was broken up into several apartments; ours was upstairs. Often we shared a central bathroom with another person or couple, but that summer we were lucky; the one remaining room down the hall did not rent. My mother and father slept in a tiny bedroom, a closet really, with the baby. Tante and Uncle slept in another closet, and I was lucky to have a whole cubbyhole to myself—that is, until the weekend when my older cousins came out to spend time at the beach. Then we were eight, stuffed into three rooms.

My mother and her sister got along pretty well—except for cooking. Despite the cramped, stifling heat of the windowless kitchen, Tante felt compelled each night to prepare a hot Turkish meal for Ovadiah, like braised, round-bone lamb, or meat-stuffed tomatoes. This irritated Mother, who said she would have been happy to serve cold tuna sandwiches until September. The minute one of them lit the pilot light on the ancient, crusty stove, insults in Spanish and English flew. They'd mutter throughout the arduous food preparation, washing, chopping, dicing, baking, and cursing, until Uncle roused himself and roared, "SULTANA!" It cut off the bickering, which was good, because it was all he had the guts to say.

It was a summer of secrets. My dad and I had a secret about going to the local pool hall together on Wednesdays; Mother and the baby had a secret language between the two of them; and I had a secret vendetta against my brother, whom I knew ruined our lives. But the biggest, most highly guarded secret was the one Tante Sultana and Mother shared concerning a relative who had made a Gentile girl pregnant. I was exceptionally good at finding things out and tried my best to disclose this story, but I never managed to piece the information together.

The way they were so hushed up about it and spoke behind their hands told me it was big. I caught words that were enticing, like "had to get rid of it" and "Gentile girls were trouble"; also, that soon she would "get it over with." The more secretive they became, the more intensely I wanted to know what they were getting rid of. But they were careful. Once, absentmindedly, Mother slipped and said to no one, "This is what happens when you fall for Christians—"

I jumped right in. "What happens?"

"Be quiet! Am I talking to you?"

I wasn't fated to know, but toward the end of August my dad went somewhere on an airplane, alone, "to take care of something." It would have been useless to ask what.

There were few kids my age to play with on the block, and I missed my friends who went to bungalow colonies in the Catskills for the summer.

I especially missed my father, who only came out on Fridays. Once in a while he surprised us by showing up on a Wednesday night, which meant he had won money at the track. I heard him whistle for me as soon as he stepped off the train, blocks away. Thrilled, I started running in the direction of that distinctive whistle — three short, one long — until his tall form came into view. Then I usually fell, hard, and bloodied both knees. But I jumped him anyway, blood, dirt, sand, and all.

On those Wednesdays, even before dinner, he took me swimming in the freezing surf, racing me into the waves. He carried me so far out I could no longer see the red square of blanket on the sand. I blubbered and screamed as he pretended to drown me. Each time he fished me out he promised he wouldn't let go again, and each time I truly believed him. He pointed across the horizon: "Look! There's England!" I followed his finger, looking, and then he dropped me again.

My father's way was to do whatever he wanted; he cared little for rules, regulations, or dinnertime restrictions. If I wanted one, even if I shivered in my wet bathing suit, the sun long gone, he would buy me an ice cream pop from the white-suited Good Humor vendor who walked the sands with a refrigerator case slung across his body. Dad whistled for the ice cream man, and, remarkably, he appeared, even though it was late. I thought this man lived on the beach because at that hour of the evening the beach was empty. My aunts told me that my father suffered awful guilt for years because he kept me out late and let me get cold.

Sometimes we stopped by Abie's Pool Hall on Beach 72nd Street. Abie was a wizened old man with tattoos and only two or three teeth in his mouth. No child, not even a teenager, was allowed inside Abie's Pool Hall at any time. Exceptions were made for the Turk. He wrapped me in a towel, and I sat in an ice-cold bathing suit in the back of the smoky dark pool hall, eating ice cream and watching Dad play.

When we finally went home for dinner, I ate everything they put on my plate without complaint. He winked at me and told Mother he just couldn't understand why she carried on about me. I was so *good*.

Memories return in color. The day I got lost comes back to me in pink and pistachio. Pistachio for the Belgian waffle filled with the ice cream that got smeared all over my white T-shirt that day and pink for the scene I witnessed that morning, the "pink incident."

I happened to catch Mother engaged in a loving embrace with my baby brother. Usually, she was careful not to display too much affection in front of me and quickly stopped if I passed by. But that morning she was so totally absorbed in him that nothing else existed. He sat in her lap as they rocked back and forth in a wooden glider that I'm sure was pink. The baby, mesmerized by her face, stared up at her, touching her. I, too, became transfixed watching them and also from the steady, gentle *she-shh, she-shh* of the rocker on linoleum.

A quick breeze sucked the bedroom curtains, baby-pink with tiny, darker-pink rosebuds embroidered on the valance, into the window where they pasted to the screen. The curtains blew out, sucked in. Even the early morning sky was a rosy pink. Watching, I started to hurt somewhere deep inside my stomach, and it frightened me. I felt like something bad was going to happen.

That's when I dropped the full glass of milk in my hand. All three of us jumped, and Mother, furious, cursed at me. Crying, I screamed back: "You called me a bad word!" Then I ran, afraid of her fury, afraid to be in that room. I don't know why I was so scared; she didn't even come after me.

So I headed for the boardwalk. Although forbidden to step foot near the ocean by myself, I was allowed to go buy ices or a waffle if I came *right back*. Not that they ever checked if I did. I waited for the Belgian waffle to be toasted and packed with pistachio ice cream then walked to the penny arcade. I shouldn't have gone inside, but I did anyway, taking my time, trying to lick each side of the square waffle faster than the ice cream dripped. I watched boys play skee-ball and shoot-'em-up games and was soon bored to death. Finally, reluctantly, I headed home.

I had walked up the porch stairs and opened the door before I realized something was wrong. It looked like our house, but it wasn't. I smelled unfamiliar cooking and heard foreign voices talking. Somehow I had become disoriented and taken the boardwalk ramp on the wrong block. This was easy to do; each street was identical with similar two-story rooming houses lining the block. The same thing on the next block, and the next. I was probably only one or two blocks away from my house, but each time I went back up the ramp I turned right (or left) when I should have gone the opposite way.

By the time I traveled down the fourth wrong ramp I knew I was lost. I don't think I panicked immediately, but when a passerby asked me where I lived, I said I couldn't remember. Something told me I'd get into big trouble if they found out I got lost, so I told the lady a lie, that I wasn't lost, really, I knew how to get home. Nona's prediction, a whole year and a half after she died, had come true.

The trouble with a clairvoyant's vision, and the thing people don't realize, is that, except for moneymaking cup-reading sessions or movie plots, the reader, no matter how gifted, can't take you the whole way. While they may really *see* an event in your future, they can't accurately predict *when*, exactly, that event will occur. So, simply by *knowing*, the course of your life won't change. Not that I remembered her prediction anyway. Had she also told me, "Stay away from gypsies," I might have had a different experience entirely.

I wandered around some more, dazed, unable to find our house. My legs ached more than usual from all the walking up and down ramps and porch steps, and I had to sit down and rest. Bad cramps in the back of my legs, and accompanying exhaustion, became another cause of guilt and recriminations for my mother. She, as well as my aunt, neglected to pay attention to my complaining about the on-and-off aching pains, especially when walking up stairs. They laughed when I whined about it, calling me *selosa*, jealous, because of the baby. "All for attention," Mother said.

Afterwards, and for the next two decades, the mysterious leg cramps were a topic she wouldn't let go of. Mother was tormented thinking she could have prevented my polio if only she had listened. If only she knew. Like a fortune teller's prediction. The Council held regular Turkish coffee sessions about it, with Aunt Allegre sitting at the head of the kitchen table in silent, tight-lipped judgment, even though doctors never confirmed that muscle pains prior to the acute stages of the disease portended polio. Everyone was ignorant when it came to explaining the origins of the disease. My leg cramps were catalogued as another piece of polio's unsolved puzzle.

The old-lady gypsy motioned with her finger for me to come in. I had started to cry, sitting with my knees up under my chin, rocking back and forth, when I heard her call, "Little girl!" They had been watching me wander back and forth in front of their house for some time. I knew they were gypsies the minute I saw them. Once a similar-looking family, also wearing colorful skirts and head scarves, had taken up residence in a storefront adjacent to Joe's Religious Book Store on 170th Street. Whenever I passed I peeked in, although they had covered the windows almost entirely in red construction paper. I'd press my face to the glass to see what they were up to; usually, they were eating and laughing. The men were always home.

"That's because gypsies don't work at real jobs," Mother said.

"What do they do?" I asked.

"They steal wristwatches and little girls. Stay away."

Shortly, they were evicted, and a boring leather goods store took their place, but while they lasted I found them fascinating to spy on.

The Rockaway Beach gypsies laughed a lot, too. When I walked in, they laughed, but I didn't feel that they were making fun of me. I felt as if I were being welcomed. It was a ground-floor apartment with its own entrance adjacent to the porch steps of a big old house. The door had been left open, probably because there were so many of them crowded into that one room. I saw at least two old women and one *very* old man who looked like a skeleton. I guessed he was head of the family from the way everyone brought him things. The older women wore red-printed bandannas similar to Grandma Behora's *yemeni*, minus the spangles, and everyone was sitting on the floor, eating. One woman ripped off chunks of bread with her teeth, making tiny pieces for the toothless grandfather to swallow whole.

Who knows what calculations went on in my seven-year-old brain? I can only guess that, right from the start, I felt comfortable with these people. There was no element of fear or insecurity, and I thought: I have found a real family to live with. My decision was made. I no longer felt lost. Secretly, I vowed to be good and not get into any trouble, so they'd love me and keep me always.

Even their language felt a little familiar. Although I couldn't understand a word of it, I kept hearing the harsh zh sound, like that of our own Spanish, in their conversations. Then two younger women who had been arguing quietly in a corner got louder, and their words erupted into a fight. I felt right at home!

There was a girl about my age who I decided would be the sister I had always wanted. When they brought my brother home from the hospital, I was crushed, hoping it was a mistake. My new sister coughed profusely, never once covering her mouth. Each time she coughed I wished her, "Oras buenas!" Good health! It was a customary blessing when you coughed in our house. The old woman laughed when I kept repeating it, and she patted the mattress next to her, for me to sit down.

She handed me a demitasse cup filled with pale tea. I hated tea, but I drank it to be polite and also because it looked just like our Turkish coffee cup. Later, when they pounded me with questions, Mother shaking my shoulders so hard I thought my head would fall off, demanding to know if I ate or drank anything with those "filthy gypsies," I lied and swore I did not.

I don't know how long I was actually with them, but it was long enough for the card-playing men to change positions. One of the boys strummed a banjo that reminded me of Uncle Jaime's oud. He sang to himself in a soft voice, and even though he sang the same tune over and over, nobody told him to shut up. They may have looked a bit strange, but I thought they seemed *happy*.

That day I forgot all about time, of which there are three kinds: there's running time, when the day just goes by, ordinary, with nothing special happening until you go to bed; there's fast time, when you're having so much fun spending the day with gypsies that time escapes, and you can't believe how late it got; and there's stopped time. This is time no child should have to experience, and soon enough it's the kind of time I would endure. This time happens when your parents are having such a brawl you think it will never end or you're in hospital time. That's when minutes pass so very slowly you can see the second hand on a watch actually slip down a notch. But when you look again, hours and hours later, it's still, unbelievably, at that very same notch.

In fast time I had no idea that it was late afternoon by the time my new friend-sister took my hand and said, "Let's go." When she got up, I saw that she was so skinny her slip of a dress could fit two girls. She had dark circles under her eyes, dirt rings around her neck, and grayish quarter-moons under her fingernails. Just then I heard Tante Allegre's disgusted whisper in my ear: "*Filth!*" I didn't care what color her neck was. She liked me. We stepped over her relatives and, hand in hand, made our way to the boardwalk.

On our walk I noticed the sports section of the *Daily Mirror* scattered open on a bench. Impulsively, wanting to impress her, I snatched it up and showed off by reading out loud, as Dad had taught me, the names of horses racing that day at Aqueduct Race Track. She seemed pretty impressed, especially when I told her I was not yet in third grade.

By then everyone on our block, Beach 70th Street, was searching for me. Aunt Allegre, who lived one block over, on Beach 71st Street, had been notified. She ran back and forth in front of the ocean, fearing the worst. Other Turks and even strangers raced up and down the boardwalk calling my name. My "gypsy adventure" was a big topic among the busybodies for the next few days.

I had only wandered as far as Beach 78th Street, actually, but for the panic it caused it could have been Bulgaria. My friend—if she had a name, I don't think I ever knew it—had an endless supply of dimes and pennies she didn't mind sharing with me. I had seen her scoop them out of a big sack in their room. She knew how to play every game in the penny arcade, including winning skee-ball every time. I was thrilled she paid for everything because a part of me knew, if I ever saw my mother again, that this would please her.

My mother loved money, always talked about having it or being "treated" to things. Pleasing Mother would become a theme in my life and also something I would never be able to accomplish. I had something to prove even at seven, even before I could put a name to what that meant.

Sultana spotted me first. She might have cried, "Thank God!" or "There she is!" I don't know. I just know I'll never forget the *sound* of their screams. The girl and I were in the process of having our fortunes told by the mechanical granny in the glass booth, even though I tried to tell her to save her money, that my dead nona had been the real thing and had told me not to spend a dime on fakes. Just as the little white cards popped out of the slots, before we got a chance to read our future, I heard them.

It was the call of the Bedouin women of the Sahara, and I'm sure they heard it there, too. Everyone on the boardwalk stopped and turned to stare. I froze in place, and so did my friend. Dumbly, we watched as two middle-aged, heavyset women, not far from where we stood, rocked and cried, wringing their hands and alternately pulling their hair. People gathered around but made a space for them as they advanced toward us on those stout legs.

I hoped it meant they were happy to see me! I braced myself for the onslaught of hugs and kisses and turned to tell my friend who these hysterical women were, but she was gone. The gypsy girl had simply evaporated. They grabbed me, crushing me to their bosoms, kissing me everywhere. Then each one took a turn examining me, holding me at arm's length to see if I was okay.

"De tu kaza no te mankes!" they said in unison. May you never be missing from your home!

There was that auspicious Ladino blessing again. Suddenly, my joy over feeling loved and missed came to an end. As I stood cushioned between their bulging bellies, they proceeded to slap me back and forth like a Ping-Pong ball, calling me a million names in mixed Turkish and Spanish: "Hija del werko!" Daughter of Satan! "Mazalbashiada!" Lower than a low-luck individual! "Espantozika!" Fear bringer! And more.

I never saw the girl or her gypsy family again. Daily, I searched for them, memorizing some thing, like a strange-looking tree stump or a colorful porch towel, so I wouldn't get lost a second time. But I never found them. The entire clan just vanished.

Life got a little harder for me after that. Mother subsequently hired two surly teenage girls to "watch" me. I hated them, and they definitely didn't like me, pinching me hard whenever they felt like it. They warned me not to tell or I'd get worse. They whispered constantly, heads stapled together, shutting me out of their "secret" conversations. Often I was forced to sit still in the heat while I watched them braid and unbraid each other's hair. This was much worse than being lonely. Whenever I could, I slipped away, even though I paid for it later.

On Sunday of Labor Day weekend the Turks on our street threw their annual block party that officially marked the end of summer. There were cheese and spinach borekas, meat pies, raki for the grownups to get drunk on, and plenty of pastries from the Greek and Turkish pastacheros. Someone hauled out a scratchy old phonograph and that same Port Said record album we had at home, with the half-naked woman on the cover. Then some Turk would begin to chant like a Muslim called to prayer, and the belly dancing began.

There were always a couple of belly dancers in the crowd, young women who were born to undulate. My father danced with all of them.

I have pictures of him bending back double or lifting sultry, dark-eyed women high in the air with one arm. He threw his back out doing this every summer. People came from all over the Rockaway neighborhood to see our Turkish party. Mother got disgusted when the non-Turks tried belly dancing, inviting her ridicule in Spanish. The party lasted all night.

But by noon on Monday it was as if it had never happened. There wasn't a trace of food, streamers, paper lanterns, cups, or spoons anywhere. All decorations were put away for next year, and everyone was in their bungalow or apartment packing. They had had enough summer.

Everything that happened to me that year is etched into sensory memory: the salt-smell during low tide, the hot-hot sand that involuntarily made my feet jump, and the creamy taste of a melting pistachio waffle. Each year I'd take the roaring surf back home with me in the form of a certain graceful shell that contained the whole ocean inside of it. Cupped to my ear, in my familiar bed, I'd fall asleep with the sea.

Entire days were spent by that sea, on that beach, until the skies turned violet and not one person or blanket remained. I can see and hear Tante Sultana plunking her beach chair in the sand, opening her arms wide to greet the ocean, and crying, "Aire! Aire!" as if it were the first time she'd ever smelled ocean.

Despite my baby brother and the unexplainable, crushing jealousy he produced that gripped my heart, the Summer of Gypsies was my best summer. It was the last time my body felt like me. I would soon forget what feeling physical was like.

You weren't supposed to admit it, certainly not to your friends, if you were anxious for school to start. I couldn't wait. I wondered who would be in my class, what teacher I'd have, and which books we'd read. By then I longed for my Bronx bedroom, which always appeared smaller to me after the summer. Mostly, I wanted my school supplies, especially the new, unmarked, salt-and-pepper notebooks to write words and poems in.

Who could have known, except maybe my dead grandma, that third grade would begin without me?

De el ke tuvo y no tiene, adjideate. Pity the
one who once had and no longer has.

LADINO PROVERB

4 ❀ Contagious

We assembled in the cafeteria on a brilliant day in May 1954, just before
Memorial Day weekend. The old public school building steamed in an
early, murderous heat, as only New York buildings do, and thin rivulets
of water, which she blotted with a folded pink hanky, ran down the
sides of my teacher's face. Even the dull-painted, mucous-green walls
seemed to sweat with a greasy shine.

They had flung open every window, but no matter how I gasped for
it no air entered. We stood breathless, row after row of kids, shifting
from one foot to the other, trying to avoid each other's body heat by
"accidentally" knocking into the girl or boy in front so as to push him
away; he then knocked into the kid in front of him, and so on. My thin
summer dress stuck like glue to the back of my thighs, and in front of
me I saw that Howie's pale-blue shirt had turned a darker blue in the
middle, pasted with sweat to his back.

A nurse and a doctor sat side by side at the head of the row. The
nurse held a huge needle like a gun ready to go off. Before each shot
she spurted liquid from the needle into the air. Some crybabies sniffled;
I deny being one of them because a photographer with a camera in front
of his face was circling the cafeteria snapping our pictures, and I didn't

want to come out like a baby. I loved having my picture taken. We were to be dismissed as soon as we got our injections, so I tried thinking of that as I stood still, melting.

When he got to our row, the man taking pictures said, "Stick out your arm and smile, *like a big, happy cheese!*" which we did, then he blinded us with white. I kept on smiling, as if I couldn't *wait* to get that ten-foot needle jabbed into me.

Earlier, before we trekked to the cafeteria, Mrs. Golden announced to the class that we were very very lucky to have been chosen for a "special test" that was going to help children everywhere. She never called it an experiment. This test, she said, would end a terrible contagious disease, and we should be proud of ourselves for taking part in it. We would now be known as "Polio Pioneers." We had even dressed up for inoculation day.

Some of us may have been lucky. The word luck, *mazál* in Ladino, was a word I'd hear all too often in the coming months. As they say: *mazál no puede fuir dingunos de su destino*, no one escapes his destiny. In early September, right before third grade, during the Week of the Six Days, a holy week prior to the Jewish New Year, my fate was inscribed in the Book of Life, and I came down with that "terrible contagious disease" Mrs. Golden had alluded to.

I was the last kid in America to catch polio. Or so my family believed. Teams of research scientists sacrificed over seventeen thousand rhesus and cynomolgus monkeys, devoted three decades, and spent millions to develop a viable vaccine, but they were too late for me. I and thousands of other *povres*, luckless souls, caught it during the last big epidemic of 1954, even as the results of the first successful field trials to test the new vaccine were being evaluated. By 1955 ten thousand fewer cases were diagnosed, and by the end of the 1950s polio was virtually wiped out in this country.

I fell sick soon after Labor Day. There was little known then about how one actually caught polio, but some doctors thought that I probably had been incubating the virus back in July, when I complained about those aching calf muscles. My mother and her sisters, even my dad, tortured themselves afterward. Not so much with the why of it but with the how: *How* could I have caught it?

Another possibility, obviously: the family of gypsies that day I got lost in Rockaway—not so much that they were dirty but more in the belief that they put a curse of infection on me. Then, too, the Council agreed, I could have become ill when Nona Behora predicted it—at that exact moment. She read it in my cup, and what they saw in the cup was the Word.

I could have picked up the bug myself by foraging in garbage cans, a nasty habit of mine, looking for "treasures." One time, inside a trash bin near the boardwalk, I found a single black suede high-heeled shoe that I thought was beautiful. Impulsively, I carried it home as a gift for Mother. She loved shoes; all she had to do with this one was clean it up a little, and maybe one day we'd find the match. I was shocked to get smacked for my generosity.

My mother, father, and both aunts went back and forth among themselves trying to figure it out, not just when I first got sick but for years afterward. Mostly, it went: "That *brúsha*, that sorceress, made it happen!" from Mother. Dad was sure I caught it at the beach and that he was partially to blame. Of course, he labeled my mother *shasheada*, distracted, and accused her of forgetting about me: "You didn't watch her good!" he said. This she already believed.

It happened during Mother's regular mah-jongg game, on a warm September evening. The actual moment of collapse—when I was "stricken," as they dramatically put it—remains vivid. I had trouble walking all day and also the day before, feeling that my knees were buckling. I tripped a few times. I didn't say anything because I thought they wouldn't have paid attention anyway.

The privilege of building the two-tiered wall of ivory tiles in front of each player's rack was given to the child whose mother hosted the game. I loved mah-jongg and was learning to recognize the tiles as they called them out: "Three Bam!" "Two Crack!" "Mah-Jongg!" Sometimes, if Mother was winning and in a very good mood, as she was that night, she'd let me walk around the table with the "bettor" and choose a probable winner.

But that night I barely made it down the short foyer without falling and had to hold onto both walls. Every step felt strange; these, I thought, are someone's else's legs, not mine. My knees buckled, I straightened them, they buckled again. Then, at the card table, as I busily turned over the tiles, like you were supposed to before mixing them together and building a wall, I simply folded, like an accordion, and dropped.

Three women, including Mother, played that night: Pearl, the dentist's wife, Allegre's daughter-in-law, Cousin Dottie, and Mother's best friend, Bernice. They were short one player, so I looked forward to walking around during the game, "betting" on the winner. They were all good, fast players who smoked throughout, and the air in our living room was dense from stale cigarettes. I was finding it hard to breathe before I fell; first I got hot, then I felt cold. Finally, I lay in a heap on the carpet, dazed and unable to move. Nobody helped me either.

"Get up!" Mother said, finally. I could tell she was annoyed that I hadn't done my job of wall building quickly; we were a speedy bunch, with no use for *avagarikos*, slowpokes. Finally, Pearl suggested that maybe I wasn't kidding. Only then did my mother take a good look at me.

"I'll give you one more second to get up, or you're going to bed!" she said. But this time her voice cracked. I looked up at her. We locked eyes. Mother stamped out her cigarette.

I can imagine how terrified those women were when they realized what was happening. Except for Bernice, a tall, immaculately dressed "businesswoman," as Mother referred to her, they had children who'd come into contact with me. Dottie and my cousin Allison, who was my brother's age, were always in and out of our apartment. And Pearl's husband, Dr. Steinberg, had his fingers probing the inside of my mouth just the other day.

I had on long-sleeved pink flannel pajamas dotted with bright-red strawberries. I'll never forget them because I fought against wearing them, whining about it being too hot—which was true—for winter pajamas. These pajamas, like other items I later searched for, mysteriously disappeared after that night. Mother was known to overdress me in her attempt to ward off drafts. Pearl even remarked, "Why is this child in winter pajamas, Rose? It's not exactly February, you know. Look at her; she's dizzy from the heat!"

This particular scene—the building of the interrupted ivory wall, the women's chitchat, their thick cigarette smoke, and my warm strawberry pajamas—is etched in memory, sharp as the delicate bird that is chiseled on a Flower tile.

I lay there waiting for someone to help me, holding in my clenched hand either a Soap or a Red Dragon tile that I had pulled off the table when I went down. I did not let go of this mah-jongg tile until I passed out, and that's probably why I hallucinated over them in the days that followed. The Soap, a blank white tile with a blue border around it, visited me first as a doorway and next as a "cigarette man's" placard, like the ones union strikers wore on their backs picketing or advertising Chesterfields in front of the Luxor theater. The Red Dragon, my favorite tile, became a predictably large dragon and then a smaller one in dreams, always ominous.

I couldn't move my legs. I remember thinking, right before I lost consciousness, how strange that was. In fact, nothing on me moved, not even my fingers, but I wasn't immediately aware of it. I just felt so tired. Any minute now, I thought, I'll get up and finish building the walls. My eyes blurred before the blackness came but not before the realization that somehow, again, I had gotten into big trouble and would get the *haftonáh* of my life for it. This was my fear, and it was well-founded. Like a cascading wall of mah-jongg tiles, all our lives smashed open.

The women fled, Dr. Hirschfeld was called, and the next thing I remember is waking up in my own bed and seeing his scowling face bent over me. I asked him if I was sick and what time it was. The doctor sighed and shook his head. He didn't look as grumpy as usual, nor did he answer me. That question marked the beginning of my obsession with Time. In coming months I would persistently ask the time of whomever came near, wherever I happened to be.

The doctor backed up, away from me, and did the strangest thing when he left: He tried to close the bedroom door so that it clicked shut. Didn't he know we *never* closed doors? Not even the bathroom door. Dr. Hirschfeld tugged and pulled, but of course it wouldn't shut. There were a thousand coats of paint on its frame and moldings. Behind the door hung all our bathrobes, two winter coats, a hooded snow jacket, and a bath towel, all on one hook. With his final yank the door shut three-quarters of the way, and all the clothing tumbled to the floor. He stumbled over it on the way out, sliding a little on my brother's flannel robe.

I was surprised not to get one of those painful, backside penicillin injections that he was famous for, as he didn't have the gentlest bedside manner. But, instead, he ran to the telephone in the foyer, and next thing I heard was him barking at Mrs. Bloom to get off the party line she shared with us. Even with a headache that felt worse than any I'd ever had, I smiled. Every day Mother and Mrs. Bloom battled over ownership of the phone line, each one insisting that the other end their conversation and hang up first. Mother insulted her, calling her the vilest Spanish names she could think of, and "talkative bitch," among other things, in English. Nothing fazed the old lady; she never backed down, and she never hung up first.

Mrs. Bloom, however, was no match for Dr. Hirschfeld. He freed the line right away with a final, booming "Geb acht!"

During the next few hours scenes went in and out of focus. It was early morning, yet, curiously, our house was ablaze with lights. Everything seemed to be out of order and confusing until the ambulance came; then I was awake and alert. Two tall attendants, a man and a woman, in white uniforms and face masks, took me out. They moved so fast there wasn't time to be frightened. Before I knew it I was on a stretcher heading down the stairs. They threw a sheet over my face and hair.

I felt as if I were sliding off the stretcher. Scared I would bounce down the stairs feet first, I instinctively shot out my left arm and grabbed for the banister. That's how I knew that at least one part of me could still move. They shoved my arm back under the sheet, I stuck it out; they pushed it back, I worked it out. This went on two or three times. Then I tried to blow the sheet off my face because I couldn't breathe right. It made them mad.

"Is she stupid?" the woman with the strange accent spoke. I had never heard an accent like hers; she was Filipino, as were all the doctors who examined me in the next twenty-four hours. The man said nothing.

So I kept still, not wanting to be stupid, praying not to suffocate. As we approached the lobby door, although it was quite warm out, I felt cold—colder than at any other time in my life. Why, I thought, am I outside in winter without a coat? From afar I thought I heard my mother wailing.

At the time I caught polio nobody knew how the disease spread. General opinion was that it thrived in water, which was the reason why public pools and a lot of beaches around the country customarily closed in summertime during 1952 and 1954, the years of the big epidemics. Many thought the virus was airborne, that one just had to be in the vicinity of somebody who harbored it in order to breathe it in.

The polio virus itself was quirky and a mystery. There were more things doctors could not explain than they knew for sure. Like why, in some households, the children caught the disease immediately from one another, while in other families only one child caught it, or a mother or father, but the rest of the siblings stayed well. While I lay paralyzed but able to breathe, teenage twin sisters, both in iron lungs, watched each other die; across the country a healthy boy attended the funeral of his identical twin brother, who did not escape the virus. Out of a brood of seven children six might have caught polio, while the seventh never got it. And many times people caught polio who never even knew they had it because it masked as a bad flu virus. These lucky souls completely recovered as if they had had only a common cold.

Everyone thought dirt was the culprit. Long after the known cause of the disease was made public, and it was determined that the virus passed through the gastrointestinal tract and wasn't airborne or carried through contaminated water, people held onto the belief that if they were scrupulously clean they could avoid it. Polio and filth were synonymous. The worst-case scenario was that of neglect: If you weren't clean enough, you might have contributed to your own child's terrible illness.

What wasn't done for me that should have been? Was I kept clean enough? Watched carefully enough? Apparently not, or I wouldn't have foraged in garbage cans or spent a whole day with gypsies. Did I eat properly? Certainly not; I ate poorly, had to be cajoled into it, and then ate little. Especially, did Mother ever let me borrow an item of clothing from a friend? This her sisters constantly grilled her about.

The Spanish Jews from Turkey had a long history behind the borrowing of clothes. When they arrived in America at the turn of the century, along with all the other immigrants, including Eastern European Jews, our people were really a minority among minorities, the poorest among the poor. From the time they stepped on the boat in Greece, Turkey, or the Dardanelles, they kept to themselves, stayed away from Ashkenazim and apart from other Sephardis who weren't from their hometowns. One odd thing was that many fell ill with disease and died in greater numbers than Ashkenazim who lived under similar slum conditions.

A cause for this, Sephardic leaders thought, was because the Turks purchased used, secondhand clothing from peddlers that was probably contaminated with disease. The problem of infection and illness got so bad, finally, that the editor of a popular Ladino newspaper, *La America*, posted a warning to his readers to immediately stop the practice of buying used clothing from strangers. This might have saved the lives of some families.

Contamination notwithstanding, the simple, scientific truth was that the polio virus, unlike other contagious diseases, actually flourished in clean, developed countries like ours, where good hygiene was practiced. We were a super-sanitized society and had been for decades, which made us more susceptible to disease. The population had no immunity against polio, as in other, poverty-ridden countries, where children were protected simply because sanitation was poor and they were constantly exposed to disease.

None of my family gave a damn about scientific information—not then, not ever. Aunt Allegre believed that everything could be prevented with *limpieza*, being immaculate, which she was. Sultana was sloppy but usually didn't worry about anything. Mother wasn't a fastidious housekeeper by any means, but of the three she was the most terrified of disease and knew that all people carried it. She believed everyone was contagious.

This affected her personality and embarrassed me. I did not know how she could act so rude to my playmates, so ill-tempered toward them and children in general. She didn't trust the health of a single kid in our building nor in surrounding buildings. She also didn't favor me playing with strange kids in the park. It's a wonder I was allowed to attend school. If a friend let out a sudden sneeze or looked as if they were about to, she snatched me away. Pestilence, *germs*, lurked everywhere, including inside those who appeared to be healthy. Of course, this made me a target for taunts. Kids enjoyed putting their faces directly in front of mine and fake-sneezing: *Ha-choo!* spitting right on me.

The only thing I knew about contagion was that if you played with a friend who had the chicken pox you'd catch it too and you'd itch all over. If you walked around *deskalsa*, without shoes or slippers, a chill would creep from the bottom up. If you sweated excessively while playing ball, well, *sudados*, the sweats, were just as dangerous as the chills. And if you tried on someone else's shoes, your toes might rot. I recognized early on that my mother was crazier in this regard than my schoolmates' mothers, but what could I do? If a girlfriend even *looked* pale, Mother threw her out. Once she caught me licking Harriet's lollipop and almost choked me with the collar of my dress as she yanked me away. Thereafter I did stuff like that only behind her back.

I already knew there were horrible things out there and that I'd better watch it, but I never knew exactly what those things were nor how I could prevent them from finding me. The women in the building whom Mother chatted with as they rocked their carriages always gossiped about three things: some people named "Rosenberg"; Russia, the country that could "drop the bomb on us"; and the terrible polio epidemic. My misinformation told me that the Rosenbergs, who lived in Russia, were probably going to bomb us. In school, because of that threat, we had to take cover under our desks at least once a week as part of the mock air-raid drills. Mother hated the fact that I had to crawl on the floor, but I loved it. The thought of getting bombed was so exciting! My friends and I were completely shielded from the reality of the Cold War, as we were from the details of the Rosenberg trial, their executions, and the terror of polio.

Of all the topics, when the women spoke of polio their voices lowered an octave. This, I gathered, was worse than the Bomb or Communism. Several newspapers gave weekly tallies of those felled by the disease, and the numbers, in the thousands, were astounding.

Toward the summer of 1954, as word spread that the epidemic was getting worse, I was given a whole new set of rules and warnings: Don't dare drink from a public water fountain in any park, at school, or when visiting the zoo. Be sure to sit at least one seat apart in the movies, and never share popcorn. If the theater gets overcrowded, it will get hot, and then you have to come home. Do not put even your big toe into a public wading pool, and don't play with anyone, not *anyone*, who sneezes! All that the list of "don't do *this* or you'll catch *that*" did was leave me with many more questions about sickness than they had answers for. I wanted specifics; for instance, do you turn red from scarlet fever? Does polio have anything to do with poles? (I thought maybe it happened if you leaned against a dirty telephone pole.) What does a polio body look like?

"You don't need to know about that, thank God," was the adults' reply most times. Polio was another secret in a world of them.

The year my brother, Charlie, was born, 1952, saw America's worst epidemic of infantile paralysis. It wasn't called "polio" until the field trials two years later. Over fifty thousand people came down with the disease, and I think the cycle of fear began for us then. There were awful stories every day about children dying, but I wasn't allowed to know more than they wanted to tell. Being an early reader, I did pick up some stuff just by sitting on Dad's lap while he read the *News* or the *Mirror*.

I pictured Disease as a monster with no eyes, like the one from Turkish ghost stories Nona Behora told, and later like the ones my teenage babysitters told me at night in the dark, to purposely scare me. I thought it must be like a kind of oversized hairy bug, and this image pervaded my dreams long before I got sick. I was a happy-go-lucky troublemaker by day, but I always suffered from bad nightmares and, occasionally, sleepwalking, which ran in the family.

My father sleepwalked also. For the rest of his life after World War II, he landed planes in his sleep. In the middle of the night he'd walk into the living room with his hat on, as if he were still in Greenland or Goose Bay, Labrador, and he'd guide the planes in to their safe landings. Then he'd take off his hat and go back to bed.

I dreamt often of a nebulous mass oozing into town in the dark of night; it crawled up the steep Bronx hills; it crossed the Grand Concourse; it searched and searched until it found my block and my building. Then the ugly glob—sometimes I dreamt it was a human "bomb"—slithered up the front stoop. Often it stopped at my friend Ellen's apartment one floor below mine, squeezed itself under her door, and knocked her down. On the worst nights it crawled up to Apartment 3A, my house, and found its way inside my bed, finally covering me like a blanket until I woke up yelling, my heart beating outside my chest.

The only way to stop being afraid of these things was to play them out. A bunch of us put on full-scale productions in the lobby, which was a terrific "theater" because of its marble benches and vast space. This was our hospital room and the bench our stretcher, examining, and operating table all in one. We'd fight, eeny-meany-miney-moe style, for the roles of Doctor and Nurse, but the sick Polio Child, always paralyzed and near death, was the very best part. For some reason none of us wanted to play the mother or the father who arrived at the hospital to take their child home. Probably because it was a long wait until those parts were "on."

After a lifesaving operation the deathbed child got up and walked. Always. Then, from someone's brilliant directorial impulse, we bombed the hospital—or else it was the Rosenbergs who did—creating a racket loud enough to get us thrown out to the street. In bed at night, though, I continued to wonder how it really felt to actually be as sick as the "patients" we played.

Polio's worst curse wasn't death. It was confinement and deformity. *Confined to a wheelchair. Locked into braces. He will walk with braces and crutches for the rest of his life.* These were the snatches of conversations we heard day after day. Victims of polio were left with all forms of maiming: shrunken legs, a limp, shriveled, useless arms. You didn't know how you'd be ravaged until the acute stage passed, and that took anywhere from two weeks to two months. Almost everyone who got the paralytic kind of polio was left with some residual damage. I had heard of these pathetic individuals so often over the years that when I got sick I wondered, but was too scared to ask, if either of my parents ever secretly wished I had died immediately, rather than become crippled.

If you caught polio, you'd be deformed or wind up sitting forever in a wheelchair, but even that wasn't the worst that could happen. The worst was not being able to breathe. Then you'd never leave something called an "iron lung." *That* was confinement. I could not accurately fix a picture of an iron lung machine in my mind—a chair with wheels was easy—and when I finally saw one in the hospital, it was worse than I thought.

The blessed walked out of the hospital on their own power; the cursed were pushed out. The hope for me in those early days was for total recovery. It had happened before, but if it didn't, my aunts and uncles believed—they insisted—that I would still, certainly, get married. Even as I lay near death, my physical fate as yet unknown, they talked about my future wedding. I guess that's what kept them going.

The most important thing for a girl was to find a nice *mansevo*. Their blessing, *Novia ke te vega! I should see you a bride!* was uttered after everything I did—cute, artistic, or otherwise. When I entertained by singing Sophie Tucker songs, they wished me a bride; when I belly danced, they wished me a bride; when I came home from school with a poem or a picture my teacher had praised, they blessed me *to become a bride*. After polio they never said it to me again.

Nor did anyone suggest I might become president of the United States, like that other famous polio victim. After all, I was still a girl. They did try appeasing Mother by citing Roosevelt's shining example of recovery: He walked, and so would I! There were many, in fact, most of the people in this country, who hadn't figured out what some already knew, that our late president *never* walked again. He wore two full-length braces and had canes, plus he always needed an arm to lean on, so he was really *confined to a wheelchair*. Roosevelt perpetrated a major sham in his day and did a terrific acting job of "passing." Helpers, who traveled everywhere with him, kept him propped up at podiums during speeches. All his life Roosevelt denied being a cripple. He acted as if he'd never had polio or else as if it was over and done with. In a few short years I'd act the same.

We were such an extroverted bunch, so physically oriented, so crazy about dancing, singing, and acting out pantomimes of friends and relatives, that the thought of one among us being hobbled was absurd. What about dancing? This was a big question. Our family gathered nearly every Sunday to watch me belly dance in our living room. They clapped and yelled *Opa!* as I spun around in my miniature blue costume, with its multiple blue veils, a replica of Little Egypt's. I was, after all, the sultan's favorite, and the Dance of the Seven Veils was my best number.

The haunting question, and much bigger issue, was not whether or not I'd ever dance again but whether or not I'd *walk*. What were all the blessings for, those prayers of protection, the *Mashallás* that repeatedly invoked our God, plus Allah, and all the spirits from Beyond? Why hadn't the countless Ladino incantations, muttered while chomping their curled forefingers, warded off evil green-blue eyes that looked upon me? Why hadn't the red ribbons, cloves, garlic pouches, and *pooh-pooh* spits in my face saved me from what no one in my family could face, the possibility of me being a *kósha*, lame for life?

Actually, we already had a *kósha* in the family, a woman named Regina, who was a third cousin to me, who caught polio as an adult. When they spoke about her, it was in Ladino only, the language used for subjects too scary in English. "Regina, the *kósha* who walks with a limp," they said, as if it were her entire name; or, "Regina who drags her leg." After saying her name, of course, they bit their curled fingers and added, "Leshos y apartados!" Let her affliction be far and away from us! I became very curious about polio then, trying to imagine Regina's walk. Naturally, I had to act it out, exaggerating my gait in how I surmised a "dragged leg" walked. Mother shook me until my teeth rattled.

"Never do that again!" Her fear was enormous.

My dad said that Regina got sick because her own father cursed her when she defied him by marrying an Italian. He not only stopped speaking to his only daughter because of her intermarriage, but he actually sat *shiva* for her, on boxes in their living room, for the full seven-day mourning period, and covered every mirror in the house with a sheet. But when she caught polio, her faithful Christian husband stuck by her and nursed her back to health. Eventually, Regina's father relented, and they reconciled. All would have lived happily ever after, except for one thing: Regina was still, would always be, a *kósha*.

Catching polio was high tragedy. If asked, what's the worst that could happen, their answer would have been "This." Word of the plight of Rabbi Sedacca's granddaughter, *la bailadéra*, the little belly dancer, who lived on the Grand Concourse, spread quickly through the Greek chorus of Bronx Turks. My grandfather's reputation was holy; most Sephardis knew him as the *tzaddik*, a man of charity and kindness, who performed *meldados* for people, the *kaddish* prayers for the dead, in their homes. A lot of people in the community owned one of his handwritten prayers of protection, sewn into pieces of fabric that he himself had pinned on their clothing.

Prayers were said for me daily in Sephardic synagogues from Brooklyn to Istanbul. Above the Luxor Movie Theater the card players at the Sephardic Social Club held a special meeting to discuss the tragedy and what could be done for our family; they took up a collection. My two Christian friends, Valerie and Karen, went to church with their mothers and lit candles for me. News of my sickness and the accompanying fear that always went with it rushed like an electric current through town. A yearly public dread and once-distant epidemic had become personal.

Families who didn't know us, and those who did, panicked. Everyone knew someone who knew a friend who had a child that knew me from school or had once played on my block. If anyone else in my school caught polio during that September or went through the same ostracization our family did, we never heard about it. All we knew was that people referred to 1410 Grand Concourse as a tainted building where "that little girl caught polio." There were rumors that people moved out, and, because this actually happened around the country during polio season, it was probably true. People relocated in order to stay a step ahead of the virus.

Our closest neighbors, the ones we interacted with every day, bought industrial-strength disinfectant and scrubbed down their doors, as if that would bar the microbes from seeping in. But they were resigned to their fate, figuring they lived so close, they were finished anyway. All the neighborhood held its collective breath, expecting polio to claim another victim. Some parents tried to avert it by keeping their kids home from school the whole month of September, even though I hadn't been inside the school building in over three months.

Family doctors and local clinics found themselves catering to hysterics. Mothers stormed their offices demanding some kind of preventive treatment. No one was brave enough to visit Dr. Hirschfeld's office in the lobby of my building, but his other office, two blocks over, was mobbed every day. Everyone lined up to get very painful injections of gamma globulin, a blood protein that acted as an antibody and sometimes offered a short-term immunity to polio. They begged for double doses. One day crabby Dr. Hirschfeld got so fed up with panicked parents that he shooed them all out and closed the office.

The Salk vaccine was minutes away from being perfected, but the wait was excruciating. Only second-graders, the age group most often stricken, had been inoculated, but after I caught it everyone wanted the shots, experimental or not. There was at least one person in each household sure he or she was coming down with it: mothers, fathers, babysitters, delivery people, and building superintendents. Each soul believed itself to be symptomatic, had muscle aches, neck pains, and imagined fevers and chills.

That fall mothers with children in PS 64 mobilized. Some telephoned round-robin, relaying the latest information and gossip, while others joined the Mothers March on Polio, a positive-action highly publicized media event that President Roosevelt had begun in the 1930s. Movie stars and politicians appeared locally in person and on TV and radio, urging people to donate money for the development of the vaccine. During my hospital experience I'd meet a couple of these celebrities myself. Magazine and newspaper photos featured stylish, middle-aged women in neat suits and little hats, gathered around the likes of Grace Kelly, Lana Turner, Elvis, or some other famous personality.

Those who didn't make it into the spotlight went door to door on their own or in groups throughout their neighborhoods, collecting for the March of Dimes. Bands of women trekked up and down flights of stairs every day, and, as added incentive for people to give generously, they carried with them large posters of adorable boys and girls on crutches, wearing metal leg braces. These beautiful, crippled children stood proud and straight as possible or sat in wheelchairs, which heightened their tiny vulnerability. All were highly photogenic; they were picked for that.

One poignant poster showed a semi-toothless, freckled boy in a cowboy hat, standing with a crutch under each armpit, smiling bravely. "THIS FIGHT IS YOURS!" was the caption under his picture, and in the background stood a huge, scowling GI in combat gear with rifle. The "FIGHT POLIO!" poster girls, in their delicate, puffed-sleeve dresses and matching hair ribbons, couldn't have been prettier. One look at these courageous little people, with their luminous wide eyes and their own braces as badges of courage, and your heart caved in. Children who, in another life, would have surely modeled clothes or tap-danced their way to fame and fortune.

Thank goodness for those posters. Although I was carefully guarded from seeing one, eventually I did, and that's how I know what I looked like. Otherwise, I never would have; Mother made sure that no such pictures of me were ever taken.

Months later, after all contagion had passed, these women, the same involved and dedicated volunteers who collected door to door, snubbed my mother when they met her in stores or on the street. Some, like Ellen Schumacher's mother, even crossed to the other side when they saw her coming. Either these "friends" lacked the ability to offer a comforting word, or else they retained a permanent, irrational dread of the disease. My mother never got over it. She kept a yearly, running grudge list of those who avoided her because of me and dosed them with her most powerful *maldisyóns*, verbal curses.

The family needed a target to which it could assess blame. My aunts blamed the vanished Rockaway gypsy family, my father blamed my mother, my mother blamed herself, and they all blamed Dr. Jonas Salk for not having his lifesaving vaccine ready in time for me. Although she never managed to prove it, and despite the fact that she went deep into a belief system that supported Turkish superstitions, my mother suspected that the field trial vaccine had given me polio.

There was that significant day in our kitchen, in the winter of 1954, when finally, after much deliberation, Mother signed the consent form from PS 64 that allowed me to participate in the now-famous blind study to test Salk's vaccine. Along with the rest of the children who made history as Polio Pioneers, my parents *requested* that I be inoculated with the experimental serum. That was how it worked; it was a vaccine trial that may or may not save your child from contracting polio—who wouldn't want to try that? Although the field trial was strictly a voluntary participation, and it was never referred to as an "experiment," we truly were the subjects of one.

It worked like this: A certain number of kids in one group received Salk's newly developed killed-virus vaccine, while the same number of children in a separate group got a placebo. Apparently, people had faith that the new vaccine would work because the entire second grade participated. Almost half a million children received the actual vaccine. Something like 10 percent, a much smaller group, got the placebo.

My mother had grave doubts about this blind study for several reasons: One, she felt, rightly, we were being used as guinea pigs; and, two, she wouldn't know until many months into the future which group, real vaccine or placebo, I had been part of. So she dallied a long time before signing the request. Because they considered her, la Amerikana, to be the "brain" of the family, and because her older sisters always looked to her for advice, she couldn't ask their opinion. My father just shrugged and left it to her, as usual: "Whatever you want to do, Rosie," he said.

I remember her sitting at our kitchen table the day she signed the school form. The table was beige Formica with a large, dark-brown diamond shape in the center. My father brought it home one day as a surprise for her, and Mother hated it on sight. They fought bitterly about that table because she knew he won the money for it at the track. When he offered to smash the top with a hammer so she wouldn't have to look at it anymore, she quit finally. We ended up keeping it anyway.

She sat there on the day of the signing, her morning coffee in front of her, the usual cigarette between her fingers, reading and rereading that school letter. She tapped her pen on the white paper, put it down, picked it up again, bit the tip of it, and twisted her mouth comically as she pondered what to do. This was her routine every morning for a week before she signed that letter. Finally, my teacher asked me if I was or wasn't going to be a Polio Pioneer. Of course I didn't want to be left out!

I heard her sigh as she scribbled what she'd forever call her "cursed signature." Muttering under her breath in Spanish, something about making crucial decisions on her own, she signed. For the rest of her life my mother made no decision, big or small, without first agonizing over it. And by the time she demanded to know which group I had been in, vaccine or placebo, it no longer mattered. I was already in quarantine, paralyzed from the neck down.

Months later a letter from Washington DC confirmed that I had been in the group of kids who were given the true vaccine. All my friends were in the other group and got the placebo. None of them caught polio.

Many things would never be adequately explained, certainly not to Mother's satisfaction. Throughout the years doctor after doctor patiently reiterated that the vaccine probably saved my life; that having the true serum in me helped me to "come back" from total paralysis or had saved me from the treacherous bulbar polio; that if they had only known in May how to pace out the three necessary doses; that in other controlled groups the placebo children had all gotten polio; and, finally, that she should be immensely grateful that my brother didn't contract the virus, too. That, and only that, offered some comfort.

The night before I became paralyzed, I had been drinking out of a bottle of Coca-Cola, and my brother kept begging me for a sip. In an unusual moment of sisterly magnanimity, I passed him the Coke behind Mother's back. My mouth had sucked the neck of the bottle an instant before Charlie swigged from it. Science, imperfect at best, was unable to explain my brother's natural immunity to polio, but his not catching it, we all knew, was the only thing that kept Mother from going over the cliff.

Not every hospital took polio patients. The serious cases from our area were sent to the Willard Parker Hospital of Communicable Diseases, in New York City. An ancient structure built at the turn of the twentieth century, it had hosted the likes of "Typhoid Mary" Mallon, committed there in 1907, as well as many victims of a 1948 smallpox outbreak. The tuberculosis patients, I soon discovered, were also sent there, as were the thousands of polio victims turned away by other hospitals.

The paralytic polios and the ones with the terrible bulbar polio, which affected the lungs, were housed in the Scarlet Fever Pavilion of Willard Parker. That's where I was, in quarantine, in a tiny, solitary room, too grim and dreary to be real. For ten days or more I lay flat and motionless, unable to move my head, right arm, or either leg. Only my parents were allowed to see me that first morning, very briefly. They came in garbed all in white, including face masks that covered everything except their eyes.

A couple of days later, or a few hours—I lost all track of time—the rest of my family, like a parade of ghosts, visited. One by one they filed into the isolation room and stood against the wall, as far from my bed as possible. I didn't recognize anyone because of the masks, but I knew my dad was there because he was the tallest. And then everyone left. It was the last time I saw my mother until I was transferred, three weeks later, to Lenox Hill Hospital.

For the first twenty-four hours white-clad attendants came and went, taking enormous amounts of my blood, glass after glass, with them. So much blood! I thought I must have only a little bit left. I'd watch the tube fill up dark red and hope it was the last time. It never was. Various nurses came in and out; every so often one would press hard on my tummy and slip a cold pan underneath me while she waited. When nothing happened, she'd press hard again, sometimes getting mad, and say, "You'll have to pee, you know." I was more than confused.

A tray of food was delivered three times a day, although I sure didn't want to eat. Anyway, I would have had to swallow lying down if I did, and there was nobody to help me. The person who brought the tray I never saw. She passed it to a nurse who put it on my bed stand. There were many among the hospital staff who refused, out of fear, to enter a polio room.

There was a pervasive, pungent smell of disinfectant always, and it took away any appetite I might have had. I did not know that every time someone on the quarantine floor died, which was every day at least, masked porters came and for an hour scrubbed the general area with disinfectant. Silent, unsmiling nurses entered my room only when they brought the meal tray or had to change the sheets and of course when it was time to torture me by pressing hard on my stomach with a clenched fist, insisting I pee. It never varied: Always the same nurse and helper changed the bedding, a different one brought the tray, and a third tried to force me to pee. None spoke to me or told me what was wrong with me.

When a week or so passed and I didn't die—I had heard them say, right outside my room, "This one may not die"—a new gang of doctors marched in to examine me. They flipped back my nightgown so that I lay naked in front of them; I cringed from shame, closing my eyes, as if in doing that, they wouldn't see. Next thing I felt was something sharp. One of the doctors was methodically sticking me with a safety pin everywhere.

"Do you feel that? How about that?

I felt it, and it hurt plenty, which, strangely enough, made them happy.

"Good! She feels something! That's very good!"

Not one of them spoke to me or looked into my eyes when I finally opened them. I'd discover that rare was the doctor who looked a polio kid in the eye. It was easy to see how I got the impression that I had done something really bad this time to warrant such punishment. Sticking pins in my legs and running cold instruments up and down my calves and the soles of my feet became another daily ritual while in isolation.

The night of that first day, and every night thereafter, even when I didn't consciously know it, my dad was there. He'd come whenever he was able to get away or just if he wanted to, at any hour, often with an angry nurse trailing behind him threatening to throw him out. I still developed a fear of the dark, but I can't imagine what it would have been like if he hadn't come. This was the first time, the only time, in my life I'd been left totally alone and without a familiar face within earshot I could call out for. After a few nights the nurses quit following Dad down the hall and left him alone; either he tipped the night nurse five bucks, or else he brought her a lamp or an ashtray. Throughout my ordeal, in the hope I'd receive the best of care, my father paid off doctors and nurses whenever he could, with bronze or silver pole lamps, with smart desk lamps, or with lovely gold filigree, leaf-shaped ashtrays that he had meticulously polished at the factory.

When conscious, I waited an eternity for my father's visits, distracting myself by watching the nightly parade of roaches climb a trail up the wall. I fought off the creeping terror by counting, first, the roaches then numbers, from 1 to 60, from 60 to 160, and up to 560. I tried hard not to cry, but sometimes, despite my resolve, a little drop leaked out and found its way into my ear. I never let go completely.

The rules were that my dad could stay as long as he didn't touch me or get too near my bed. "Sure," he said, then the minute the nurse left, he ripped off the white face mask, threw it on the floor, and kissed me. I knew he traveled far to get to Willard Parker from the Bronx and that when he came from the factory in Lower Manhattan he was tired, so I never asked him why he was late. I don't know where he got the energy. Some nights he arrived after one a.m. Each day, just as I was about to let go and bawl, sure that he couldn't make it, he showed up. He never disappointed me.

Somewhere inside the ancient Scarlet Fever Pavilion an angel hovered. I struggled, moment by moment, but lived. While awake, I didn't feel that sick, nor did I have a lot of pain—that would come in a few weeks, when I got the Sister Kenny "treatment." But I was amazed at how tired I felt even when doing nothing, and I worried that nothing moved except my left arm. I was a righty! What if my right hand never worked again? It seems bizarre how desperately I fought to not cry. This was extremely important, to show everyone that I was grown-up already and not a baby like Charlie. I instinctively knew, perhaps, that my stoic father needed to see me holding on, too. So I held on, maintaining a bravado I'm sure I did not feel.

The nightmares I had at home were nothing compared to the ones I suffered in quarantine. I'd fall off, and dreadfully large, undefined shapes would envelop me, loom over me, until I jerked awake. Shadows gathered around my bed, disappeared, and reappeared. I couldn't tell night from day, so wanting to know what time it was became obsessive. From that time I developed a penchant for collecting clocks and watches, one for every day of the week.

But the most frightening thing was what was happening inside my body. Not being able to move my legs or wiggle my toes terrified me. Dad promised me that the minute I could move them they'd take me out of quarantine and put me with other girls, so I figured I had to try harder. I tried, but my neck remained stiff and painful. Mainly, I focused intently on the closed door and willed my father through it.

Isolation Ward was the way station between life and death. Overall, less than one polio in ten died, but in a city as big as New York or Los Angeles, that meant hundreds or even thousands of kids and adults. Twenty-five percent of those deaths occurred in the first twenty-four hours, which explained why they let my entire family in that first day and never again. Only after I lasted a month were they certain I'd live; 90 percent of deaths occurred during the first three weeks.

Spinal polio, the kind I had, usually didn't kill its victims, but it often ravaged them, even causing quadriplegia. Desperate families resorted to settling for the least of the worst: "At least she doesn't have bulbar" was an oft-repeated phrase on the wards. Bulbar polio attacked the respiratory muscles so you couldn't breathe on your own. It killed 50 percent of its victims.

As the many hours, days, then weeks passed, my condition slowly improved. I slept better, drank milk through a straw or ate a vanilla-chocolate ice cream cup that my father made the nurses keep in their private refrigerator. Sometimes they'd bring it to me late at night before he came, and with my good hand I'd lick the ice cream from the inside of the lid, which often revealed a picture of Gene Autry or, if I got really lucky, my hero: Hopalong Cassidy.

The more days I stayed alive, the higher the window shade on the one window was lifted, as if near-death called for total darkness. I looked forward to the light and also to the morning nurse who inched that shade up each day. She was pretty and gentle, with blonde curls falling out of her cap, and when she talked to me she looked into my eyes. She assured me that we were still in the month of September, another question I must have asked dozens of times. But she, too, avoided mentioning what sickness I had.

I began to know morning from night and good nurses from bad. My morning nurse had no stripes on her cap; the no-stripes caps were much kinder than the one- or two-stripes caps. By the time I got to

Hospital Number 3, I had a good education about nurses' personalities, and none matched the characters from one of my favorite books, *Cherry Ames, Practical Nurse*.

One day my bed was moved so I could look out the half-open window that faced the wall of another part of the hospital. Every so often a ray of sun glanced off the dark brown bricks and lit up my dingy room, reminding me of the outside. The weather was still warm as summertime, and I liked being near the open window—at first. Soon I became aware of a horrible sound; directly above my room people were coughing, spitting, and clearing their throats, as loud as if they were next to me in bed. It went on all day, every day. When they hacked and retched upstairs, I too choked and shuddered, swallowing hard so I wouldn't throw up.

I guess I was in quarantine for about two weeks. The average stay was ten days to two weeks, although some were there for three, depending upon the hospital. To me it felt like two years; I was positive I'd been abandoned there forever. No one ever confirmed exactly how long I lay confined in the isolation wing. They couldn't "remember." When asked, they'd say, "Don't think about it!" so I'd shut up. I got the message: Don't talk about or remember *anything* about polio or the hospital experience. I couldn't figure this out. Polio had been such a big news item *before* I got it, why clam up after? But, then, nothing made sense anymore. It was as if I had lost my place while reading a book and could not find my way back to the story.

My mother, meanwhile, was engaged in her own life-or-death battle. Shortly after they wheeled me into quarantine, she crumbled. When she learned that the official diagnosis was really polio, she abandoned any veneer of composure and started screaming. They escorted her out of the hospital and nearby vicinity fast. At home she raced through the apartment like a figure skater gathering up all Evil Eyes and amulets that had been placed in our dresser drawers for protection then dumping them in the garbage. "Doomed! Doomed!" she cried. It became her favorite phrase.

Modern, fast-mouthed, and sophisticated—what my generation later called hip—she nonetheless succumbed to fortune teller predictions, superstition, and old-country ideas of retribution. Her deep-rooted belief wasn't so different from that of her sisters', but Mother took it a step further, convinced that someone had admired and praised me, had envied my beauty, and had therefore deliberately put a treacherous spin on the wheel of the Turkish zodiac, cursing our entire family with the worst malediction possible: El Dio ke te tome a ti y a tu padre . . . May God take you and your father and the mother who gave you birth, and the midwife who received you . . .

Only a top-notch enchantress who knew the special medicines and elaborate ritual healing prayers could extricate us from the mess "they" cursed us with. Devastating diseases like mine called for women healers who made use of both common and strange ingredients, like sugar, saliva, salt, candles, mumya powder, nail parings, hot lead, urine, cloves, ashes, and even the forbidden oil of a pig. We needed Turkish women who were familiar with the ancient Tres Yaves cures, the Prayer of the Three Keys, which was sung or recited . . . One to open, one to close, one to remove all harm . . . There were long medieval verses that survived from ancient Spain to Istanbul and made their way into the houses of prekantadoras like my grandmother; powerful, spooky spells, like the Prekante de Kulevra, the Cure of the Serpent. But who was still alive to recite them? In her prime Behora had known how to perform all these rituals. Mother couldn't come up with a single candidate knowledgeable enough to meta la mano, pass her hands over me and reverse my illness.

Over the course of the next few weeks and months she bought into this skewed thinking more and more, becoming embittered and irrational. Her personality changed entirely. Even her facial features changed; the corners of her mouth seemed to turn down much more than before. And God help anyone who referred to me as "lucky." Of course, in this epic tragedy I surely was, but no one had better use that word in front of her.

She stopped answering the door and the phone and every now and then tore a chunk of hair out of her head as her own mother used to do when distraught. Unable to console her or listen to her awful wai-wai-yoos, woebegone wailing, friends and family fled. My father couldn't take it all and headed for relief to the hamam, when he wasn't with me at the hospital. No one, not even Allegre and Sultana, her constant companions, dared approach her.

Although she stayed away from my hospital room, my mother, nevertheless, became mentally entwined with me and obsessed with curing me. For good reason. Being a rabbi's daughter, she was well aware that in Sephardic ritual prayers the naming of the sick person and the mother of that person were recited together. As the Talmud says, "all incantations are recited in the name of the mother." From her side we got the mystical- cabalistic; from my father's side, the magical-shamanistic. It didn't matter. Neither side knew what to do, and my condition knew no solution. We were "doomed."

When she wasn't obsessing over shamans and curses, she was bad-mouthing the vaccine field trial promoters. Her cast of heavies changed at will, but it was a pretty constant list from which she ranted a litany of accusations: her dead mother-in-law, the sorceress, plus the rest of Dad's ill-starred clan; Mrs. Peltz, principal of PS 64, for putting children's lives in jeopardy; ugly old Stella-the-witch, our tailor; and various Turkish and Egyptian cousins, fresh off the boat, with their respective foreign infections. Most of the time, though, the biggest culprit was herself.

"What *werko*, devil, guided my hand the day I signed that damned form?" she asked a thousand times.

My aunts told me that this period in our lives was the most terrible, frightening time any of them had lived through since those terror-filled days in 1910, four years before they left for America, when gangs of *Cristiano* ruffians chased them through the streets of Çanakkele and pelted them with rocks. Every year during Passover or Easter my aunts, uncles, cousins, and other Jews in town came under attack, accused of ritually murdering Christians and of eating Christian babies or drinking their blood. These, Aunt Allegre said, were dark days, when they were forced to lock themselves inside barricaded houses until the rioters were done. The severity of my illness, and the fact that I was the youngest girl of the three sisters, brought back their deepest fears of annihilation.

For the rest of her life Mother believed she had done something very bad to deserve having a child so sick. But what? Clearly, she was being punished, and no one could talk her out of it. At age seven I did not understand this phenomenon of self-blame, nor did I think things were that bad. Even when I heard Dad, beside my bed, whisper in Ladino, "The Sixth Plague of Egypt is upon us!" I didn't worry, although it confused me. I was too young to recognize that all of us, my mother, my father, and I, had turned a corner.

Oddly, Mother and I lived parallel lives. We were both cut off from the world and felt deeply alone, we were scared of what was coming next, and we were paralyzed as far as being able to change our respective situations. But I discovered, at about the same time, a resolve I hadn't known existed in me. I knew, for one thing, that I was going to try to get out of bed, no matter what the doctors said. Every time they made their rounds I clenched and unclenched my weak left hand, vowing that I would *get out of bed*.

I kept pushing my terrible imaginings toward the back, even as my fighting spirit emerged in front. Foremost, I wanted to know what happened to my mother. I kept asking, but no one would say. Whenever high heels echoed down the hallway, I prayed they'd be hers. I worried about that ruined mah-jongg game, which, had she won, would have paid her double because she was East. Could she still be mad at me for that? When I said my prayers I vowed to God to be a good girl from now on and not give her so much to worry about. Other times I feared she had caught my sickness or the kind of cold that they said killed Nona Behora. But my father said no, "She's not *that* kind of sick." What other kind was there?

The Turks always say, *Grande mal es el no saver*, The great harm is not to know. And so it was with me; neither the pain of my stiff neck, nor the frustration of being paralyzed bothered me as much as ignorance. No one would tell me what had happened to my body nor what was going on with the rest of my family. Where was my little brother? On the morning the ambulance came, Cousin Lorraine was the first relative to arrive. She was my favorite older cousin, and when I heard her voice I expected her to come into the bedroom to see me. Instead, she left almost immediately with Charlie. Did that mean that she was mad at me, too? And if my brother was at Aunt Sultana's, then Mother didn't need a babysitter, so she would have been free to come to the hospital. Nothing was going right or as I expected.

Everything to do with time becomes approximate in hospitals. Their favorite word is *soon*. I lost all respect for that nebulous, meaningless word, especially when they told me I'd go home "soon." I missed being home but not as much as I missed knowing the facts, like *why* I couldn't go home. I had always been a question asker, even when I got no satis-factory answers or got slapped for asking. Now I really *needed* to know. It made me afraid not to, and this kind of fear was also new. I didn't recognize my own voice, wobbly and low, as I called out to nurses, to anyone. When one of them finally responded, I got scolded for crying or was given a mini-lecture about how there were other children much much sicker than me who didn't cry at all. I didn't care. Even being chided by a cold nurse was better than not having my door opened at all.

I knew I was sicker than the time I had a horrible case of the measles and my vision got blurry, but I never suspected polio because no one ever said the word. "She gets a bad case of everything," Mother once told a neighbor. "Bad grippe, flu, chicken pox, measles, you name it." But with polio they didn't name it. The other mystery was, why couldn't *el germano*, the German, as my father called Dr. Hirschfeld, cure me with a shot of penicillin like always? No matter how sick, he'd come up, give me a shot, and in a couple of days I'd be jumping around. I innocently believed that he, like any doctor, could make me well. They always had in the past!

Even with an experience so scary, one surpasses a point in Fear when, because it floods you entirely, you're wrapped in it and therefore numb. It was better sleeping; when my eyes opened and I became alert, I got agitated. Then my world was reduced to listening and waiting.

It must have been about ten days into my stay in quarantine when I felt an achy sensation in my right arm and found that I could open and close my right hand. My fingers came back, too, and it was delightful being able to move them. My first thought was how happy Dad would be, and my next was to ask the nurse for paper and pencil. For some reason she said, "Not yet."

Little by little, parts of me returned to somewhat normal. I still ached all over and could not yet sit up straight by myself, but gradually I could turn my head without pain and also eat sitting up. I didn't want the food, but at least I didn't have to fall into it anymore. Before, the only way to eat was on my stomach. They'd flip me over, and my weakened arms would tremble as I struggled to support myself on my elbows. It was so hard to stay like that. More than once I collapsed face down onto the food tray.

Nurses didn't have time to cajole me into eating. They were busy with an overflowing isolation ward, running from room to room up and down the halls all day and night. I wondered why they would always run instead of walk; I had no idea of the hourly crises they faced on the ward. Still, the nurses discussed my case as if I were deaf and dumb and didn't know they were talking about Mother.

"She needs you-know-who at mealtime."

"Just at mealtime?"

By the end of about two weeks I was totally alert and moving—except for my legs. They didn't work at all, though the doctors kept insisting it was good that they hurt when poked with pins. I was completely ready to go home, begged for it, but it wasn't to be. One morning when my father was there, a doctor pulled him outside and told him that I would never walk again. He delivered the bad news fast, just like that. Because they were right outside my door, I heard everything.

He told him I had no quadriceps muscles in either leg, that they appeared to be dead, and that soon my legs would atrophy from lack of use. He tried to explain also about motor neurons, damaged spinal nerves, shrunken muscles, and other residuals of polio, but my father's face must have registered something that made the doctor stop talking.

"Have hope," the doctor said, "but get her a wheelchair anyway. It looks like she'll need it." He added that I could leave Willard Parker soon—not to go home but to another hospital where they administered Sister Kenny's hot-pack treatments, which were often successful in reviving dormant muscles.

"And there's physical therapy, too. You know, kids can fool you." The doctor went on to say that I was very brave . . . miracles happen . . . I was lucky to be alive . . .

Then his voice trailed off, and he sort of shouted at Dad: "Sir, do you understand?"

Oh, he understood, all right. My dad may not have known that *atrophy* meant "shrink" or what *dormant* stood for, but he was smart, and I know he got the picture. I wondered why he didn't ask the doctor some questions or at least call him crazy. Of course, I couldn't see his face, so I didn't know how shaken he was by it. Speechless, he shoved the doctor and took off.

It was as common for parents to receive devastating news like this in hallways, cafeterias, or visitor lounges as it was for my father to run off when he was furious. I would hear doctors or other hospital workers deliver dreadful prognoses, sometimes right in front of a victim, and then be off again on their rounds. Because polio was so unpredictable, many verdicts were premature, but in the majority of worst cases, like mine, the medics were right.

I'm sure they didn't intend to be brutal, but they were, and so mothers, fathers, aunts, and grandmothers promptly fell apart. Most of the hospital workers then were appallingly ill trained and emotionally unprepared for handling such an epidemic, not to mention family members. Nor did they know much about polio's legacy, as the virus never followed a specific course in any two people. It was near impossible keeping up with the sheer number of cases admitted each day.

When he came back, I saw from my father's face that he wasn't going to talk about what the doctor had said at all. And, besides, he didn't believe a word of it anyway. From the beginning he never accepted, and wouldn't let me accept, being paralyzed for life. "They told me you're gonna walk outa here," he lied.

He wasn't going to tell Mother about the wheelchair either. I'm sure he planned to come up with something clever and would have, as he was a wonderful liar. But he needn't have worried about shielding her because she already knew. Earlier, as if it were a coordinated effort, Mother received a call from a hospital social worker informing her that the NFIP, the National Foundation for Infantile Paralysis, had deemed me an eligible candidate to receive a brand-new wheelchair, free of charge. A permanent chair. One we never had to give back. One I could have for the rest of my life.

"This should make things a bit easier for all of you," the woman said.

A double whammy, it spelled out to the world that, one, I would never walk again and, two, we were poor enough to get charity.

"I guess you're telling me we're just lucky," Mother hissed, and hung up.

All over again, she drenched herself in blame. This was too much for her. She had been preparing herself to come to the hospital, but after that phone call she had a setback. Her thread was thin anyway because of the undercurrent of accusatory finger-pointing. Certain Turks had let her know their feelings: If Sephardis were tough enough to make it through Attatürk's revolution and flee to America, how could one of them "let their child get so sick"? Good mothers prevented these catastrophic illnesses; they know not to cut off a child's hair during *primavera*, springtime, when germs present themselves. No wonder my resistance collapsed!

When I asked for my mother, I was told to concentrate on *my* job, to get strong. I didn't want to "let everyone down," did I? I had to "fight hard," and, if I did, maybe I'd even *walk*! And it starts with *never crying about anything*. "Crybabies stay in bed forever," the nurses told me. I was not even supposed to feel one bit sad because that was called sulking. Sadness would gladly wait a few years for me, they knew. For now the Polio Pioneers had to have courage!

Guts. I heard the word so often that by the time I was ten it had become my mantra and middle name. All of us, every kid in all three hospitals, was brave. Courageous. Gutsy. During grueling physical therapy when they taught us how to walk on our metal legs between parallel bars, then how to fall, then how to get up, we were brave; in the giant whirlpool tub filled with hot, pounding water, we were brave; during the slapping of boiling-hot wool on our inert legs, we were brave; and when holidays came and went and we had to spend them on the ward with strangers instead of at home with family, we were brave and cheerfully sung Christmas carols with the volunteers, even when we were Jewish.

I would learn how to press my lips tightly together to keep back screams, and I don't remember any roommates putting up much of a fuss either. *Cowards* screamed, not the polios, not even when they yanked our legs and pulled on our contracted muscles to stretch them. Why weren't we all screaming, *Get me out of here?* I'll never know, but surely a lot had to do with the times and those fighting heroes of World War II and Korea. We survivors of the most dreaded virus aligned ourselves with them, and so it was perfectly natural for some of the crippled poster children to be photographed with those soldiers and fighter pilots as dramatic backdrops. Like them, we had earned the respect of the entire country. Everyone was proud of us. We were winning the war on polio!

The parents who visited weren't so brave. Many fainted in hallways and could be heard screaming at all hours of the night. Guts, I learned, was synonymous with youthful innocence, raw naïveté; cowardice was simply knowing too much. The few among us who did cry, carry on, and make life harder for the hospital staff were labeled "sissies" or "troublemakers," and nurses attended to their needs last. These kids saw their true plight and wanted out: out of bed, out of the ward, out of being totally helpless. They were smarter than we who just shut up and took it. These few kickers and screamers were wise to the tragedy that had struck them down, and they knew that polio was the worst thing that would ever happen to them. The rest of us were on a blind mission. I wanted very much to get better and win the war, really, I did. But I wasn't sure exactly how I was supposed to "fight" to do it.

A few days before I left the quarantine wing, my tante Allegre paid me an unexpected visit. Magically, she appeared beside my bed wearing a mouth mask but not the white gown. She couldn't kiss me yet, but her eyes conveyed the same love for me that was always there. On my forehead she placed that big hand that cooked me the best feta cheese omelets and then whispered, "Hanúm de la tante!" as usual. I was still the star of the harem! Tears ran down her cheeks, and then I started to cry, too. What a relief when she didn't tell me not to!

Tante slipped something underneath my pillow and told me to leave it there and not let the nurses throw it away. It was a three-times folded handkerchief containing walnut shells inscribed with Hebrew characters that I assumed were prayers. Another old remedy for serious illness, which, somehow, gave me hope.

I asked my aunt why, when I didn't feel that sick anymore, was everyone still sad? Choked with emotion, all she could repeat was, "Mi alma! mi alma!" My soul! My soul! Then she had to go. The visit did wonders for me but was very hard on her and took its emotional toll, according to my cousins. I had no idea how dangerous it was to venture into a quarantine area. All I know was that the visit strengthened my determination to get up and walk. Nobody was going to tell me not to! I had disappointed everyone by becoming so sick, but I knew now that my favorite relative still loved me as much as before. That's the moment I became aware of my personal "guts." When she left and I was alone again, with no one watching, I let myself cry for a long time.

Although I begged, when they changed the sheets the next day, the handkerchief disappeared.

I came through the dark passage that was Willard Parker into a brighter space but not before one further Willard Parker initiation. It was the night of that happy day when the morning nurse told me what I wanted to hear, that I was being moved to another part of the hospital because I was no longer contagious: "You're so much better," she said, "that now you can have other girls to talk to!"

It wasn't exactly going home, but at least I was getting out of that horrible, lonely room with the roaches and the upstairs hackers. I didn't realize that my loneliness was so complete that it made me catch my breath, as if I'd been running fast. I had spent at least two weeks in a stark room, without a toy or a doll and only my father's visits to connect me to the outside. My stuffed animals and other toys, any personal items from home, were thought of as contaminated and weren't allowed. Parents were supposed to destroy anything that a victim had held or played with prior to confinement, so if you were admitted with your favorite blanket, teddy bear, or the doll you loved, it was immediately confiscated and burned, and you never saw it again.

Hospitals are worlds unto themselves. It does not take long to get used to the particular smells and sounds of daily life, as everything runs by routine. I would find this comforting, eventually; sick people do not need surprises. Meals were always served at the same time; washing rituals were completed in the mornings; snack carts came around two hours after dinner, every night. Lights stay on twenty-four hours a day in the hallways, so it's never pitch-black, and you know it's 4 p.m. by which nurse walks in. That is why when something bad happens on a ward everyone, except those in a coma, are aware of it.

In addition to the coughing and choking upstairs, I had become aware of strange noises coming from the room across the hall: a cacophony of whooshing, whining, suction, and bubbling sounds. There was also, from time to time, a loud clicking sound, kind of like galloping horses. It was the iron lung room, where portable respirators the size of small cars mechanically breathed for those whose diaphragms or throat muscles, or both, had been paralyzed by polio.

"You are very lucky not to be in there," the nurses said. "Those kids can't breathe on their own." A mere cold, and one could die in a few minutes from not being able to sneeze and properly clear her passageways. Most of them had had emergency tracheotomies the moment they were admitted and couldn't speak; they had tubes coming out of their noses that kept oxygen bubbling and flowing. But they were alive, some barely, and what I didn't know was that one or two of them died every day.

If an iron lung stopped, the person inside it stopped also. The bulbar polios imprisoned in them suffocated. Most of the time the iron lungs' steady, mechanical rhythm was soothing, and it lulled me to sleep, not unlike the sound of subway trains. It was the mysterious clicking sound I wondered about, until the night when all the whirring, whooshing, and whining and muted clanging just stopped. I had gotten so used to it that the sudden silence jerked me awake.

Nobody knew what happened: it was September, still hot and humid, and it had just rained. There could have been an electrical storm in the area that caused the power to go out and stay out for too long. The world across the hall went silent. I, too, automatically held my breath, waiting. Then the sound of a hundred horses.

Pandemonium ensued. Even in iron lungs they fought to live. With no use of their limbs and too weak to scream, kids and adults learned to click with their tongues to attract attention. When they needed something, or especially if someone in the room was in trouble and was gasping for help, whomever was able to began clicking. Twenty, thirty, forty tongues at once frantically clicked against the roofs of that many mouths, and they made quite a racket.

Nurses came running, first a few feet, then lots of feet. Any time an iron lung stopped, or when they took a patient out of it briefly to clean it, they had to hand-pump oxygen into the person. When the whole roomful of lungs stopped, every soul in there needed help—fast. Parents, visitors, whomever was around ran to help; nurses dashed back and forth, calling out to doctors and to other nurses. More came running: aides, hospital workers, electricians. The running was punctuated with cries of "Help!" Equipment banged around in the hall.

I lay there waiting, terrified, knowing instinctively that something terrible was happening. I, too, stopped breathing, hoping that familiar whirring music of the lung machines would start again. I knew it was finished when I heard women weeping and then other voices calming them. Finally, the sound of a bed—the iron lung machine?—being wheeled down the hall.

The tragedy took over the night, and by morning two children were dead. I heard someone in the hall say that a kid's "skin had shriveled up." I didn't know that was code for their heart giving out, but the thought of skin shriveling was bad enough. Nobody knew if they would have died anyway or if the power outage caused it, but it was light out before things got back to normal.

A few hours later two nurses came and wheeled me, still in my bed, out into the hallway. I stared into the open doorway of the iron lung room, which was now calm and quietly rhythmic, and I could not believe how many oblong, beige-and-white metal canisters filled that room. Maybe fifty, wall to wall. And each one with a little head sticking out of it. Like cars in a parking lot, the iron lungs were on wheels, lined up in rows.

Each lung had a mirror attached near the patient's head so he or she could see what was happening in the room. During the emergency the night before, a nurse had gone down row after row of machines flipping mirrors, so that the people inside them wouldn't be able to see someone else dying.

As they paused to straighten my sheets, I stared, unable to look away. One of the kids happened to be facing my way, and she smiled at me. Before they pushed me down the hall, I managed to smile back.

My new room was definitely more cheerful, and it had two windows. There was another girl in it, too, but she slept a lot, so it wasn't much better than being alone. Now, they said, I could have a doll—only a new one, nothing from home allowed. But all I wanted was my composition notebook. A big worry of mine was that I was missing so much school. How would I ever catch up?

I finally lost patience. That night, when he tried to leave, I grabbed my father's shirt with my good arm and wouldn't let go. I cried, wanting to know when I'd go home, and "soon" wasn't good enough. He didn't have the heart to tell me I was about to be transferred to another hospital called Lenox Hill. I saw him struggle with it, trying to tell me, but he couldn't get it out. Finally, like during their weekend brawls, when he'd had enough of fighting with Mother, he ran.

"Your father isn't supposed to sleep in the chair, you know!"

It was my roommate's voice; at least then I knew she had one. My father had apparently come back in the middle of the night and was dozing in the corner chair. The morning nurse was surprised to see him there, too.

When he stood up he leaned over me, gripping the bed rail so hard I thought his white knuckles would pop open. His eyes that morning were dark and sad, just as on the first day, when he blinked at me above the white mask. Not the most articulate person, when emotional, he became even more tongue-tied. Finally, in Ladino, he said: "Dio, dala mazál, y echeme a los perros!" God, give her good luck, and throw *me* to the dogs!

I felt sorry for him and sorrier that I had cried the night before. Impulsively, I stretched both arms out and lifted them up, high as I possibly could, to show him how much stronger I was.

"I gotta go to work," he said. "But here, *para sus palavras.*" To write your words.

Inside I was thrilled to find four sharpened pencils and a brand-new salt-and-pepper notebook.

1. Rockaway Beach, 1954

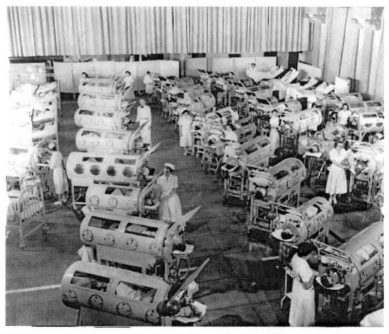

2. Polio Pioneers, 1954. Courtesy of the March
of Dimes Birth Defects Foundation.

3. Typical Iron Lung Room, 1950s. Courtesy of
the March of Dimes Birth Defects Foundation.

4. Nona Behora, fortune teller, ca. 1952

5. Tante Allegre and Doris, on the Concourse

6. Lorraine, Brenda, and the hidden brace

7. Sultana and
Ovadiah

8. Vic and Rosika,
just wed, 1943

9. Executive secretary, Knopf Publishing

10. Turkish dancing at a bar mitzvah

11. Bellina the Belly Dancer

12. The author at seven

13. The Council: Allegre, Rosika, and Sultana

14. Bellina Dances with abandon to the record *Port Said*

15. Miss Rheingold Beer, 1958

16. Cousin Jacques from Port Said

5 ❀ *Grace*

The warm September breeze drifted through our open kitchen window, carrying with it, from Sheridan Avenue on the east, throughout the alleyway that led to the Grand Concourse on the west, the excited voices of neighborhood children on their way to school. It was the first day. Mother stood by the window, watching. She heard their high-pitched shouts, their laughter, and also their mothers calling out to them, to the Susans and the Davids and the Michelles, to be careful crossing and to please stop running in their new shoes.

Soon the streets grew quiet again. All the children were at school, where they were supposed to be, all parents were back inside their apartments enjoying a second cup of coffee, and the resident sparrows on our fire escape resumed their morning symphony. From below came only muted sounds of distant traffic. In this peaceful setting my mother walked to the stove, knelt in front of the oven, and shoved her head deep inside.

Whether it was a mock-suicide or a real attempt, we don't know; nobody is even sure about whether or not the gas was turned on. Thing is, we didn't have that kind of an oven anyway. Half the time we couldn't even light the pilot light. Dramatic in the best of circumstances,

Mother's grief over my catching polio had culminated in one hysterical, desperately theatrical act. Luckily, Cousin Dottie happened by at that moment. As usual, she knocked twice before entering, walked in, and saw Mother there—actually, she found herself staring at my mother's backside. I imagined my cousin, with her bleached-red beehive hairdo and her stiletto heels that tap-tapped down the foyer, turning the corner to the kitchen and seeing her aunt crouched in that awkward position, head and torso stuffed in the stove.

"I gave her a good shake," Dottie claimed, "and told her you needed her more alive than dead!"

I needed her, period. I had woken up that morning in a new place, ensconced in a big room at Lenox Hill Hospital on Manhattan's East Side. They must have moved me in the middle of the night because I had no recollection of being taken from Willard Parker in an ambulance, although that's what happened. All I know was that I found myself in yet another unfamiliar circumstance, and my father was nowhere around. But I didn't panic because there was one other inhabitant in bed next to me, a girl with hair so white-blond it looked as if it might shine in the dark.

"My name is Alice," she said, "and this is Jesus. Do you know him?"

She thrust what appeared to be a necklace or chain of small, pale-blue beads in my direction. At the end of the chain dangled the figure of a little man, whom I could just about reach if I stuck my arm out all the way.

"Jee-zis?"

"Not Jee-zis!" She was horrified at my dumbness. "You have to say it this way: Jee-zus! Like that! If you say it right, I'll let you hold him."

I said it, and apparently right, because Alice flipped the necklace my way. I caught it with my left hand. The hanging man had both arms stretched out, and his legs were crossed, as if he needed to go to the bathroom and was holding it. Alice said that her grandmother brought him from Rome.

"Don't you have rosaries?"

I admitted I didn't have any, nor had I ever seen a necklace like hers before in my life. But I did say that my favorite aunt's American name was also Alice.

"If you pray to Jee-zus," she said, "you'll walk. He heals people, you know."

Well, I certainly wanted him in that case! I had become really tired of being bedridden, quite restless of late, and wanted nothing more than to walk. Every day I thought about walking, wondering why I couldn't do it yet, and why it was taking so long. Also, I had been thinking up ways of doing something about it. So I shoved the little hanging man under my pillow before Alice could change her mind.

At least Lenox Hill was a much better place than the previous hospital. In fact, it was a palace compared to what I had just left. We were in an open ward, and our room was big enough for six girls, bright, and with a large window. Hospital workers and volunteers came and went, bringing us chewing gum or books and magazines from the hospital library. I didn't care at all about eating, but even I could tell that the food was much better, too. Nurses' aides in blue dresses with no caps took care of us and paid us more attention than the nurses did. They washed us and sang to us some mornings. One even polished my nails pink one Saturday, just for fun. She taught me that if you run cold water over nail polish it dries faster, a lesson I never forgot. Life was so much better that I recognized how lonely it had been up until then. I told my father that I loved Lenox Hill, but, surprisingly, he looked sad to hear it. Still, he went out to find the nurse's aide who polished my nails and tip her.

By the end of the week two other girls joined Alice and me in the room. One had broken her neck in a car accident and wore a thick white body cast, and the other's legs got crushed when a huge sign fell off the top of a store. My dad told me that the sign-girl's father had offered Dr. Deaver "five grand" just to fix his daughter's legs, but the doctor refused, saying that if money could buy those things he'd be a rich man. All of us were sick, but in various stages of recovery, and we became fast friends, the kind that you make in those particular situations. We felt as if we'd known each other forever.

Even though she was ten and I was about a month shy of my eighth birthday, Alice and I were close; she was my first, and would always remain my best, hospital friend. Thanks to polio, we were in the same boat. The nurses called us "the redhead and the blonde" because we laughed and talked nonstop, sitting up in our beds with our legs stretched out in front of us, feet propped against wooden boards to keep them straight. Alice convinced me that we wouldn't be in bed for long, that Jee-zus was going to "fix us" any minute now. I had my doubts, but she sounded so *sure*.

My new friend told me about novenas, what happens in church, and how miracles occur when you least expect it. Also, she told me she wore a bridal dress on the day she married Jee-zus. I was duly impressed, especially since I thought you had to be much older to get married. If either of my Christian friends made communion, I didn't know about it, but I did recall groups of girls dressed as little brides strolling the Grand Concourse from time to time.

There was a lot I didn't know. Alice looked skeptical when I insisted that I had never in my life said something called a "Hail Mary," and she made me swear I wasn't lying when I said I didn't know that Jesus's mother was a holy virgin. She asked me how many names of saints I knew—none—so she went down the list and recited them for me. So many! I tried to memorize some, concentrating as if it were the most important lesson of my life. In return I told her how I could belly dance with zills on my fingers that clicked and described the blue chiffon, multi-veiled costume I wore.

"And I had a blue stone in my belly button, to keep off the Evil Eye!"

"You mean really *inside*?"

But she was most impressed with the stories of how my grandmother brought dead people back to life with hot lead and her very own hands.

Alice's mother came every morning and stayed all day. She never lost faith that her daughter would soon walk. She'd arrive with Alice's white ice skates slung over her shoulder, as if the two were about to leave for Rockefeller Center's rink. Completely sure that Alice would get well, Mrs. Cook talked of the trips they'd take when Alice got out and about how much shopping they'd do. I had gotten used to not having my mother around, but seeing the Cook's camaraderie brought a new sadness that I bore silently. I knew Mrs. Cook felt bad for me. She brought me homemade cookies, comic books, or pairs of socks, when she came, just like she brought Alice, and she encouraged me to pray to the hanging man for everything I desired.

Something told me that Alice was worse off than I was. When the pin-sticking doctors came around and poked her, she never cried "ouch!"

like I did. They'd frown and shake their heads. Not that they were helpful; again, I wished my nona was alive to come to the hospital and fix us both, something she was good at. Alice loved the story about Nona's secret bowl from under the sink, the one that she heated balls of lead in, and how the magic fire it created cured bad sickness. Mrs. Cook would listen politely and smile if she were there, occasionally saying things like, "Oh, dear!" or "My goodness!"

"You must have loved your grandmother very much," she said. But I had the feeling that she didn't believe the stuff about the lead-popping ceremony or Grandma's magical powers.

Every night before she left, Mrs. Cook took a little blue book from her purse, and then she and Alice recited prayers from it together. When they got to the part where you say, "Amen," I joined them in saying it, too. Then, she kissed her own hanging man, and they both made the sign of the cross. I learned to do it, but I would get good and slapped when I did, later, at home. I know Alice needed her rosaries more than I did, but, as long as she didn't press, I wasn't giving them up.

My father didn't care what kind of necklace they gave me. When I first slipped it out from under my pillow and said, "This is Jee-zus," he examined it, turning it over and over in his big palm.

"Very nice," he said.

I told him that Jee-zus was going to heal me and help me walk if I prayed to him every day and said his name correctly.

"So pray!"

Dad was a practical man. "Here," he said, "this will help, too."

Wrapped inside one of his handkerchiefs were a bunch of blanched almonds, and each almond had strange-looking symbols written on it. He made me eat all of them at that moment, even with the ink on them, as he watched. It seems that my father had traveled all over the city looking for a fortune teller that some of the Turks told him about who knew what words and mystical symbols to write on almonds. This was supposed to cure a child of illness. At least there was nothing to keep hidden under the pillow that the nurses would throw out, which they were very fond of doing.

There was no end to the remedies Dad tried in order to get me out of that bed. One night Alice's father came by very late, and the two of them met. Mr. Cook had just returned from a place called Lourdes, in

France, and he had brought back something very "blessed," he said, to heal Alice's legs. From inside the breast pocket of his coat, he removed and carefully unwrapped a small bottle of "holy water" that he then bathed his daughter's legs with. My father, who watched intently, was interested.

"Hey, Jack, any of that stuff left over for my girl?"

My dad called everyone "Jack," from gas station attendants to ushers at the Luxor. He was never embarrassed about not knowing your name, and it didn't seem to bother Mr. Cook, either, who generously gave us the rest of the holy water. I did not want that cold water splashed on me, but I had no choice; my father bathed my legs with it anyway. He made me laugh as he did it, by muttering one funny Ladinoism after another, under his breath: "Kon pedos no se boyadeya wevos!" One cannot paint eggs without farts!

This made no sense, literally, of course, but I knew he meant, "We have to try everything, no matter how silly or unpleasant."

Every other day we went to something called hydrotherapy, the first in a series of new and often fearful hospital experiences. You couldn't ever show any overt fear. Nurses and physical therapists referred to it as "adventures." Those who could sat in wheelchairs; the others were rolled on gurneys to an elevator that led to another elevator and finally down to what seemed to be the bowels of the hospital's subbasement. If I took the trip today, it probably wouldn't seem so far away and involved, but when you're seven a large hospital is as vast as an airplane hangar.

By way of a series of labyrinthine tunnels we entered a muggy room that had in it a Hubbard Tank, one giant silver vat shaped like a butterfly, plus another smaller vat. Dressed only in our panties, the girls were put into a canvas sling and airlifted into one tank, while the boys, also half-naked, were lowered into the other. The worst part for me was being hoisted toward the ceiling. I swung there, high up, practically naked, with nothing to hold onto. I'd close my eyes and wrap my arms around myself in order to feel my own body heat. It wasn't much better than the time I was carried downstairs on the stretcher, covered with a sheet.

Then there was the moment when the sling tipped, and I was *sure* I would plunge headfirst into the vat. It wasn't unreasonable; our therapists didn't seem to be paying attention. They were talking and laughing among themselves while each of us was lifted. I knew that by the time they saw me fall it would be too late. My hanging man was always with me on these excursions. I wanted every god imaginable to protect me from the ropes breaking.

Once I was lowered into the water, it wasn't so bad. One of the therapists was already standing in the vat, waiting, and the rush of the whirling water against my legs felt good. They felt strong, like they used to, and they moved with momentum. During hydrotherapy, after I got over the fear of being lowered on ropes, I felt as if I could leap up and run out, just like my old self.

Those of us who were making progress graduated from hydrotherapy to swim therapy. For this we were wheeled down to a basement room not so far away as the vat room. I had never even been in a swimming pool before, as we had always gone to the ocean at Rockaway Beach. I wasn't happy wearing red hospital shorts and a too-big T-shirt, but I had no choice. Some of the girls had beautiful bathing suits.

In general I loved the water, even when it was icy-cold. The hospital swimming pool was much warmer than the ocean, and it felt good to be buoyed up, feel light of body again. One therapist would hold me under my belly, exactly like Dad did in the ocean, while one behind me moved my legs in a kicking motion—what I'd be doing myself if I could have. She didn't let go like my father did when he wanted to scare me, yet I trusted the therapist a lot less. In my heart I knew he'd never let me drown; with her I wasn't so sure. They'd laugh at me and say "Good!" when I insisted that soon I'd jump into the pool myself, without their help.

On one such therapy day they announced that a real movie star, an Olympic swim champion who had actually won a gold medal, was visiting our hospital for the sole purpose of meeting us. She was going to teach us how to float on our backs so that someone else's hands wouldn't have to hold us up. Right away, I didn't like it. I asked to be taken out of the pool. It was as scary to think of a stranger letting go of me in a swimming pool as it was to imagine the ropes breaking over the whirlpool vat. Besides, I knew I would not float. The staff calmed me down, pointing out that no one else was balking or seemed in the least afraid. Still, I did not want to see the famous swim star. I prayed she'd get lost on her way to the hospital or forget to show up.

Until that time my only celebrity experience was with Buffalo Bob Smith on *The Howdy Doody Show*. It was Mother's dream come true when they picked me, out of hundreds, to sit in the Peanut Gallery on live television. I loved the show—we all did. Every day at five o'clock thousands of kids sat rapt in front of their TV sets and waited for Buffalo Bob's familiar question: WHAT TIME IS IT, BOYS AND GIRLS? so that we could scream back: IT'S HOWDY DOODY TIME! When the windows were open, you could hear every kid in the neighborhood bellow it out. I was excited, too; I was actually going to meet Clarabell the Clown and Princess Summerfall Winterspring in person.

"You're a natural for television," Mother said. That morning, for once, as she brushed my hair, she didn't yank it off my scalp.

My mother liked to say out loud that I had "the face of a cameo" and a "perfectly chiseled nose." This I heard over and over for as long as I can remember, along with the other "compliment": "She *looks* like him, but she *thinks* like me!" People would laugh at these quips, but I never understood why. I knew that she hated her own long nose because she said that, too, often enough and bemoaned her fear of fixing it. Once she even put a fifty-dollar deposit on a nose job and then lost her nerve and the fifty bucks at the last minute.

I was often reminded of how important it was to have "good features" like mine. "You have the face of a cameo," she'd say, but unsmiling, so I wasn't sure if that was a compliment either. There was an old woman in our building who always wore a cameo pin on her coat, and, chiseled or not, it looked to me like a sickly-white old lady's face.

Whatever it was that landed me on *The Howdy Doody Show* didn't matter; I won the fight for which dress I'd wear—the hated Scotch plaid or my new lavender one with the dark-purple trim—and Mother even kissed me that morning, a rare event. But sitting in the Peanut Gallery turned out to be very different from watching it on TV. I guess because I was tall they sat me in the last row, scrunched between a fidgety girl in a white dress, who kept pulling it away because she accused me of sitting on it, and a sweaty boy who smelled sickeningly of too much Brylcreem hair pomade. The studio lights were so white and blindingly hot that it wasn't long before I felt like I had to vomit.

At home Buffalo Bob smiled during the whole show, but in person he seemed so unfriendly! In fact, he looked *mean* as he strolled up and down in front of the Peanut Gallery, squinting and searching through the rows of kids for . . . something. Nausea rose up to my mouth again, and I swallowed hard. Then, maybe because I was afraid of throwing up on television, I started to cry. I wanted out of those jammed, stuffy bleachers and away from mean Buffalo Bob and what seemed like five thousand screaming kids.

Just then, Smith noticed me. He scowled. In one swift motion he pointed straight at me and jerked his thumb, giving the usher the signal to take me out. It was just two minutes before we were to go on air. I cried harder. Soon Mother was brought into the little room offstage where they had taken me, and I didn't like her face: shocked and then furious. Everyone at home, all my aunts and uncles, cousins, neighbors, and friends, anyone who had a TV set, was tuned in to watch my television debut. She wouldn't even look at me on the subway ride home. Both our moods were the exact opposite of how they'd been going down to the studio. Uptown we were dead quiet.

My aborted TV appearance, for some reason, came back to me on that particular swim therapy day. I just knew that the floating lesson would not go well either. I'd get these "feelings" from time to time, like my nona did. Like hers, they came from nowhere or happened anywhere, when I least expected, and I often got a stomachache from it. Naturally, my aunts weren't at all surprised that I had them. To the Turks that some among us were clairvoyant was taken as fact.

The swim star's name was Eleanor Holm. I had never heard of her, but they said she had won a gold medal in the 1932 Olympics. She was older than I thought she'd be, although she couldn't have been over forty, and very pretty. Her dark hair was tied back, away from her face, and she wore a smooth, one-piece, black bathing suit. I was fascinated by her long, muscular legs and by how she dived effortlessly into the pool, barely splashing the water, gliding from one end to the other in no time, like a seal. But there was something about her I did not trust.

The other kids had no problem swimming with an Olympic champ. She held each child in turn as they lay on their backs, her hands supporting them from underneath, and showed them how to float above water. Everyone got a fast ride around the pool, too, and loved it. And one or two actually floated for some minutes on their backs while she took her hands away. Not one face went under water.

I begged to go last, hoping she'd get tired. As each kid finished and was floated back to the side of the pool, I'd change places with whoever was behind me until, finally, there was no one left. It was my turn, and I couldn't get out of it. I remember the flicker of annoyance in Holm's eyes when I said I did not want to float. It was just a blink, but I knew she was tiring of my protests.

"Just relax," she said, "and you'll float like a dream."

I made her promise not to take her hands from underneath me. I did not want to see the ceiling nor lay on my back on top of water.

"Even if I take my hands away, you'll float! You'll see!"

All the others were shouting, encouraging me to go ahead and do it, pressuring me not to be a baby. And the swim star was fast losing patience. "You'll see, honey, it's *easy*. I won't let you sink!"

I didn't believe that for one minute, but what could I do? Everything was all right for a couple of minutes while Holm glided around the pool with me in her arms, smiling as if she were being filmed. The rest of them clapped because I had finally let her hold me; they thought I was floating. She held my body just above the water and circled the pool easily with me a few times, like a waiter carries a plate. Then, right in the middle, we stopped.

"Don't go!" I begged. She went anyway.

First, a moment of peace as I focused on the ceiling, where sparkly little dots danced and shimmered, as if reflected by the water. Then I sank like a stone.

I think I hit bottom. As I went down, I saw Holm's dark eyebrows knit together in a frown, more puzzled than angry. Her mouth opened really wide and stayed that way. Maybe she said something, I don't know. All I heard was *glub blub*, as I sucked in chlorinated water and choked.

Six hands grabbed me from all sides; they pounded my back, turned me around, and shook me. Holm kept insisting, over and over, "That has never happened to me, *never*! No one has *ever* gone down . . . I don't understand it! You're not supposed to sink!"

I didn't trust her from the start, but I vowed to make a bigger fuss next time someone tried to convince me that they'd "hold me up," in or out of the water, when I knew better. The good thing, though, was that the mishap got me out of swim therapy for a week.

All the polios, those who were still paralyzed and those who were getting better, had treatments and therapies; many also endured more serious procedures, like spinal and other orthopedic operations. Sometimes they took dead muscles from the front of the leg and switched them with stronger ones in the back, like hamstrings to replace quadriceps, for instance, in the hope for more function. Or a foot would be stabilized into a permanent, rigid position so that it would no longer "drop" when the person walked. Occasionally, these experimental procedures worked well; often the surgeries only maimed the victim further.

Many of us lost a lot of weight in the hospital, especially after the acute phase of the disease was past. I lost about twenty pounds, which did nothing to add to my pale, polio-ravished appearance. As they wheeled us to hydrotherapy, X ray, or for more surgery, we glanced at each other in passing, broken, patched-up, emaciated—though brave!—little kids, and we smiled and waved at each other. Whenever I saw someone my age swathed in bandages or encased in a huge white plaster cast, I felt so lucky that it wasn't me getting operated on.

But nothing, not even my near drowning, got me out of the Sister Kenny treatments. This was routine therapy at Lenox Hill, and not even the holy water from Lourdes, my hanging man, nor a shiny silver mezuzah could stop it. Everyone dreaded it. Sister Kenny was an Australian nurse who believed that muscles paralyzed from polio could possibly be revived if they were stimulated with wet heat, and often it helped relieve painful muscle spasms as well. The pioneer nurse traveled around the country during the epidemics, demonstrating to nurses and doctors, some of whom laughed at her methods and distrusted them, how the treatments were applied.

Kenny didn't believe in putting lifeless legs into splints, a common practice then, claiming that it caused weak muscles to atrophy. Although she rarely got the credit she deserved, a lot of polios were helped, even healed, by the hot-pack treatment, which was credited with the return, in some cases, of significant muscle function that otherwise might not have occurred. That is, if you could stand the ordeal to begin with. They never came right out and said that wet heat definitely reinnervated weak muscles, but my doctors believed in the treatment, and neither one of my legs shrank in size from disuse. Enduring the procedure was so awful, though, that, had I known my father gave his permission for it, I'd have been very angry with him.

Everyone in the beds suddenly stopped talking mid-afternoon each day, when the aluminum carts rattled toward us. Laundry tubs filled with water were plugged into an electrical outlet in our room to heat up what would become steaming-hot woolen cloths. Then, just at that temperature, they'd be placed on our paralyzed legs. Futile as it was, some of us hid under our sheets as the cart approached. These flannel cloths were so hot that the nurses couldn't touch them with their bare hands; they had to be fished out of a cylindrical pot with a stick or tongs. This burning misery stayed on, usually, until the flannel turned cold. Then you'd be shivering—but not for long. In a half hour or so the nurse returned, and some freshly boiled flannels were applied.

The badge of a courageous child was taking the Sister Kenny treatment as hot as they gave it without weeping or whimpering. I'd compete with myself every day to do better than the day before and not make a sound. But even the boys cried out, it was so painful. Only Alice, lying there like a fallen, white-haired angel, while clouds of steam rose off her calves, kept smiling. Chief Nurse Murphy loved her for her stamina and praised her to the heavens, but I suspect that Alice barely felt the heat. As for me, I would forever loathe the smell of wet wool; it made me queasy. In wintertime, whenever my coat got soaked with snow or rain and we hung it to dry in the bathroom, I'd shudder. I couldn't go in there; the smell reminded me too much of those boiling cloths and the agony they caused.

The hot-pack treatments gave me a whole new set of nightmares. One night, maybe because I had been talking to Alice a lot about Grandma, I dreamt I was in her apartment, carrying a tray of Jordan almonds, water, and Turkish coffee around the room for company. As I passed her the *tavla*, it fell out of my hands, and everything on the tray broke. Scalding coffee splashed on my legs. Like most dreams, it seemed so real that I screamed for the nurse. Fully awake, I was astounded to realize that my legs actually *were* burning and tingling. Then I saw that while thrashing around I had knocked my pillow to the floor and with it the hanging man who had been underneath. A dilemma: Do I call for help and risk getting Nurse Cohen, or do I try to fetch the necklace myself?

Nurse Cohen was different from all the others. She had a reputation among the wards of being cruel and even of striking some children, plus she did not like me from the start. I didn't know why; there was just something about me that angered her. When she looked at me her eyes narrowed as if she were trying to figure out what I'd done wrong. I prayed that she wasn't on duty the night Jee-zus fell because I knew she'd be mean to me no matter what, if just for being up so late, and, most likely, she'd take my necklace away.

Lots of times the nurses chose to ignore us, even though we knew they heard our calls. Their station and the nurses' lounge were very close to our room. Those of us who couldn't sleep would listen to the late-night shift laugh and talk about their lives, their boyfriends, and where they had gone on dates. They consumed bags of potato chips, my favorite food, night after night. The rustling of the bags and their crunching made my mouth water.

The radio in the nurses' lounge played all night, some of the new rock and roll songs, like "Shake, Rattle, and Roll," and also dreamy 1940s music, like "Mood Indigo" and "Moonlight Serenade." *The Glenn Miller Story*, a nostalgic movie about the famous bandleader, had just come out, and most of them had gone to see it. They also talked nonstop about Marlon Brando, who won an Oscar for *On the Waterfront* that year. If it weren't for the lounge next door, I wouldn't have believed that our nurses had lives away from the hospital. Most of the time I only saw the stern, unsmiling side of them, in their white caps and starched pinafores. But late at night they were just ordinary women who went to the movies, danced, and visited places in the outside world that I barely remembered existed.

Everything was quiet the night I made my journey, so I decided not to call for help. Of course, all the other girls were asleep. As usual, I was the only one up; I never made it through a night without some calamity. Either I peed the bed and had to lay in it until someone decided to change it, or else I had a screaming nightmare. But this night something different occurred.

I simply couldn't leave the hanging man on the floor until morning and go back to sleep. I had to try to pick him up. I began to strategize how to do it. My bed was a good distance from the floor, pretty far for me to fall. Also, if I made it out of bed, how would I ever get back up? I needed Nona's eight ball, in whose murky liquid the right answer to every problem could be found.

I closed my eyes and concentrated: What would the eight ball say if I asked it, should I now get out of bed? The answer it most frequently gave seemed to whisper from the walls: *It seems so . . . It seems so . . .*

I wasn't a fearful child, which was why I got into trouble a lot; my curiosity often tempted me to do stuff that I shouldn't have. Once I even stole a jar of bubbles from the bin outside Joe's Book Store, on my friend Ellen's dare. I knew stealing was wrong, yet all she had to say was, "I have bubbles, and *you* don't!" I took them, and then I waited under my bed all afternoon, terrified, for the police to come and arrest me. Tante Sultana called me *werka,* devil, for doing it. No matter what the consequences, I could never resist a challenge.

I should have been scared to get out of bed simply because it had been almost a month since I walked. But I wasn't. It was because I, like Alice, also believed in the little hanging man. I felt she knew what she was talking about when she said that Jee-zus would see to it that I wouldn't get hurt. I had no idea that this was what people referred to as "faith." Also, Hopalong Cassidy, my cowboy hero, a Man of Action and Integrity, had many creeds; one was: "Only through hard work can you succeed. Don't be lazy!" It would be very hard work to get out of bed, I thought. Hoppy will certainly be proud of me. And that was it. Whenever I decided to do a thing, my habit was, at the moment of decision, to stop doubting whether or not I could.

Getting down was easier than I thought. First, I swung my legs over the edge until they dangled; I had done this before while doctors banged on my knees with their rubber reflex hammers. At that moment, as my life hung in limbo, a tune I later learned was called "String of Pearls" happened to be playing softly next door. I knew that everything in my life was going to change if only I got out of bed, hopefully, for the better. I had to do it! There was Grandma's voice in my ear again saying, *Try it, hija! Try it!* And suddenly it felt good, right. I felt like jumping.

Still, I hesitated. What a long way down! What if Nurse Cohen heard something and came in? She'd box my ears, her favorite punishment for girls she didn't like, or worse. I looked down, and there was Jee-zus, patiently waiting for me. He was all tangled up in the blue beads and lay upside down, like the Hanged Man on one of Nona's tarot cards. According to my grandma, if you drew the Hanged Man card, and if it faced the tarot reader when she turned it over, that meant you were suspended in indecision about some problem. Nona's advice for that was "sacrifice." You had to give up something, she said, for something else. Then you could "pass from one phase of life to another."

So, I sacrificed safety and jumped. Actually, I sort of slipped to the floor; the pillow broke my fall. There I lay, stunned, half on, half off, the pillow. First thing I grabbed the rosaries. Then I struggled to stand up, forgetting for a second that I was supposed to be paralyzed. Sleepy, and swaying a little with dizziness, I stood nonetheless, amazing myself as what I did began to sink in. I was actually *standing*. I held on to the side of the bed and looked around; nobody woke up, no nurse appeared. But I *was standing*! My knees started to shake from fear—too late, I was already up on my feet.

I took a tentative step to the side—so far so good. Then I took another and another. And then one more. I did not fall. I *walked*! Of course, I had to try no hands, so I let go, which was a mistake, and fell backwards on my head. Then I was in a predicament. Again, I had the option to yell for help or try to get up one more time. By that time, though, I was much too tired from the effort. All I could manage was to flip over on my stomach and crawl to a chair, dragging my legs behind me. The whole time I never let go of the hanging man. I couldn't believe it, but he and I made it across the room.

Getting onto the chair posed another problem. There was only one possible way to do it: somehow I had to get on my knees and turn around, which I did. Then, with my back to the chair and both hands on the seat behind me, I lifted myself up into a sitting position. It took three or four tries. Finally, there I sat, safe but extremely tired. I learned to perfect that little maneuver, and in a few weeks' time I'd demonstrate it over and over for the other kids in the Physical Therapy room at the Rusk Institute.

There was nothing left to do once I made it into the chair. I had no choice but to stay there until morning or until a nurse entered, which-ever came first. Exhausted from my little excursion and relieved it was over, I felt giddy with the feeling that I had accomplished an impossible physical act. I had never thought about my physicality before the experience of illness. I just lived in my own body, ran to catch a ball, jumped up and down, fell a lot, got scraped knees and elbows, and never gave it a second thought, all the stuff kids do in the course of a day. Now getting from bed to chair had become remarkable. This act of daring was another new thread that would be woven into my character. In the future I would be happy only when attempting the hardest, or nearly impossible, physical feats. It would give me an almost perverse excitement to do so, especially when told, "You can't."

Delighted at my own achievement, I carefully wound the rosaries around my fingers like I had seen Alice do and fell asleep upright in the chair.

When Luella, the nurse's aide, found me in the morning, she just assumed neglect: "Oh, honey, did somebody leave you here and forget about you?"

"No, I walked!"

She laughed, giving me that squinty-eyed look that people give liars, and carried me back to bed.

I knew no one would believe me, so I didn't tell anyone at first, not even my father. But every night, the minute I thought the time was right to do it, I got out of bed and practiced walking. I fell a lot. I had a bunch of red and blue bruises on my legs and hips. By the fourth night I made it to Alice's bed and woke her up. I scared the heck out of her, but she was excited for me.

"It's Jesus!" she said. "It's a miracle!"

Who was I to argue? A bigger miracle was that Nurse Cohen still hadn't found out about it, although Luella figured out what was going on. She didn't tell, but she was worried about my bruises and thought it time to come clean. She made me promise to tell my father that day, or she'd have to tell Nurse Cohen.

"You don't want her to find out before your daddy sees you walk, do you, honey?" The aides knew Cohen's reputation.

I had been saving the big news, hoping to be able to walk across the room to my father without holding on. I was almost there, but Alice couldn't hold out a moment longer; she broke down and told her mother. Mrs. Cook cried at first, and then they both said a million Hail

Marys over me. I wanted to get out of bed right then and show her how I did it, but she wouldn't let me.

A strange thing happened that day; Mrs. Cook couldn't *stop* crying. She kept looking from me to Alice, back and forth, and I believe she had a revelation that her daughter would never walk. If Alice thought so too, she didn't let on. In my opinion Alice was braver than any of us, well tempered and quietly stoic. No matter what she knew, Mrs. Cook continued to bring the ice skates to the hospital every day.

The night I walked into my father's arms I was so anxious about doing it that I couldn't eat. He had arrived earlier than usual, during my supper. When he saw my food tray untouched, he went out to get me a candy bar, and while he was gone I got off the bed. Alice covered her eyes; she couldn't bear to see me fall.

He walked in, saw me standing, and stopped, mouth open. Then he pushed his hat to the back of his head and got down on one knee. For a minute I thought he'd cry, like when Behora died, because his face crumpled up. He recovered fast, though, smiling that ear-to-ear grin he was known for, and opened his arms for me to walk into.

"That-a girl! I knew you'd do it, I just knew!"

Carefully, I walked toward him—well, let's say I took some teetering steps in his direction—without holding onto anything. I think I could have made it into his waiting arms, but he met me halfway and grabbed me so hard that his hat got knocked to the floor. For once he didn't care.

"Wait'll your mother hears!"

Then I confessed. I told him how I had practiced every single night by getting off the bed all by myself and how I would sometimes fall asleep in a chair until the morning. All the while, though, I worried that Nurse Cohen would find out and box my ears, and I finally admitted this to my father.

"She would never touch you!" he said. "And who cares about her, anyway? You're walking! You keep it up, and I'll go tip her or something."

So typical of my father: There isn't anyone who can't be bribed with a monetary gift. As it turned out, we had both tragically underestimated the night nurse's cruelty.

It didn't take long for word to get around that I was the "miracle" of a ward filled with polio kids. Doctors, nurses, nuns, and the hospital priest came to see me. Some just wanted to touch my hand or face, for some reason. New doctors kept getting added to those already making rounds; they gathered by my bed to test my reflex responses and watched while I took a few shaky steps. I couldn't go far without my knees buckling, but each time I walked I silently prayed to my hanging man to keep me from falling. I got very tired from all this exertion, but no one could deny I was walking unassisted.

They determined that I'd definitely need braces and crutches, yet every doctor who ever saw me, then and later and throughout the years, was astounded at how I functioned. They all said the same things, words I got weary of hearing so many times: "Incredible!" "Amazing!" "Impossible!" And: "How do you *do* it?" I had dead quadriceps in my left leg, as those nerves never rejuvenated. Still, I walked. I was prepared, too, for doctors' discomfort and skepticism when they heard "miracle." Some laughed; some got disgusted. Thank goodness for those like Dr. Deaver, a kindly, heavyset man who was loved on the polio wards for his ability to calm and appease mothers. He was one of the few who told my father: "There is more we *don't* know than things we do. Perhaps it was a miracle after all."

Now that I was up on my feet, Dr. Deaver arranged for a "brace man" to visit and fit me with leg braces, plus something called a "Milwaukee Brace," which I did not like the sound of at all. He explained that those things would keep me straight and help me walk even better and for longer periods of time. Now there was an end in sight to hospitals. I wanted to go home for my fast-approaching eighth birthday in early November. If not then, perhaps, they said, I'd be discharged in time for Thanksgiving.

The Milwaukee Brace was as ugly and uncomfortable as I had imagined. It was a neck-to-pelvis contraption with leather straps and metal sides, very cumbersome, and hard to get into. Two nurses had to do it, and I usually made such a fuss that they were happy to wait until my father came so he could do it. For as long as I wore that thing, at least six weeks, my father was the only one able to get it on me.

With the Milwaukee, two full-length metal leg braces, and crutches under each armpit, I walked, or, rather, I jerked down the hallway, kind of like the Tin Man in The Wizard of Oz. Up and down the length of the hall I'd go, with my dad and a physical therapist behind and alongside me, clutching the back of my pajama pants in case I pitched forward. Soon, Dad promised, I'd wear real clothes, but I knew that, no matter what I put on, I'd still look like a walking robot in that ugly body brace.

I loved being the center of attention. While I wasn't about to be spared from the hot-pack therapy to come, nor from painful pull-and-stretch muscle exercises, I was admired and respected by the staff for my spunk. Suddenly, I was even Nurse Murphy's favorite.

"There's a good soldier!"

If Alice minded being second place now, of course she didn't let on.

Polio had again fooled the doctors. A rebound like mine, a whole month past the acute stage, rarely happened. There were many suppositions, but the doctors couldn't agree on any one thing that caused it. Some thought it was the Sister Kenny treatments that helped to revive and loosen up my contracted muscles; others scoffed at it and called it bunk. And then there was that tiny band of believers, Alice and myself included, who knew the truth about certain unseen forces. As the professionals tried to figure out why it happened, I got up every night and practiced walking, my little man tucked neatly inside the breast pocket of my pajama top.

A few days after my walking midnight miracle, Mrs. Cook showed up accompanied by her parish priest, a man called Father Thomas. He was young, quite pale, had dark hair, and wore wire-rimmed glasses. He stood by my bed, hands clasped in front of his black suit, and looked at me for a long time without speaking. It felt very strange having him stare at me like that; I didn't know what to do with my own eyes and kept shifting them from right to left. Other hospital priests had come by from time to time, asked me what my religion was, and, when I told them "Jewish," they usually just wished me well and left. Father Thomas was different. When he finally spoke, he asked:

"Child, do you know what has happened to you?"

"I walked."

"Oh, it's more than that. You have received grace from God. High grace. Do you know what that is?"

I said yes anyway, hoping he wouldn't question me further. Then, hands folded in prayer, the priest and Alice's mother knelt together by my bed and bowed their heads. They stayed on their knees for a long time. Meanwhile, Alice, eyes closed, prayed from her bed.

"I'm Jewish," I said, when they finally stood up. Apparently, that didn't matter at all. I had been given something good called "grace," and that, I learned, was the miracle.

Father Thomas was very smart and knew all about the Sephardic Jews from Spain. In fact, he knew more about us than we did. He sat on my bed and asked if I wanted to hear a story "about your people." I, who loved stories, said sure, and his turned out to be really interesting. They were about the Spanish Inquisition, about martyrs who could not be redeemed and torture chambers and people who were "relaxed." This, the priest said, didn't mean "rested." It meant that the head of the Catholic Tribunal relaxed them, or handed them over to another bunch of people who then tortured them by burning them up in fire ceremonies that everyone witnessed in the middle of town.

The victims were Jews, he said, called "penitents," who were forced to march through the streets of Spain wearing yellow vests and hoods. I loved these exciting, new stories, but I didn't admit to the priest that I really didn't get what "marders," "tribes," and "penny-tents" had to do with me.

In Father Thomas's opinion I had been blessed, not a few days or a couple of weeks ago, when I came out of a near-coma, and not even when I first walked, but I had actually been given grace a very long time ago, probably hundreds of years.

"You, my dear little girl, have been marked; long marked for a blessing."

Most likely, he said, I was a descendant of conversos, or "New Christians," Jews who had truly converted to Christianity during the Spanish Inquisition in order to not get tortured and burned.

"They became Catholics, and they remained Catholics forever," he explained, "throughout the centuries." And that was why the Lord blessed me. "The ones who went back to their old religion, rest their souls, they died horrible, horrible deaths."

I begged him to tell me how, but he wouldn't. "The important thing," said the priest, "is that the Jews of Spain, your ancestors and your father's ancestors before that, always had a great affection for our Lord, Jesus Christ. They believed in him, thought him an honest man."

So, I was a brand-new Christian! That was great news; now I could have Christmas presents and Chanukah presents. I was happy for Alice, for Jesus, and for myself. All my friends, I knew, would be so jealous when I celebrated Christmas. I was positive that now Mother would allow us to have a Christmas tree. All of this kind of made sense to me. For one thing there was that Greek convent on the island of Chios where my aunts had been educated, a place they never stopped talking about. Of course, this meant that they were New Christians too but kept it a secret. Their faces undeniably changed expression when they mentioned the Greek nuns, the statues in the monastery, the elaborate tapestries, and all the statues of saints scattered around the grounds. And the way they always added, "But when it came time to teach the catechisms, we went out! We always went outside!" made me think that they felt guilty for not *wanting* to go outside. I had it all figured out.

I told the Father about my tantes, about how every time a nun passed on the Grand Concourse they'd twist a button around on their coats, mutter a Ladino prayer, and make me do it, too. He didn't know anything about button rotation, but he agreed with me about them being New Christians. That might certainly be true.

"A wonderful thing," he said, looking at my hanging man. "A wonderful thing."

Subsequently, an even bigger miracle took place. Word of my walking, the hanging man necklace, the holy water, and all the other Christian stuff inevitably got back to my mother. Instantly, she snapped out of her lethargy. This was just the catalyst, a good fight, that she needed. Her daughter, the granddaughter of a prominent rabbi, praying with *rosaries?*

I'd been waiting a long time to hear her step. Then, just like that, there she was, tall as ever in the doorway, in her forest-green in-between coat, her beige beret with the short black feather sticking up on one side, and black suede gloves. The green coat accentuated her red hair; it seemed brighter than I remembered. She took off the gloves and slapped them a few times in her palm. I saw she was trying hard to smile, and she almost pulled it off. But, smiling or serious, to me she looked good.

We all stared at her—we couldn't help it: Alice, Mrs. Cook, the broken-neck girl, the sign-girl, and an aide who had been filling the water jugs. Behind Mother, right at her heels, stood an angry-looking security guard, breathing hard. He had chased her upstairs when she ignored his command, in the lobby, to stop. She kept on walking and was proud to tell the story of her defiance as she made her entrance onto the ward. It was eventually added to her repertoire of adventures.

"The guard yelled, 'Stop, Lady, or I'll shoot you!' And I yelled back, 'So shoot!' Did he think he was going to keep me from seeing my child, no matter *what* time of day it was?"

I didn't doubt the exchange for a minute. Mother turned, gave the guard one of her "looks," and, grumbling, he backed out. Whatever sickness she had was gone, and obviously she was all better. Even so, something told me to hide the rosaries.

My mother seemed thinner to me. She worried that I was, too: "Why aren't you eating?" was her first question. She had brought me a big piece of Tante Allegre's delicious spinach pie, and, though I had no appetite for it, I made an attempt to nibble a piece to make her happy.

"And here's a present from me." She unwrapped a small, silver rectangle on a chain. It was a *mezuzah*, an exact miniature of the kind we had bolted to our front door at home. She showed me that inside was a tiny scroll with holy words written in Hebrew, and then she fastened it around my neck.

"This is what you should be wearing, not that . . . that thing. Give it back."

"I won't!" I shoved the beads further under the pillow. I would fight to keep him — my hanging man wasn't going anywhere out of my sight. Mother and I locked eyes, just like we'd always done.

"Never show it to me again," she said.

Later, when Father Thomas came, he was delighted to meet Mother. He bent his head toward her, saying "God bless you!" a couple of times in his cheerful way. Mother was unimpressed.

"Yeah, you too."

"Your young lady here certainly has spirit, doesn't she?"

"Yes, of course! Have you ever known a Jew without it?"

She leaned in close to me: "Listen. They've been trying to convert us for thousands of years. You are the daughter of a Jewish mother, who's the daughter of a rabbi. That makes you 100 percent Jewish, and you will *always* be Jewish, no matter what *bavazhadas*, nonsense stories, people tell you. Period."

And that was the end of it. She never mentioned the rosaries again.

My mother took charge and changed some things for the better. Although my dad threw a few fives around for the aides, and all the nurses loved him because he was so good-looking, he usually came at night, often arriving very late, and rarely saw how it was for me daily on the ward. First, she saw to it that I got ice cream every day with lunch and somehow schemed to have them bring lunches to her and to Mrs. Cook, too. Next, she corralled every single doctor who ever examined me for the lowdown on my walking situation. She came to the conclusion that I would have no more spinal taps, no splinting, and definitely no casting, as casted limbs often caused the muscles to shrink. For this I would always thank her, as neither one of my legs atrophied.

But the bad news was there was only so much they could do at Lenox Hill. If I really wanted to walk "like everybody else," I'd have to go to the Rusk Institute on First Avenue and the East River for extensive physical therapy. The last thing I wanted was to be in yet another hospital, and I refused to listen when she brought it up, putting my hands over my ears. I craved nothing special, only the ordinary things: to be home for my birthday, have a party and eat ice cream cake with my friends, wear a brand-new dress, and play pin-the-tail-on-the-donkey. But in the back of my mind the phrase "walk like everyone else" stuck. I knew that if I went home now that wouldn't happen.

Mother's final mission was to find me a rabbi. She found two, one young and one very old, who both visited me every day. I didn't care for the old one with the long beard at all, and he knew it. His beard smelled like garlic, and I kept drawing farther back from him as he spoke. He stopped coming after a few days. The young one wasn't that bad, but I didn't like him nearly as much as Father Thomas. He didn't smile much, nor did he tell me good stories. And for some reason I was embarrassed and felt my face go hot when he rocked back and forth at my bed, reading the Hebrew prayers while Mrs. Cook and Alice watched. He'd then stop suddenly, open his black book at random, and talk to me in English about "mercy" and "abandon." I had no idea what he was talking about. Or else he'd tell me things about my grandfather that I already knew, like how his name, Sedacca, in Hebrew meant "goodness and charity."

"I know," I said, sullenly. I was not very nice to him.

One day, to combat his boring chanting and *davening*, I pulled out the hanging man from under my pillow and dangled it in front of the rabbi's face: "Do you know Jee-zus?" I asked. "He helped me, and that's why I can walk now."

A faraway look came into his eyes, and they opened wide. He took a step back from me. After a few minutes of silence he said, "Little girl, I pray for *shelemut* for you and for wholeness and completeness. *Shabbat Shalom!*"

With that the rabbi clapped his book shut and left. I never saw him again.

My hair had not been washed in nearly two months. This wasn't uncommon; the polio wards were full, the nurses and aides were short-staffed, and children were in hospital so long that parents and relatives couldn't hang around all day, every day. Most had resumed their natural routines. For many of us getting shifted around and placed in awkward positions in order to have our hair washed in bed was a painful, if not nightmarish, proposition. The iron lung polios sometimes went months with greasy hair.

Because my birthday was a few days away and I was doing so well, it was decided that I should have a bath and a shampoo. This was a big event. I was taken to a large bathroom on the same floor that I hadn't known existed until that moment and put into a regular bathtub that stood on four curved legs. The hot water felt so good on my itchy scalp; it was fun and normal being in the bathtub again. And there I soaked, feeling normal. And soaked. And soaked. Though she said she'd be back in "a little while" to take me out, the nurse never returned.

I have no idea how long I was actually in the bath, probably over an hour. My fingertips had been shriveled for a long time, and the water was no longer hot. I now seriously mistrusted anything that had to do with water and the people who put me into it. In fact, I hated water. It brought only trouble, and, worse, it meant total helplessness. I shivered, and my teeth chattered. It was clear that I'd spend the rest of my life in a stagnant bath.

I realized, just like the times I swung in limbo over the whirlpool vat, and when the famous swim star let me sink, that I could not get out by myself. I felt trapped and, at the same time, incredulous that I could do *nothing* about my situation. Nothing. I stared at my dormant legs, so still under the cloudy bathwater. They were the same legs I always had — that is, they looked the same. Nothing had changed in appearance, except they didn't work. Why didn't they? Why couldn't they move? I was angry at my legs for this. As if separate from my body, they had called a strike and deserted me, taunting, "You can't walk without us!"

I called out once or twice, but no one came, even though the bathroom door was partially open. I had already become accustomed to waiting; it was my newly acquired skill. Not that I hadn't always known about it. Mother would stop to talk with a neighbor on the street, and then talk and talk, while I fidgeted, squirmed, and pulled at her sleeve. "Wait!" she'd say. And I always had to wait for dessert until after the awful okra or green peas were finished. But there was an end in sight; now waiting was ongoing, every day. And I never did waiting well. I wasn't nice about it, like Alice, a nurse's dream. If they forgot about her, she just kept on waiting, silent and peaceful. She never called twice. From my time in two hospitals I was learning that the more demanding you were, the longer you'd have to wait.

Down the hall a radio played a catchy tune. Music is the bookmark for the various junctures in our lives that become memory. The song comes on, and we're back in the era. Forever, taking a long bath would be associated with the Chordettes singing, *Mr. Sandman . . . bring me a dream . . . bom bom bom bom . . . make him the cu-test that I've ever seen . . .* By the time I was rescued, the radio, somewhere not far away from that bathroom, had the chance to play it twice, and I knew the words by heart . . . *and tell me that my lonely nights are o-ver . . .*

With my fingertips now bone-white and with goose pimples all over, I forced myself to sing along with the sixteen-bar, *bom bom bom bom* refrain, just to keep distracted. "Mr. Sandman" stayed in my head for weeks; I'd hear it when I woke up, I'd hum it all day, and it ran through my head until I fell asleep.

An unrepentant nurse finally rushed in, hauled me out of the bath, wrapped me in a couple of towels, and raced me back to my room before anyone figured out she had totally forgotten about me. I was shaking and cold but very very clean.

For my eighth birthday there were exceptional gifts and special visitors. My roommates looked on jealously as I opened the best surprise: a

Hopalong Cassidy watch with a picture of William Boyd, the actor who played Hoppy, big as life on the dial. He stood there in black and white, a hand resting on either gun, as if about to draw. Adding to its beauty, the big hand and the little hand glowed in the dark. When I held it up, they gasped. The card read, *Hoppy Birthday! Love, Hoppy and the Gang at the Old Bar 20.*

When I asked Dad if Hoppy really sent it, he swore, dead serious, that he had: "Who else?"

I adored Hopalong Cassidy, far more than the freckled-face, silly-looking Howdy Doody, and I never missed his TV show. Except for my father, I thought Hoppy, in his black cowboy suit and hat and white necktie, was the handsomest man in the world. I loved his white horse, Topper, too, and even his friend Lucky. I touched the watch's face all day, thrilled. But along with good gifts came birthday disappointments as well. I did not get the expensive Hopalong Cassidy bike that I'd begged for. I half-expected my father to walk in wheeling it that day, and the fact that I might never again ride a bike didn't occur to me. I just figured they couldn't afford the sixty bucks for it.

My father denied, for the next five years, that he was the one who sent me birthday and Valentine's Day cards from Hopalong Cassidy. They were signed, "Love always, Hoppy," had no return address, and contained the sweetest sayings and messages, like "Thinking of the prettiest Valentine, Love, Hoppy" and "Your birthday means so much to Hoppy!" Mother told me that the postmark came from Manhattan because that's where Hoppy's agent worked. The cards made me feel loved just when I needed it most. The thought that Hoppy, busy in Hollywood with all the things a cowboy does, took time to remember my birthday thrilled me. And even when I got older and knew for sure that they didn't come from Hollywood at all, but a place much closer to home, I was still surprised to know who really sent them.

I never took the watch off. I placed its box under the pillow next to the hanging man, and the Timex watch with the black alligator band and Radiolite dial, sent by my aunts and uncles, went into the drawer of my nightstand. I was comforted to have two watches; that way, if one of them suddenly stopped, the other would be able to tell me the time. Often I'd awake at night just to make sure that the Sworn Enemy of Crime and Cruelty was there, glowing, watching out for me.

Another treasure came from an unexpected visitor, a distant cousin through marriage, named Fina Gallano, a talented, well-known portrait painter. She had painted many faces, some famous, some ordinary. Aunt Fina had also endured a great sadness in her life. Her only daughter, at just my age, eight, died after a terrible case of the measles. When Mother spoke of it or mentioned Fina's name, she did so reverently. My mother said Fina was "gifted and a *grand* lady." And then she'd sigh. Because she neither looked nor spoke like any other Sephardi we knew, including rich ones, I called her "Fancy Lady."

The artist wore beautiful green eye shadow and dark-red lipstick the day she came to the hospital. She had dressed up, she said, just for me. As if I were important. Even the nurses wondered about her; she was tall and had on a royal blue suit and a luxurious, sable-brown mink coat, the kind Mother wanted. Her dark-brown hair was worn in a bun at the base of her neck; she wore it that way all the years we knew her. I tried not to stare too long at the big brown box she carried from Saks Fifth Avenue. I knew it was for me.

Aunt Fina stared, though. She studied me, head cocked to one side, for so long I began to twitch. I didn't realize that that's what painters do; they stare and study. Finally, she put the box down.

"Would you like me to show you?"

Slowly, dramatically, the Fancy Lady unwrapped my gift: a matching two-piece outfit in gold paisley. I had never seen a dress like it. Then she formally presented it to me, laying it in my lap.

"For you!"

It had been so long since I wore real clothes. I didn't know what to say or if I should unbutton my pajama top and try the blouse on. She read my mind.

"You *don't* have to put it on *today;* just remember, you *won't* be in hospital clothes for the rest of your *life.*" Aunt Fina spoke like that, in deliberate, clear sentences, stressing every other word and enunciating perfectly. "This can *be* your *new* back-to-*school* outfit."

It was the loveliest dress I'd ever seen. I had forgotten about clothes, about picking out skirts and tops the night before, for school. But I knew I'd never forget this gift or the way she spoke and how she presented it to me. The skirt and blouse were so pretty that I, too, would be again. I'd wear dresses, this dress, and go back to school. Sadly, I outgrew the outfit before that happened, but for sentimental reasons I kept it for years after it should have been given away, not wanting to part with the memory of how I got it.

Before she left, as if she were folding a queen's robe, Aunt Fina repacked the dress and put it at the foot of my bed. Then she stepped back to admire me again, holding my face in her perfumed hand. She told me that my time in bed would be "so brief—why, it is nearly over!" I hope I managed a thank-you. I was in such awe of her that I was often speechless around her. But she played more of a role in my life than anyone knew. When, at thirteen, I wrote my first real poem, Fina gave it to an author friend of hers, a woman named Esther L. Schwartz, who sent me her book, *How to Become a Professional Writer*. Inside the book, too, was a note that read: "I told a writer friend about your poem, and she liked it so much that she autographed this book for you." Signed, *Fancy Lady*.

That a real, true author wrote, inside her own book, words of praise for my poem was another incredible gift and one that gave me encouragement to keep writing.

Mother missed Aunt Fina; she had already left by the time my mother got there, but she put her hand to her throat when she saw the dress. It made her cry. I was used to that; I didn't get it, but lately everything made her cry. Sometimes I, too, cried along with her, not knowing why. Mother carefully rewrapped the dress and, although I didn't want her to, took it home. I would have liked to keep it there a couple of days, just to look at.

Two more visitors that week were my Uncle Albert and Aunt Vicky. It was mid-afternoon after whirlpool, and I was exhausted. Maybe because I was lying down, I looked sicker than I was. My aunt's big, dark eyes opened wider when she saw me, and I noticed that she kept as far back from my bed as she could. She looked nervous the whole time she was there. I still wasn't used to not being kissed; before, I had to beg my uncles to stop planting a hundred wet, slurping kisses all over my face. Even though we weren't in the contagious hospital anymore, the ones who weren't outright afraid to come were still scared to get too close.

Uncle Albert and Aunt Vicky were quite a pair. She was considered beautiful, an olive-skinned Sephardi, who acted cool and aloof. The both of them fascinated me with their interchanges. Mother was jealous of Aunt Vicky's nose, which she confided to me had certainly been "fixed." She looked down on her, called Vicky "the janitor's daughter" when she talked about her, because Vicky's father was once the super of a building on Washington Avenue. "Al and Mrs. Capone," Mother said. Maybe that's why my aunt acted stuck-up, to get over that.

When she addressed Uncle Al, my aunt did it in a deadpan manner, sounding a lot like Keely Smith talking to Louis Prima. She'd say outrageous things without ever changing her expression. For instance, one time when I was riding in their car on the way to a wedding, my uncle got lost. If it were my mother, she would have immediately started bitching and accused my dad of being a bad driver. But Aunt Vicky, cool as ever, just kept on filing her nails, as if she hadn't noticed we were on some back road in the middle of Long Island. Finally, so low I didn't think I heard right, she said, "Al, would you please drop dead?" I tried not to, putting my hand over my mouth, but I had to laugh. My father would have gone crazy. My uncle didn't even react; he just kept on driving.

Uncle Al told me he had brought me a "big surprise," although I saw they carried nothing. He then unlocked the wheels on my bed and pushed it toward the window, jamming it into the sign-girl's bed. Luckily, she wasn't in it at the time.

"Maybe the genius shouldn't move her bed," my aunt said, in monotone, expression unchanged. I laughed. I could never understand why my mother hated Aunt Vicky so much. I always thought she was very funny.

He didn't answer, of course, but instead turned me around so that I could see out. In that way he was exactly like my father: They both did whatever they wanted, when they wanted.

"Look down," he said. I looked. There, in the street below, were my three cousins, Sandra, Alan, and Larry, waving frantically in the direction of my window. They were dressed for winter, in heavy jackets, hats, and gloves. Winter already? In our hospital room the temperature never changed. Sandra, a couple of years older than me, was the tallest of the three. It looked, from where I was, like she wore a white fur hat that I'd never seen before. The three waved and waved. When they finally got tired, they stopped for a second to rest then resumed with jumping jacks.

It was the first time in over a month that I'd seen children who weren't sick. Another thing I had forgotten about: jumping jacks and bulky winter clothes. I started to wave back and then stopped. I knew I could see them, but they were too far away to see me, even though Uncle Al said they did. He had first come up to my room when I was in the whirlpool and judged exactly where, downstairs, they should stand. He thought I'd be happy seeing my cousins—Alan and Larry were so handsome, my friends loved it when they visited—so I didn't want to disappoint him, but the visit had the opposite effect. I thought about it long after they left, too. It was at that moment, by the window, that I acknowledged for the very first time that I was different now from all my cousins. I knew it for certain, but I didn't want to be different. And, just as fast, I promised myself that, even if that was true now, one day I would do much better jumping jacks than they did.

Maybe Mother sensed what I was feeling because she got angry when I told her how I saw my cousins "in the street."

"Some surprise!" she said.

As it turned out, my Uncle Albert's attempted kindness caused more trouble than even he could have guessed. Soon after the visit my father took a *punto*, an injury to his "point of honor," when Uncle Kelly and Aunt Lee didn't visit me in the hospital like Uncle Al did. A huge rift formed between the brothers that lasted for the next thirty-five years. Eventually, he'd hate Uncle Albert as well, for other things, but for now it was just Kelly, and he stopped talking to him because of it.

As the Thanksgiving holiday approached, the ward took on a festive look, and everyone seemed to be in happy anticipation of something. They pasted cutouts of turkeys and silhouettes of pilgrims on our door, and I began to feel excited as in years past, when I couldn't wait for the holiday to come. The one ritual our family kept to was going, all four of us, even the baby, to the Macy's Thanksgiving Day Parade. Even Mother got up that day early enough to catch the subway down to 34th Street and find a good position at the curb, so we could see everything. I loved the heart-pounding drums and the marching bands that my brother slept through, which I watched from on top of my dad's shoulders. I had no reason to think that I wouldn't go to the parade when I got out of the hospital. I didn't know that the only reason Mother went was to see, and have me see, the Rockettes close up.

My mother was obsessed with line dancers, especially the Rockettes, although she also loved the June Taylor Dancers on "The Jackie Gleason Show" and would wake me up if I was sleeping to see them or any dance act on TV that I might miss. I knew she had this career in mind for me by the way she'd push me practically into the street when they were about to approach. The cops always had to shout at her to get back. There were so few times my mother got enthusiastic that I let her push and pull me; it was better than her being her usual: annoyed with me.

It was natural to think that the holiday caused such palpable excitement, but I was wrong. It was the "special visitor" coming to visit the polio ward whom everyone was anxious about meeting. We knew it was a man, and, whoever he was, the nurses were especially revved up. In fact, they were a little crazy with it. The cleaning and straightening up began as early as six o'clock on the morning he was to arrive. This was "a *real* movie star," they said, but they were still mum as far as telling us his name.

I was fed up with surprises and with celebrities. I couldn't think of anyone I wanted to meet except, of course, my idol, Hopalong Cassidy. But I had no expectations he would come from California to visit a hospital in Manhattan. Somehow my father would have found out about it and told me. I just wanted him to get there already, as the nurses' state of electrified anticipation was rubbing off on me and making me, and everyone else who wasn't comatose, dizzy.

Aides and janitors zipped in and out, back and forth, all morning, washing and scrubbing; they even washed the window. Every five minutes a nurse popped her head in the room to make sure our beds were straightened and we weren't eating in them. Finally, they dumped all the wilted or dead flowers and brought in a few new arrangements, which smelled fresh and sweet. Taking no chances, our room was sprayed with a perfumy floral mist. It smelled overwhelmingly better than the ever-present disinfectant.

I had never seen anything like this cleanup. Our drab hospital room was transformed; it sparkled. We shined, too. Those of us who could brushed and fixed up our own hair; aides groomed the others. I became envious of one girl in the room who had long braids. As I watched a nurse plait them, I suddenly wanted my old hair back. I didn't even have a mirror in my drawer, nor did I care, until that moment of movie star madness. I wanted to see what I looked like; I wanted to get dressed up and wear patent leather Mary Janes. New pajamas, not that I had a pair anyway, wasn't enough. I had a feeling Mother should have left me the paisley dress from Aunt Fina. That would have been a perfect celebrity outfit.

By noon he still hadn't arrived. They kept pushing up the time, until it was two o'clock. We were all yawning. The flowers were still fresh, but my roommates and I were drooping a bit. Then, when we least expected it, squeals from the staff alerted us to the fact that he'd come, trailed by an entourage of white-coated doctors, giggling nurses, and other hospital people in suits. In addition, the movie star had his own little group tagging after him who stuck close by his side every step of the way. The whole group sort of all moved as one body.

Of course, it wasn't my Man of Action, Epitome of Gallantry and Fair Play. Instead of a handsome cowboy in black was an ordinary-looking guy in a plain white shirt and dark coat. Alice and I exchanged baffled looks, but, naturally, she kept her mouth shut. This *couldn't* be the someone famous!

Dramatically, with a sweep of her arm, one of the floor nurses stepped forward, something she'd been waiting all morning to do, and presented him: "Girls, I'd like you to meet *Marlon Brando!*"

Her eyes opened really wide as she pronounced his name.

"Who?"

The word slipped out before I could stop it.

That year Brando won an Oscar for *On the Waterfront.* He was apparently a heartthrob, one of the hottest actors around, and I guess they expected us to be thrilled that he chose to visit us polio kids. Brando also had an interest in playing the part of Jonas Salk in a movie that was under consideration in Hollywood. Salk himself was fast becoming a celebrity. Fewer and fewer cases of polio were being reported, thanks to his now 90 percent effective vaccine. There was actually an end in sight to a dreaded contagious disease, and Jonas Salk, more than any Hollywood star, was America's number one hero.

The whole crowd around him hushed as Brando made his way around our room. He took his time, walked slowly, paused in front of each bed long enough to scribble something on white paper handed to him by an assistant, who never left his side. He spoke a few words directly to each girl, but I couldn't hear what he said because his voice was so low. When he got to my bed, he nodded at me, she handed him paper, and he began to write.

The whole time I had been clutching a real celebrity's birthday card, hoping by some chance it might be him. I thrust this in Brando's face: "Do you know Hoppy?"

My unexpected question made him blink, several times. I'm pretty sure he didn't smile, but he made some kind of mouth movement. After I'd seen him in a few movies, I realized that it was that Brando half-smile, half-sneer he was famous for.

"No," he said.

The nurse who had introduced him flashed her eyes at me twice, like a headlight, indicating I should not have asked him that. Brando finished signing his autograph, handed it to me, and moved on. That was the last I saw of that scrap of paper; Mother confiscated it—which was fine with me—the minute she saw it. She was crushed not to have met Marlon Brando herself, and I'm certain she would have had a conversation with him if she'd been there, no matter how many officials tried to stop her. The autograph stayed in her jewelry box for years; she showed it to everyone in the world, and I wouldn't be surprised if, when I wasn't around, she said she met him in person.

No one told her about the Hoppy question I asked, but I didn't get away with it anyhow. The floor nurse with the headlight eyes made sure she removed the chocolate pudding with whipped cream dessert from my dinner tray before they brought it to me, every night for a week.

I had gotten so used to Lenox Hill and hospital life that there were times when it felt like my new home. I was reasonably well fed, and no one forced me to eat; I had friends, notebooks, my diary, cards, and gifts. There weren't many surprises anymore, which was a relief, and I knew what would happen at each hour of the day because hospitals run on a strict regimen. The routine was so familiar that, when they brought a new girl in, the old-timers, like Alice and I, were able to reassure her by reciting what her daily schedule would be.

But I was getting bored. For one thing the day stretched out too long until my father got there. My mother read two newspapers all the way through when she was there, and when she finished she took them to the nurses' station, where she'd spend time chatting with them and waylaying doctors.

It was mid-November, and they said I'd go home any day. Until then I had to figure out how to amuse myself. The sign-girl went for surgery and never came back, so I don't know what happened to her; the broken-neck girl had her cast removed and seemed fine. The day she was discharged she jumped up and down on her bed until a nurse put a stop to it, and I was glad to see her go. Later that day their empty beds were filled with two new recovering polios who, like Alice and I, had almost been in time for the vaccine but not quite.

I asked Alice one day, "Do you want to go home?" She never seemed bored, lost patience, or got irritable, even though it was apparent that she wasn't going to walk. She did progress into a wheelchair, but that was it. This was how she answered my question: "Teresa of Avila says that God fills our needs, and those who have patience will attain good things."

"Yeah, but there's nothing to do!"

"Patience is a real virtue, you know."

Patience. What a meaningless word to an eight-year-old. Lucky for me, I wasn't a clairvoyant like Nona, or I would have seen just how much waiting was in store. My condition meant an incarceration of waiting, although I'd fight to the death to change that whenever possible. Impatience, some doctors said, was a trait that actually benefited me because I refused to lay back and be a cripple. They must have known how frustrating it would be to wait for something that would never happen. But how could they tell me that? It would have deflated my spirit. I learned how to wait like anyone imprisoned anywhere learns—because I had no choice. I would never take to waiting as sweetly as Alice.

Doing stunts and pranks helped ease the boredom. I felt closer to Alice now, and the other girls in my room, than to my friends at home. We shared secrets and invented what we thought were interesting, involving games to play from bed. One of them was called "Catch the Washcloth." We'd throw a wet washcloth from bed to bed, but if you missed, even if it landed on the sheet, you were punished by having everyone throw her wet cloth in your face at the same time. Another game, called "Snow," involved balling up as many tissues as we could accumulate and flinging them around the room for a snowstorm effect.

We laughed so hard at the look on the nurse's face when we called her in and she saw the mess. Once one of them even slipped on a wet washcloth, which of course was hilarious. Most of them were good-natured about our games, even though we gave them a lot more work, but there were a couple of nurses who weren't. And when they got mad enough, they paid us back, usually by holding up our lunch or dinner trays for half an hour until the food got cold.

Mirth or conspiratorial carrying-on got dampened the minute Nurse Cohen came on duty at four o'clock. Often she'd arrive earlier so that she could inspect the rooms, making sure everything from floor to window was orderly. Predictably, she was the only one I came into contact with who wasn't thrilled with my progress, and she certainly wasn't tolerant of pranks. That I could have gotten hurt walking around at night, on her watch, infuriated her; it made me the focus of her bullying.

I knew that, no matter what I did, this particular nurse was not going to like me—not that she was overly kind to anyone. It was as if she disliked taking care of sick children altogether. And, though most of us will, at some point in our lives, encounter a Nurse Cohen in the guise of an overbearing boss or supervisor, her innate character was far worse than that, bordering on the inherently mean, the likes of which I'd never meet again. Unfortunately, I was slated to know the punishment she meted out to patients who thought themselves "little miracles."

She caught us at the washcloth game only once, which was enough to get my ears boxed. Her face scrunched-up with rage, fists balled, she stood over me and punched. Had I known she was on the early shift, I probably wouldn't have tried it. I was the only one punished; she made me the example. My ears rang and burned; they stayed red, too, for a long time afterward. I thought I'd be deaf from it forever.

"You think that hurts?" she said, when she was done, her face really close to mine. "That's nothing. You think you're so cute walking around in the dark, getting all bruised up and making tissue messes that I have to clean! You better watch it! I've got your number!"

She scared me more than I wanted to admit, but I thought she was just trying to keep me obedient. It worked. I was appropriately afraid of her. Nurse Cohen told me that if she ever caught me out of bed at night I'd be "sorrier than sorry" and that, then, "not even Jesus" could rescue me. Still, I felt compelled to get up and walk in the middle of the night and took a chance during the day by continuing to think up creative games to amuse my roommates and me. I got away with most everything, until the one time I didn't. Unfortunately, I misjudged Nurse Cohen in thinking that boxed ears were as far as she'd go.

It happened on a weekday. It had poured the night before and all that day, steady pounding against the windowpane. By three o'clock it was so dark outside it looked like nighttime. Most of us had had no visitors because of the weather, except of course for Alice, whose mother always came, and we were deliriously bored. It got even worse after dinner, as the night stretched out endlessly before me. Hours would pass before my father came, if he came. We were all restless; I was more so than anyone. I thought how I hated the rain, how I wished it would snow because snow was prettier, and that's when the idea came to me. Looking around, I saw that everyone had a little jar of talcum powder on her nightstand. The Amazing Powder Pillow Game was born.

The idea was, we'd sprinkle talcum powder all over our pillows and then dive into them as fast as we could to come up with a face full of snow. The first person to pop up was the winner. The only trouble was, we didn't just sprinkle the powder on our pillows; we *poured* it on. Everyone, that is, except me. My fatal mistake was that I wanted to watch the others get white-faced; I didn't want to myself. I only pretended to dive. Maybe, if my face had been powder-clogged also when we were discovered, she might have spared me.

How hilarious are the simple games. I called, "On the mark, get set, GO!" and the agile girls twisted around, dove into their powder-covered pillows, and came up as fast as possible. How funny and ridiculous they looked, sputtering and with bone-white faces! You couldn't help laughing your head off. They looked like a roomful of ghosts in beds — except for me. Then things turned bad. One of the girls began to choke on the powder she sucked in, couldn't stop, and soon they were all coughing and choking. This only made me laugh more, but, as my Tante Sultana always said, "Riyas muncho hoy, yoras mas muncho a la mañana": Laugh a lot today, and you'll cry ten times harder tomorrow.

Two passing nurses saw the chaos and the girls' distress and rushed in to help. I found that funny, too, and it produced another wave of laughter that I rocked back and forth from. When, finally, the choking girl vomited, at the moment Nurse Cohen entered the room, I was laughing so hard I neither saw nor heard her come in. She barely glanced at the strangling girls but headed straight for me.

"I see that our little ringleader is having a *wonderful* time of it, while her roommates *suffer*." At the word *suffer* I stopped. If ever the expression "the smile was wiped off her face" meant something, it was then. I was in trouble.

It took a while to clean up all the powdery mess and make sure that the girls' passageways were cleared. For a bright kid, although I was in a hospital, sick, I had little awareness of physical danger and even less insight about that nurse's character. I was perceptive enough to know that she disliked me but not savvy enough to know how much. I was nervous, until about two hours had passed. Then I figured Nurse Cohen was so busy she forgot about me. I congratulated myself that I had gotten away with it, again.

When Nurse Cohen came in pushing a wheelchair, even when she parked it by my bed, locked it, and, too sweetly, asked me if I would please get into it, I didn't suspect anything, but I knew enough to say no. I refused to get in it.

"Well, then, let me help you," she said. Swiftly, she scooped me up, and before I knew it we were whizzing down the hall, pretty fast, past nurses who went by in white blur, past the big-tub bathroom, until she stopped at a door just around the bend. Then I knew what was coming.

"Please," I whispered, "please."

But she wouldn't listen, and that was all I could get out before my throat closed and I was rendered mute.

I don't think the nurse said anything; she just pushed my chair inside and quickly locked the door. I faced pitch-black darkness. No matter how wide I opened my eyes, I couldn't see a thing. *This is the Dark Room,* I thought, before I panicked. Thanks to a sliver of light under the door, in a few minutes my eyes got accustomed to the blackness, and I could make out shapes. That was even worse. They were ominous-looking, looming shadows. I was alone in the Dark Room all the kids whispered about—just the bogeyman and me.

There's a good reason many cultures scream and make deafening rackets or dance around clanging pots and pans and loud instruments in order to chase away demons. Noise in itself is good; it means life. Anything, at that point, would have been better than the dead silence surrounding me. I tried but was unable to manage a decent scream; all I could do was croak helplessly and shake uncontrollably. Why I couldn't scream baffled me. I, with such bellowing, healthy lungs, who shrieked well enough to thoroughly terrify my brother and bring Mother and my aunts running. I had gone beyond fear and had just *stopped*.

I sat hugging myself in the wheelchair, as still as I could be, my mouth open but soundless, my hands tightly clenched, and my heart jumping out of my chest. I had no hanging man, no Hoppy watch, no Evil Eye amulet, nothing with me to protect me from the enormous monster shapes in front and all around me that would at any moment begin to move, to devour me. But what could I do? What *should* I do? I had always come up with something whenever I got into trouble, and even in Rockaway, when I got lost, I did something—I kept on walking. That life was over. It dawned on me that I could not get up and run. Maybe I'd never run again, meaning I'd forever be at danger's mercy.

I felt the weight of overwhelming helplessness; I felt like a baby, younger than my brother, whereas a day before I was proud to be a grown-up eight-year-old. Although trapped in a small area, I probably could have shimmied the wheelchair around until I faced the door and then pounded on it. Wild-eyed with fear, I didn't even think of doing that. Also, in normal times I'd have climbed up on top of things, kicked and screamed, carried on. But, then, "normal times" were past, or I wouldn't have been in a wheelchair. Cohen knew that the Dark Room's legend would paralyze me more than polio could; she counted on it.

The Dark Room became, for me, the dividing line. Not the moment of collapse at Mother's mah-jongg table nor being whisked away by ambulance and not even my abandonment in isolation, but this was it, the incident by which I would forever gauge all bad, humiliating, or potentially terrifying experiences. Whenever I'd get in a jam, I'd ask myself, is this a "Dark Room" situation? And 99 percent of the time, because the answer was no, I'd get the courage to tackle whatever problem was in front of me.

I finally wept, slopping tears into my open hands that were in front of my face, so I could keep peeking through my fingers at the shadows. I rocked back and forth so hard in my chair, it moved as if it were being pushed. Snot and spit ran down my chin onto my pajamas until I was choking, not unlike my roommates had a short while ago, from the Powder Pillow game.

It's impossible to tell how long I was locked inside that closet, which was probably an ordinary medical supply room. The irregular shapes I likened to creatures were undoubtedly instruments, bottles, and basins, maybe even the hot-pack laundry tubs and other equipment, covered with sheets and blankets. For as long as I stayed there I alternated between the dry heaves and bawling. When at last I took a raggedy breath, exhausted, and cautiously looked around, no blobby shape had advanced toward me.

These mountainous images imprinted on me and remained with me long after I was too old to be scared of the dark. The slithering glob belonging to many old nightmares had found me, and I knew he'd always come back when it got dark. Many years after that day I accidentally got locked in a bathroom stall and shocked the women outside who were trying to get me out by lustily and repeatedly screaming for help, a lot fiercer than was necessary.

I must have either passed out or fallen asleep, but when I woke up I was back in my bed, and my dad was there. The minute I saw his face I started to heave again, hard and loud enough to wake my roommates. My hysteria frightened him, but I couldn't talk to him coherently and explain what happened. Part of the reason might have been fear of his deep rage. There were things about my father that no one knew, things I heard him talk about in his sleep, things some of the uncles knew. Like the time, for instance, he knocked "some bum" down onto the train tracks after a fracas on the subway platform. I didn't find out what happened to the man. His controlled temper prevented me from telling on Nurse Cohen. I didn't care a whit about her, but I sensed my father, if he found out what she did, would get in trouble because of hurting her.

He found out anyway. My dad was a big favorite among the night nurses, and it took no time for one of them to snitch on Cohen. He hunted her down and tried to strangle her; it took several people to pry his hands off her neck. They said she tried to run, to escape to another floor, but Dad followed her and cornered her. I don't know why the nurse thought she'd get away with it; everyone knew how my dad felt about me, and he came every night.

The version my father liked to tell, and the one I also prefer, was where he slapped her across the face then dragged her down the hall to the Dark Room and locked her in.

"I stood guard by that door half the night so she couldn't get out! So the *gursurza* would know what it feels like! I should have killed her!"

Nurse Cohen disappeared, in the future, whenever she saw him coming, and she also kept away from me. I saw her every day as always, in and out of my room, going about her ordinary nursing duties, but she never talked to or looked directly at me. There were other nurses who took care of my needs, and in time I recovered from the experience. But for the rest of my days at Lenox Hill I was done with pranks.

I didn't get discharged, for some reason, until the day after Thanksgiving, but the holiday was fun anyway because I celebrated with my hospital friends. They served us a gala turkey dinner with special, turkey-shaped cookies for dessert, plus ice cream. All that morning volunteers came by with coloring books and board games for those who wouldn't be going home. Later on everyone's parents and relatives crowded into the room, and we had another party. In a way I didn't want to leave.

I had been given the gift of grace more than once during my hospital stay. It came in various guises—as a little man who hung on the end of a blue-beaded necklace; as the cool "holy water" on the back of my inert legs; and even as the sight of my dad's gray fedora, peeking into the room at just the moment I needed to see it. Grace came, too, in the abstract, as forgetfulness. A few days past the Dark Room incident, it was as if it hadn't occurred. Aunt Fina's act of kindness, her poignant gift of a dress for someone else's daughter, that made me feel pretty again, was the sweetest grace there is. Most of all, grace was given me in the courage to walk, courage I pulled from somewhere, to try though the odds were overwhelmingly against me.

They strapped me into that ridiculously bulky Milwaukee Brace, insisted I wear the two long leg braces and the clunky, ugly brown oxfords that they fit into, and then sat me in a wheelchair for the ride down. Some of the nurses kissed me good-bye at the elevator, and two of them rode down with us. As the doors closed, I waved to Chief Nurse Murphy, and she saluted me. Nurse Cohen was nowhere around.

Two of them accompanied us into the elevator and down to the lobby, but when we got to the front doors my father stopped them from pushing me out. He would keep his promise. He locked the wheelchair on either side. Slowly, but without help, I stood up. I was a bit wobbly, and one of the nurses went to catch me, but I think my dad must have given her a look because she quickly moved back. Standing tall and keeping as steady as possible, with a crutch under my right arm and Dad's tree of an arm supporting me on the left, I stepped over the hospital's threshold and walked out to the street.

Aboltar kazal, aboltar mazal.

A change of scene, a change of

fortune. LADINO PROVERB

6 ❖ Northern Lights

It was full autumn by the time I came home from the hospital, and the crisp Bronx air, that late November day, stung my nostrils. It smelled just as I remembered for that time of year, like peppermint and burnt leaves, a sensory treat I looked forward to in the fall because it signaled my birthday and the holidays after. As far as I knew, no one in our Bronx neighborhood actually burned leaves, but the steel door on the side of our building that led to the furnace room was left open more often, so the coal man could shovel the small black rocks into the shaft leading to the coal bin.

Dad drove a borrowed car I'd never seen before, a mint-green Buick with red leather seats, and I sat in the back, my metal legs stretched out on a pillow. He let me keep the window rolled down all the way from Manhattan. I saw that the majestic red maples lining the Grand Concourse had long ago laid their red and gold carpets of leaves on the ground, and most of them had been lifted up and carried away. The trees were as stark as they'd be in January.

As we approached our building, I twisted around to see whether anything else in the neighborhood had changed while I was away. As far as I could tell, all seemed intact, from Matarasso's Turkish grocery at the bottom of the 170th Street hill to the no-sign Chinese laundry at the top. The Luxor's marquee was blank, except for some scrambled black letters still stuck there, from which I could not make an intelligible word. They were preparing to change the movie; a tall ladder rested against the building.

Where did end-of-summer go? I felt, at that moment, like I had missed a lot. Just yesterday I was unpacking my carton of Rockaway Beach stuff then running downstairs to catch up with Ellen, who wore her brand-new school outfit that day, a blue-pleated skirt and a white blouse, although she wasn't supposed to. She got punished for it later and had to do the dishes for three nights in a row. As Ellen and I bounced the spaldeen back and forth playing hit-the-penny, aiming for the shiny 1954 penny placed in the exact center crack of two pavement squares, we discussed the merits and the drawbacks of having Mrs. Fein for a third-grade teacher. Thinking about that conversation, as the wind whizzed through my hair, felt odd; I wasn't in third grade, and I had no idea what Mrs. Fein was like, good or bad.

Smitty, the super, was the only one out when we pulled up. The streets were empty but for a solitary woman wearing a kerchief and pulling a shopping cart. Smitty looked older than the last time I saw her. Her thin, wiry body was bent over the threadbare patches of green we called a "garden," really two small rectangles of dirt on either side of the building, and her wild, iron-gray hair stood up like a board against the wind. When she saw us, she straightened up then ignored us to sweep brittle dried leaves and bits of paper off the steps with the same broom used to chase kids out of the basement furnace room when we wanted to watch the huge fire swallow up garbage.

Dad helped me out of the car to a standing position. The Milwaukee Brace felt as if it weighed fifty pounds. The bottom of it cut into my pelvis, and my braced legs ached from being in one position too long. Just getting out of the car wearing all those appliances was a production. It felt as if I were dragging along another person. But I managed to stand, in those clumsy, ugly orthopedic shoes, by holding onto the side of the car. My father removed his hat, wiped the sweat off his forehead, and exhaled with a whistle: "Ke moplatón!" What a dead weight!

Our building had a double stoop of four, fairly steep steps, "protected" on either side by two stone lions, painted green that season.

Then came a landing then a flight of ten marble steps to the inner lobby. But there was something else, too, that I had never noticed before: No banister! My mouth fell open. How would I climb up? I hadn't given a thought to stairs or to holding on until that moment. Even if I balanced really well on the crutches, I knew I wouldn't be able to maneuver the outer stoop by myself. No one had warned me about this; it was my first physical dilemma out of the hospital.

I stood on the sidewalk in front of my building looking up, as if at the base of a mountain. Old Smitty, hands on hips, watched as my father, in one swift motion, lifted me and my crutches and carried me up the stairs.

We lived in the back of the building, so he had to go across the length of the lobby carrying me in order to get to the rear staircase. Then there was a landing of three smaller steps before the next two flights. Technically, there were only two and a half flights of stairs to our apartment, 3A, but it felt like ten. Grunting, Dad assured me it wasn't so bad, that I weighed next to nothing, but by the time we got to our door he was breathing hard. He stopped, caught his breath, mopped his forehead again with a handkerchief, and then ran back downstairs to retrieve my wheelchair from the sidewalk. Finally, I was home.

I had lost a lot of my natural chubbiness since September. Clothes hung off my thin shoulders, and the belt of my wool skirt had to be fastened with two safety pins. Mother stood by the door as we entered, unsmiling, dragging deep on her Philip Morris and blowing the smoke out of her mouth in short bursts. I struggled past her on the crutches, trying to walk steady because I knew she was watching. From the first day my mother was loath to show any emotion regarding my physical struggles, nor did she give me any sympathy whatsoever, claiming later that she did not want to "coddle" me. She said she felt that I'd be much stronger if she "stepped back" and let me be, but that was only partially true. In fact, she was quietly fuming all the time, furious with me, with my illness, and with our whole situation in general. Usually on a short fuse, Mother had gone the opposite way, it seemed, and the heavy cauldron of resentments that rested on top of her flattened her personality.

Everybody called Mother's attitude stoicism, but I knew it was displeasure. A tiny bit of coddling wouldn't have hurt me. Never overtly affectionate to begin with, my mother's remoteness after I got polio distanced us further. She seemed at a loss as far as knowing how to balance caring for me and also leaving me alone to become healthily independent. I could not reach her at all, had never felt her approval, but I would spend the next dozen years trying to get it. The one thing Mother's attitude did do was make me push harder with everything all the time. In the end, though, our dance left us both physically and emotionally exhausted.

I hadn't yet been told it officially, but I knew that I wasn't supposed to count on anyone's help to get around. The polio motto was, and would always be: Do it by yourself, no matter how hard, no matter how long it takes. Mother must have known this, too, because she made no attempt to assist me then or in the difficult months that followed. My father was different; instinct told him when to step in, and he had no compunctions about helping me when I really needed it. But most often, out of necessity, I was forced to do for myself. I had no one to compare myself with, so I don't know how other recovering kids' parents treated them, but I flew solo. I came to depend upon my own ingenuity regarding my mobility and figuring out logistics.

Walking all by myself to my room that first day, which, luckily, wasn't far from the front door, and positioning myself where I could reach everything I needed so I could get around without falling flat on my face set the tone for all future physical endeavors. My dad would be the one to lift me, turn me, and strap me into the heavy Milwaukee and leg braces. Along with tying my laces, he'd give me moral support, love, and encouragement—when he was around. The rest of the time I was on my own.

I had to learn how to handle a body different from the one I always knew, the one I had left the house with two months before. If I forgot to unlock my braces at the knee before I sat down, which I did that first day when I made it to my bed, I'd crash backwards, metal legs flying up in the air. This happened a few times, and I saw it really upset Mother. She'd catch her breath each time, hand to her throat, momentarily paralyzed. She didn't know what to do when I became unbalanced; they were all so terrified I'd fall. None of us knew what to do. We learned as the days went by.

She had to focus on something, and my weight was a good target.

Mother stood over me, studying me, as I lay on the bed. Then she gave me her hand and pulled me upright.

"*Flaka!*" Skinny! She blinked several times behind her glasses, assessing my appearance and trying to conceal her shock at my thinness. In the hospital all the kids were similarly sickly looking, so I didn't seem so bad; at home it was pronounced. I appeared shrunken, half the size I should have been. The Turks *hated* skinny; to them it was abnormal. All our women were round, even fat, and except for Nona Behora, who had been morbidly obese, fat was fine. Thinness was associated with illness. Only the old and sick, drunken *borachos*, bums, and the poorly fed who came from derelict mothers were thin.

My aunts, who came by a couple of hours later, felt the same way about my appearance. Sultana's reaction was similar to Mother's, and, because she had never been tactful, she let me know it by gasping and plucking the skin on her cheek: "Ke me muriera yo!" Better I should die than see you like this!

That was my "welcome home." Tante Allegre, who *had* seen me practically dead in the isolation ward, was calmer but just as worried. She wrung her hands and pressed her lips together before she was able to call me *hanúm de la tante!* Her "star of the harem" looked starved; something had to be done.

So, the Council was back in session. They spent an hour in the kitchen, conferring. It was *flaka* this and *flaka* that, as if thin were the worst thing in the world. At least this they could try to fix; they had a mission now. I suspected they were cooking something up, and right I was.

From Day One home they wrote a prescription for Turkish foods and Middle Eastern delicacies guaranteed to fatten up a sick child. The forced feeding continued for months, even after my appetite returned and I'd gained weight. At least six times a day someone would ask me, "Ke kieres komer?" What do you want to eat? And at least that many times I'd answer, "Nothing." The mere thought of food sickened me, and nothing they served looked appealing. This was different from my usual pickiness over certain foods; I had lost my desire to eat totally. They couldn't tempt me—not then, that first night, not the next morning, not for many weeks to come. I didn't know why it was, either; I'd had no such problem in the hospital. Something snapped the moment I stepped through the door that made me instantly tired of food and even more tired of hearing about food.

First, they cooked the foods I'd always loved, but they also made new ones I'd never heard of. That first night Mother made me *fidellos tostados*, an angel-hair pasta dish that was a favorite of mine. Most Sephardi cooks knew how to make *fidellos*, no matter which town in Turkey they were from, because it was originally a recipe from ancient Spain. I called them "orange noodles." In normal times I'd lunge for them, hot or cold. I used to stand by the open refrigerator, grab a bunch cold, throw my head back, and slide them down my throat. Mother reminded me of how often I did this, but I sensed she was just as angry that I wasn't doing it as she had been those times I did. *Fidellos* went perfectly with potted lamb, and that dish was the first to go awry for my homecoming.

In late afternoon I smelled the pasta toasting and heard it cackling as it browned in Mazola oil. Next came the pungent odor of frying onions and then the sound and smell of searing lamb. The minute I smelled the lamb I wanted to throw up. Finally, the meaty tomatoes were added to the pasta mix—I pinpointed the exact moment they plopped into the pot—and I gagged. Swallowing a few times, I tried hard not to retch. At any moment, I thought, I'm going stop this and be hungry for lamb and *fidellos*; I'll *crave* them . . . No amount of self-talk helped. I couldn't stand the thought of eating the dish and knew I wouldn't. I spent the rest of the afternoon sipping ginger ale, gulping and swallowing.

Lamb was our staple, and we ate it several times a week, cooked in different ways. It went in soups, was stuffed in vegetables, and was molded into meat pies. The "round-bone" shoulder lamb had always been my favorite because of the *tutano*, the small center bone with marrow. To think I had once sucked that marrow with gusto was unimaginable. *Kodredo al forno*, roast lamb, was just as unappetizing; lamb the Greek way, with an egg-and-lemon crust, horrible. By the end of the frantic-cooking weekend they made lamb at least three different ways—all rejected.

Then they had arguments over *why* I rejected everything. Such lamb silliness, like, whose idea it had been to put scallions in the pot and why Greeks are healthier than Turks—why, their marinade, of course! The truth was, my aunts and my mother couldn't accept that, no matter which way they cooked it, I was done with lamb. Its distinctive odor had become intolerable.

They tried *pollo de miel* (braised chicken with honey). Not interested. Next, *peskado sofrito* (lightly fried fish), then *pitta de peskado* (fish pie), then *pitta de keso* (cheese pie), and, finally, *pitta de mina* (meat pie) with chopped meat, no lamb. No thanks. You'd think they would have stopped at that point. Instead, incredibly, they came up with yet another lamb "treat" they hadn't thought of before: *koftes*, lamb kebobs. How did I like that? I choked, that's how. I had a long week ahead of me.

But it wasn't just meat; everything was distasteful to me, even the green color of Tante Allegre's spinach pie. Eyeing the *spinaka* dotted with white blobs of feta cheese on top, and knowing that an egg poured over the pie gave it its glaze, finally made me puke. Tante Allegre was in tears again, Sultana in disbelief, and Mother furious. After all, hadn't she brought me a piece in the hospital, and hadn't I eaten it all and asked for more? Wasn't the pie the right height and consistency? Didn't it have a crispy enough crust? Look how much less spinach there is than feta cheese! How about I break off the four crispy corners, like always, and just eat those? Rejecting Aunt Allegre's food, especially, was worrisome and beyond her comprehension. But I, too, was surprised. I didn't know why this was, and I apologized for it, over and over. I just couldn't swallow.

Sultana shouted at me, senselessly, "Bre! Bre!" Allegre bit her curled finger and said the prayer for protection by rote. No doubt, a spell had been cast.

"De farto de todo, la chika!" The child is fed up with everything!

Not everything. *Arroz rojo* (red rice), not spicy, and Ritz crackers, plain, were good; in fact, they were the only morsels that got through the roadblock that had mysteriously formed at the bottom of my throat.

Cooking was the only way they knew to make me whole again. For Mother, who never could show affection and hated to cook, toiling in the kitchen was an expression of love. She was never going to be able to tell me how eternally grateful she was that I had lived to come home. Instead, she spoke more gruffly than ever and cooked for me the few things she knew how to make. Grateful or not, I wouldn't touch her *fidellos* nor her *fasulya* (string beans in tomato sauce) and wouldn't drink a drop of the *sopa de lentijas* (lentil soup). By Monday, instead of slowing down, they were cooking more—outdoing themselves, preparing *pransas*, banquets, which they'd carry in to me on trays. And if I didn't try to nibble tiny portions of everything, they cried. It made sense that ultimately, inevitably, they'd switch to desserts.

For once Aunt Sultana's *mustachudos* were mine alone. I did not have to share them with my brother or anyone. It was hard to believe that I once salivated at the very sight of the gaily printed Barton's candy box, wherein, on rows of wax paper, those moist, sugary walnut balls, Sultana's "secret" coveted recipe from Çanakkele, rested. She actually left them on my bed and tiptoed out, which told me I had permission to eat them *all*—if only I would. The candies sat adjacent to my right arm, a forbidden box I once ferreted out of Tante's lingerie drawer from underneath a pile of girdles. Stealing them from her house had been more of a thrill than eating them.

After the ordinary desserts came the exotic confections, recipes that involved real work. I was treated to dishes few Sephardis ate on a regular basis, simply because they were tedious to make. One of these was a pudding called *sutlach*. One of Sultana's card-playing cronies, a woman named Luisa, famous not for her cooking but for her dread fear of and refusal to attend funerals—never in her life did she go to one—sent over *sutlach*, the special treat sure to bring me back to health. Luisa was from Salonika, where the pudding was considered a great delicacy. Some cooks in Turkey even had a separate small oven for the purpose of making this pudding.

Fear of death or no, Luisa was a good *sutlach* maker, they all said. She knew just how to proportion the rice flour and the milk, a delicate balance, and its main ingredients. The sweet pudding took the woman over two hours to make, but, sadly, I couldn't eat a spoonful. Her time and trouble were for naught; the delicacy was wasted on me.

Next came *Torta de los Reyes*, the Cake of Sultans, a moist confection made with orange rind and almonds, so named for kings because it was that delicious. In a most theatrical procession two ladies of the harem and two sultans carried it in: Allegre, Sultana, Ovadiah, and my brother, Charlie, a little sultan-in-training.

With aplomb Uncle Ovadiah un-muted himself and announced: "Johá the fool says, *kome!* EAT!"

A nice try, anyway. As if the legendary idiot of Turkish folklore could possibly influence me. I had never not wanted sweets. The cake smelled really good, too, so I tasted it to make them happy. It even tasted good. It just wasn't good enough to actually eat.

Instead of giving up, they decided to try one more confection, Istanbul-style, a cake called "tishpitti."

"I won't eat it," I said.

"Not even tishpitti? But why? You love it!"

"I'm not hungry."

Tishpitti, a pecan nut cake, was a dessert made for the Jewish holidays and for special occasions. Some neighborhood Turk must have made it special for me and dropped it off because my aunts didn't make that, and we hardly ever had it in the house. When tishpitti was around, I was uncontrollable and invariably got smacked for eating too many pieces and getting a bellyache. I liked to grab off a chunk of the cake and try to cram it down as fast as possible, my own game of dare-you-to-catch-me-doing-this. When I saw it, though, as with the all the other treats and foods, my stomach flipped. It was too "brown," with too many little pieces in it that were nauseating. Had I ever liked tishpitti to begin with?

"She hates the flecks," Mother said. My aunts sighed.

Preparing foods that would entice me to eat became a matter of life or death. I guess it gave them something constructive to do with their time, other than worry. Within the course of my first week home my aunts and other members of the Turkish community, as well as my reluctant cook mother, had baked, breaded, potted, stewed, and chilled practically the entire table of contents of a Sephardic cookbook. We didn't even have cookbooks in the house like my friends' mothers did. The only one I ever recall seeing was Cooking the Hollywood Movie Star Way, a dusty tome that sat atop the refrigerator forever. I doubt Mother made a single recipe from that book; she was merely obsessed with all things Hollywood. I prayed she wouldn't start now.

Just when I thought they had exhausted all the Turkish, Greek, and Moroccan recipes they could think of and would quit, they came up with one final delicacy: rodanchas, a harvest pastry made for the Sukkot fall festival. These pastries were difficult to make properly and required arduous preparation time, but they had a special significance for our people.

Rodanchas were considered a "spiritual" food. They were filled with delicious ingredients, including one not so appealing to me, *kalabasa*. Squash. Often the type of winter squash that was supposed to make up the main filling was hard to find, even at Matarasso's. As a substitute filling for the big "surprise," they used pumpkin squash. Had I known that, I'd have thrown up sooner than later.

Pumpkin notwithstanding, the pastries were delicious and came with a great story. One year, when Nona Behora was still alive, our family had a dinner in honor of two newly arrived cousins from Port Said, Egypt. *Rodanchas*, because of their spiral shape, which symbolized the life cycle and the ascent of the soul into *Gan Eden*, Paradise, were part of the menu. An uncle recited seven blessings over seven different foods, including these spiral-shaped pastries, and then he told me that the *rodanchas* were considered "holy" because of their secret ingredients. All who tasted them, he said, would have *mazal*, good fortune, forever. In ancient Hebrew the word for pumpkin, *karah*, also meant "to rip or tear up," and by eating the food God tears up any harsh edicts or punishments a person may have accumulated over the year.

I thought of the pumpkin blessings story when I heard my tantes oohing and ahhing over how good the *rodanchas* turned out. I lay in bed watching the ceiling and wondering if God had had any bad feelings toward me and if He'd tear them up and throw them away if I ate a *rodancha*. For the first time since I got sick, I considered the idea of punishment connected to catching polio. Knowing how superstitious they all were, I thought they baked the *rodanchas* especially for that reason.

But even with all the spiritual contemplation, and well before the pastries had cooled, I began concocting excuses as to why I wouldn't have any. I ate up the story but left the *rodanchas*.

Weak and anemic, at the start of my second week home, I became moody and listless, not wanting to get out of bed. It was just too much trouble. For one thing I hated being awakened by my father at 5:30 every morning, before he left for the factory, to be put into the Milwaukee Brace. I was buckled, strapped, clicked, and arranged, and then he worked on the two leg braces. Fast and always gentle, the whole thing took him less than fifteen minutes, while my brother remained fast asleep in the next bed. Then Dad went to shave, and I tried to go back to sleep, but wearing all that hardware made it impossible.

I would sit propped up in bed and doze until Mother got up to make breakfast.

It was understood that my father would be the one to attend to me as far as the putting on and the taking off of my braces. Often I'd get around the ordeal by sleeping in my clothes from the day before, just so that I wouldn't have to get dressed at the crack of dawn. If I didn't do that, or get dressed in new clothes before my father was ready to put the brace on, I risked staying in pajamas all day until he got home, twelve hours later, to take it off. It wasn't that my mother didn't have the physical strength to do it; she just couldn't handle it emotionally. No one ever told me this, and we never talked about it, then or later, but I knew that was the reason I had to be dressed before he left.

He said the same thing to me every morning: "Today you'll eat good, right, kiddo?"

And every day I answered, "I'll try."

"Don't try! Do it!"

"Okay."

But day after day passed, and I could do no better than a few Ritz crackers or a bowl of red rice and maybe half a Hershey Bar. Unable to tolerate my starving to death one more minute, Mother summoned Dr. Hirschfeld. I hadn't seen him since that foggy morning long ago when he called for the ambulance. He took one look at me and began to reprimand me in his harsh German accent, threatening to send me back to the hospital if I didn't eat a full meal right away. I told him I wasn't afraid of that and that I missed the hospital and my friends there. As the doctor scowled at me, his glasses slipped down his nose, and when he pursed his lips he looked funny because of his big bushy mustache. He cleared his throat a couple of times.

Clearly, he was again puzzled by me, like in the days prior to his correct diagnosis of polio, when he came up twice to examine me, and twice he declared: "Ya! A stomach virus!" He was wrong then, and he didn't know what to say now, except "Grumpf!"

There was nothing any doctor could do for me—no shots, no pills, no treatment for what ailed me. Time, Dr. Hirschfeld told my mother, would bring back my appetite. Otherwise, I was just fine.

Of course, I was anything but fine. I felt like a foreigner in my own house and a stranger in my own body. Every day I had the usual impulse to jump out of bed in the morning, until I remembered. The moment I opened my eyes it clicked that I couldn't. Nor could I run down the one flight of stairs and knock on Ellen's door whenever I felt like it. A small compensation was that I could read and write all I wanted to without somebody yelling at me to "put the book down and go play outside."

Daytime television was so boring, and I didn't want to watch it, anyway. I wanted to run. How strange that was to think about; I had never considered running to be something I'd wish for. It hadn't been so bad at the hospital, with all the routines, therapy, and the hustle and bustle of hospital staff and visitors coming and going. All that changed when I got home. I thought I was well aware of my limitations, but I really had no idea. When the truth set in, I saw how many hours in an ordinary day are taken up with physical movement, beginning with dressing for school. The day was much too long, especially since I began it so early and stayed up late at night, not having anything to be late for in the morning. But the longest stretch of all were the hours between lunch, which I couldn't eat, and dinner, when my dad came home. Those were endless.

Spontaneity. It was the word I didn't yet know, and it was gone. I was slow at everything I did, I moved ungracefully, and I made noise when I didn't want to because of all the equipment I walked with. When I got ready to stand up, everybody knew about it and watched me. I grew to hate being watched and refused to look at anyone's face so I wouldn't see them looking at me. That my condition would require me to think before I acted wasn't at all stressed in the hospital; that I'd learn in the rehab institute. I would be taught how to do it, and it would be another hard lesson. Even so, the impulse to act spontaneously never went away.

Dr. Hirschfeld did one good thing; he ordered them to stop cooking me exotic dishes, and for that I was grateful. He said I should be treated "just like everyone else" in the family, and I should definitely join them at the kitchen table for meals, whether or not I ate. No more rice and Ritz crackers in bed. So Mother insisted I come to the table for dinner. It was the beginning of a long, private battle she'd wage over how to treat me: normal or special; like everyone else or with extra privileges because of my "condition." Her push-pull went on throughout my childhood.

I had it easier than she; as soon as I could, I obliterated the word *special* from my vocabulary, opting for *just like everybody else*. In the end we both paid a heavy emotional price for not being realistic and recognizing where I did belong. I was not special, and I was not like everybody else, either, nor would I ever be.

I complained mightily about having to sit at dinner, but Mother insisted. So I struggled to walk to the kitchen table. I took my time, every bit as dramatic and punitive as she could be. I'd fidget with the braces, as if I had trouble unlocking them, and finally, when I sat, I always made someone fix the chair or get me a pillow or something. Then I sulked some more, pushing my food around on the plate or taking tiny bites, merely pretending to eat. I probably could have gotten away with pinching my brother's arm or kicking him under the table, too, if only I felt like it. They would have let me do anything, I think, just to see me be my old self. But I brooded, sulked, and drooped, instead, weighted down with things a lot heavier than metal braces.

I felt like I was on display. When I struggled to stand up, my parents stood up. When I reached for my crutches against the wall, they reached for them, too. Always, Mother set her face in stone, trying to reveal nothing during my shuffling and maneuvering, but she couldn't help her lips from compressing slightly or her eyelashes from flickering a few times. That's how I knew it killed her when I lurched. Dad looked the other way; I didn't know if he couldn't bear to watch me walk or was trying not to break the unspoken don't-help-her rule. My little brother blinked and stared at the wall, taking his cue from them. Charlie was such a serious kid. During those early days at home all he remembers is the feeling of constant fear and not knowing exactly why.

Finally, unable to take it another second, Mother would throw down her napkin and light a cigarette, signaling, thank God, that dinner was over for another night. And the food on my plate turned cold.

I needed friends more than food. At last, some of them came to see me. First, Ellen came up, with her mother, although her two younger sisters stayed home. Barbara, the doctor's daughter, who was two years older than us, came up the day after that. And that was pretty much it. Most of the kids I played with in the neighborhood disappeared. The kids on the other side of the building didn't come up either. No boys visited me. The girls in the Astor Court, where Cousin Dottie lived, were gone as well. "They have so much homework," Mother said.

I had imagined another fantasy: that every kid in the neighborhood would be crowding into my room, dying to examine my appliances and hear about my hospital adventures. I couldn't have been more wrong.

The first thing I went to check, the moment I stepped into my room on that first day home, was if I had a message from Ellen. We had rigged up, with strings and clothespins, a pulley system that ran from her bedroom window to mine. It carried our important notes back and forth at every hour of the day or night, and we didn't even have to open the window all the way in order to retrieve the piece of paper. But the pulley arrangement was gone, and the string had been cut. My father said he didn't know what happened to it; he offered to make me a new pulley, but I didn't want him to. Our ingenious setup sure beat yelling to each other down the open dumbwaiter shaft, but for some unknown reason it had been dismantled.

I happened to be sitting in the wheelchair, running myself up and down the short foyer, when Ellen knocked and opened the door. She seemed surprised to see me in it. Her eyes got opened wider. She had to look down to talk to me, and I had to look up at her. I was finding out that a wheelchair makes you shorter than everyone, and I wished I had been standing on crutches. But Ellen looked even taller than the last time I saw her. She acted shy, too, like the day when we were three and had just met, and that made me feel shy. My friend did not know what to say to me.

After swishing her skirt around for a while and averting my eyes, her mother whispered, "Ellen, ask your friend how she *feels*."

"How do you *feel*?"

"Fine."

"Really?"

"Yeah."

They were both trying not to stare at my braces, which I found strange. Ellen would take a peek, then look up at the ceiling, then take a peek, then look at the wall. Neither of us did much talking.

"What happened to our pulley phone?"

"I don't know."

"Oh. Do you want to see how I can walk?"

She shrugged, and Millie was at a loss.

"Well, we are *so* glad you're home at last, sweetheart, really! Aren't we, Ellen?"

"Yes."

And that's how it went. They left before I could struggle to stand and lock my braces for a demonstration, as if they were afraid to see it. Two girls who could never shut up, who whispered, talked, fought, and giggled endlessly, who had so much to say that they had to rig up a pulley phone system outside their windows, were now wordless. Millie promised to come back, "tomorrow or very soon."

The same thing happened with Harriet and her mother. They'd say, "See you tomorrow!" But they didn't return. Whoever came by stayed a very short time, as if they were visiting a hospital, as if I were still sick. My friends acted unnatural when they did show up, speaking to me in stilted speech, ultra-polite, as if I were another adult instead of their friend.

I eventually learned that a lot people, both in and out of the family, were still terrified of catching polio, and some felt that stray germs or contaminants from the hospital might possibly surround me. Also, my friends had that all-consuming activity known as "school." After school they played downstairs like I used to until suppertime or went shopping for groceries with their mothers. At night they did homework. I had become an outsider; I didn't know what was going on in my class or the school, and they had nothing to talk to me about.

Because Barbara was older and in fifth grade, she was more mature than the others. She came up to see me a few times and seemed genuinely interested in my experience. She asked me a lot of questions about being in the hospital and even wrote down my answers. I felt important until I found out that her questions were mostly for a school composition she was writing about "a person she admired." It was called, "My Friend Who Got Polio," and it earned her an A.

I finally understood that I wasn't going back to school. Mother said I would be "having school," which sounded mysterious. Still, I was anxious to "have school," go to school, anything, just to be busy. All the cousins on my mother's side who lived near me were much older than I, either married or working in the City, and the cousins on my dad's side who were my age were in school. That left Charlie, three and a half. Sensing a crisis in my increasing loneliness, my father took a big chance and got me a dog.

I had always wanted a dog or cat, but Mother hated animals, so it was generally out of the question. I guess he felt she'd relent because of my condition and also be cured of her fear and squeamishness in the process.

"Why did you bring this animal in here," she hissed at him, "*why?*"

Because he was a terminal optimist. But it often made him—and me—a victim of his magical thinking. Although my dad tried to do good always, more often than not it backfired. It was very brave of him to try to make me happy with a dog, but we both knew from the start it was futile.

The first charmer in a parade of pets was a brown-and-white cocker spaniel puppy I temporarily called "Brownie." His eyes melted snow. He looked deeply into mine, and we fell in love. Brownie was so well behaved; he sat happily on my lap for hours, but, eventually, I had to put him down in order to stand up and lock my braces. At first he sat on the floor patiently, looking up at me while I tried to figure out how to walk with him in my arms *and* balance on crutches at the same time. Next thing I knew, he was gone, scurried away to find fun, like puppies do.

It wasn't two minutes before Mother screamed for someone, anyone, to GET THAT DAMN DOG OUT OF HERE! as if Brownie were a Bengal tiger. My lovely, loving cocker spaniel pup went back to wherever he had come from the very next day, although I cried and pleaded with her for hours.

Uncle Al's wife, Vicky, brought me my next love, a little white kitten, not more than eight weeks old. It was so tiny that I figured just for that reason I'd have better luck. Aunt Vicky reminded Mother that cats were a lot cleaner than dogs, that they didn't have to be walked, and that they brought the owner good luck. This last bit of information really irked Mother. Watching her face as her sister-in-law spoke, I felt uneasy and accepted that my luck had already run out. She couldn't wait until my aunt left.

"Hmmp! A new veterinarian in the family! Now what would a janitor's daughter know about cats or luck?"

The darling white ball of fur won my heart, unfortunately, as quickly as Brownie had, and I forgot all about the dog. She also looked at me soulfully, this time with green eyes and a little head that seemed permanently cocked to one side. "Whitey" was so dear and made the tiniest of cat noises, hardly a *meep!* out of her; nevertheless, Mother winced whenever she heard it. Hard to believe one could be scared of a kitten such as this. My mother was. To her cats were the same hell as dogs.

She let Whitey stay the night—locked in the bathroom, with a towel tossed into the bathtub for her bed. All night long the kitten meowed pathetically until none of us could stand it, and first thing in the morning my father got rid of her. Again, I pleaded, bargained, cried, and carried on, to no avail. As protest, I refused to wear the Milwaukee Brace.

The kind of guy who didn't take no for an answer, Dad made one more attempt to make me happy with a pet. He smuggled in a nearly full-size scraggly black dog, which he swore he "bought" in a pet store. I think he probably found it on the street but wouldn't admit it. I was ordered to "keep him quiet," and, though I had misgivings, I so wanted him that I vowed I would make it work. We were both gamblers; he bet on losing propositions most of the time, and I bet I could win Mother over.

"Blackie" was cute, quiet, and amazingly well-tempered, considering he was a virtual prisoner of my room. The arrangement actually worked—for three whole days. Blackie stayed the longest of any pet thus far, and I had new hope. Suddenly, I felt like eating again. This made Mother happy, and for that reason she may have pretended not to notice that something strange was going on in my room. Naturally, all the food I said I was starving for, everything they cooked, went into the dog. My father winked at me when he got home at night then immediately spirited Blackie downstairs for a walk. When they returned, he quickly cleaned up whatever mess the dog had made that day, and then he dumped the newspapers that were stashed under my bed. With the window opened a crack, my room was ventilated well enough that it hardly smelled. My little brother, already terrified of me, knew not to open his mouth.

I think Dad loved being complicit in a crime that had the potential to outwit Mother. And what a terrific secret while it lasted. Miraculously, the dog did not bark once. Every time my mother got near my room, I shoved the sweet animal under my covers where he obediently stayed, and if she looked in she'd see me pretending to write or read. Alas, I became much too attached to Blackie. Nothing but sadness can come out of such arrangements, and the day came, finally, when the dog trotted outside to explore the rest of the house. I wasn't fast enough to catch him.

The screams and Spanish curses that poured from my mother's mouth were awful, even for her. They must have shocked the neighbors, too, because dumbwaiters were opened, and several of them cursed us back, telling us just where to go. All that commotion made the normally quiet dog go wild. First, he ran around in circles, then he jumped over the end tables, toppled chairs, and knocked ashtrays, one full, to the carpet. More screams. He streaked through the apartment back and forth, finally barking his head off. The more Mother yelled at him to stop, the more Blackie crashed into things, until he wore himself out. Then he hid out of sight.

My father located the trembling dog behind the couch. He tried to tiptoe it out of the apartment without me seeing them, but he had to pass my room to do that, and I was waiting for them. I stuck my crutch out to stop them, and my father almost fell over it. Then more crying, begging, bargaining. Not a chance. Blackie went, and he was the final animal. Even my father gave up—almost. I refused to look at or feed the stupid goldfish he brought in the next day. They were the only living things Mother would allow. They went, too, when I would have nothing to do with them.

Word of the animal fiascoes got around. Cousin Dottie's brother-in-law, Sy Karr, a bandleader, sent me a gift of a small guitar. I think I plucked its strings a few times, still brooding over my lost animals. Again, I had no *gana*, desire, for anything. Someone even arranged for an instructor to come up and give me guitar lessons once a week, and, who knows, maybe with a teacher the guitar would have peaked my interest. In any case music had to wait. Destiny had something else in store for me.

Early into December Dad broke the news: I was going to the Rusk Institute in Manhattan so they could teach me how to walk better, maybe even without braces and crutches, and in time I'd even ditch the Milwaukee, too. I didn't want to wear that forever, did I? I would only have to stay at "the Institute," as Rusk became known in our house, for "a while," but no one knew or could tell me how long, in terms of weeks, a while actually was.

The Rusk Institute of Physical Medicine and Rehabilitation was located in Manhattan, at First Avenue and the East River, so it would have been impossible for me to come and go on a regular basis. If I did well, they said I could come home in about a month or so for weekends. The minimum stay for physical therapy was two weeks, but that could stretch to two months, depending.

"On what?"

"You know."

I didn't know. My dad must have known about the arrangements for some time, because he had a hard time looking me in the eye when he told me about it. It was typical of him to promise that I'd be "dancing by the day of Lorraine's wedding." It's not that he enjoyed fooling me or giving me false hope; he really believed it with all his heart. He never lost faith or stopped insisting to me, to everyone, that I'd not only walk better but I'd belly dance again, too, and that one day I'd walk completely *normal*. I'd fool everyone. He was an eternal optimist in all things, steadfastly going with the plus side rather than the minus, no matter what the issue. His attitude gave me that push, a raison d'être, which I might not have had, but I'm also not sure that it didn't pressure me into demonic achievement, even into attempting the dangerous. Once, crossing the Grand Concourse on crutches, I tried to outrun the cars. There was nothing I wouldn't do for my father, and he knew it. I had already proven that with my hospital "miracle" walking.

My cousin Lorraine was getting married on Sunday, December 19. Even if the worst had happened and I had died, Aunt Sultana and Uncle Ovadiah would have had no choice but to go on with the ceremony, as Jewish law forbids canceling a wedding for any reason whatsoever. The immediate family would have gathered to witness the ceremony, but there would not have been a celebratory reception. Naturally, for many reasons, they were all relieved.

Lorraine, fifteen years older than I, was planning her Sweet Sixteen the year I was born. In the next couple of years I'd get to know her better and think of her as the sister I never had. It wasn't long before I modeled myself after her. Brides, like Cinderella, were part of magical fairy tales.

This was why they all repeated, "novia ke te vea"; to "see you a bride" was the best a girl could do for her family. The highest calling. After I went to the hospital, no one expected me to even attend la boda, but, because I was doing so well, they counted on the Rusk Institute to shape me up enough so that I'd be able to walk into the chapel on my own.

"It's a top-notch place, kiddo," Dad said. "They come from all over the world for your kind of thing. They're the best in the business."

That was all he could manage, and it was a lot for him. I fought not to cry, as usual, but when it was time to go I couldn't hold it in any longer, and I gushed. Now bravery was out of the question. I didn't want to leave; I was through with hospitals, hot packs, and mean nurses. Every time my father tried to talk to me about it, I cried, and he turned and fled. Mother would stare at me, wanting to say something, I know, but unable to.

The Sunday I was to be admitted to Rusk a pall came over the house. My parents had at least one good fight every week, usually on Sunday, but that hadn't happened since I'd been home. They both acted oddly subdued together, unlike their old selves, almost like Barbara's parents. While they didn't discuss books at the dinner table, like Dr. and Mrs. Hirschfeld did, they were at least civil to each other and more soft-spoken. That in itself was scary; surely, Charlie and I had never seen it. Oddly, I missed the loudness that was unique to them. It was strange without everyone talking or yelling at the same time. Even in early morning, her worst hour, Mother's mood was bearable, where once it had been beastly. You couldn't even talk to her before breakfast. And my father hadn't been so restless of late either. He had not gone to the Turkish baths in months. All that would change.

That morning, before we left, Dad chain-smoked Lucky Strikes. He sat by the window holding his head up with one hand, listening to Turkish wailing music instead of the upbeat chefti tellis we usually danced to. A cloud of smoke surrounded him, but Mother ignored it. Normally, when she had had enough of his cigarette smoking, she'd grab his Luckies and throw them down the dumbwaiter. Then I'd have to go to Jaffee's to get him two more packs when she wasn't looking.

Finally, he could no longer tolerate the silence in the apartment. He jammed his hat on and bolted, yelling over his shoulder that he'd be "back in two minutes." He did come back soon then went out again.

That went on all afternoon. Our front door opened and closed, opened and closed. He kept finding excuses to leave the house for something or other, like he had to go "pick something up," until my mother couldn't stand it and told him to either stay in or go out for good.

I tried to eat the tuna fish sandwich Mother made me for lunch—at nine o'clock in the morning—but it was no use, and it was a big relief when my aunts and uncles came over. But they, too, had long faces. They were only able to stay for a short time. No one knew what to say to a kid who was devastated about going to the hospital.

"It's not a hospital," my mother said. "It's different, you'll see. It's much better."

But I knew she hadn't ever been there, so how could she know?

Neither of us spoke as my father strapped me into the brace. He scowled, so I knew he was upset. I also knew that I had to at least pretend to be brave for his sake. That burden I had to carry, for some reason, so I did. We bundled up well, and Mother walked us to the door. For a second, when I looked at her face, I worried she'd break down. Harsh as she was, I liked it better than the thought of her hysterical. She had neither kissed nor hugged me yet, and, though I wanted her to, I couldn't ask. She adjusted my hat, and then brusquely, in Spanish, she commanded me to eat. I nodded, although we both knew I probably wouldn't. Finally, after staring at each other a second more, Dad lifted me up in his arms and carried me down the stairs.

"Arvoles pekan, ramos yoran . . ." I heard her say. The trees sin, the branches wither. I didn't understand. Then she closed the door really fast.

We clunked downstairs, and when we got outside I saw that it had begun to snow. It was that time of year when it's nearly dark by 4:30, and for some reason that made me happy. Little white flakes dotted the windshield, fast making a velvet sheet. He drove like that, with the windshield all white, until we couldn't see out at all, and he had to turn the wipers on. Their droning rhythm soothed me. I sank back low in the seat and went as far away as I could, almost immediately. I had gotten used to doing this when doctors examined me and touched my body. If I concentrated, I found I could actually be someplace else: running with a kite on the beach or playing with dogs in a field. With the darkness, the snow, and the rhythm of the windshield wipers, I was almost there.

I closed my eyes and thought, No one can annoy me to eat. I had two hand-me-down Nancy Drew mystery books that I could almost read; I had my "secret" rosaries with the hanging man; I had my trusty Hoppy watch with the glow-in-the-dark hands and my favorite book, *Christmas in the Country*. Even though I had long outgrown this Golden Book, I loved it still because it was the family I wanted. They all go to visit Grandma and Grandpa in the country for a perfect, snowy Christmas. I envisioned the hens in the barn making corn garlands for the Christmas tree, while Betty and her grandma stitched cranberry chains to decorate it. Of course, the cows would wrap presents, and the little brother, out in the forest with Grandpa, would chop down a suitable spruce tree.

"We was thirty-one guys who volunteered," Dad began. "They dropped us one night by parachute into sixteen feet of fresh snow. We had no idea where the hell we landed."

My father's voice in the stillness startled me out of my reverie. We had approached the 181st Street Bridge, and it was fully night.

"A few guys lost their nerve to jump; they had to be pushed out of the plane. Goose Bay, Labrador. That's where we were. The jumping was easy compared to what came later. They didn't tell you nothing. Not before you went, not while you were there. You was just an army air corps volunteer. That's all you knew."

My first thought, as I listened to his story, was that Mother would criticize his grammar. Under her breath she'd probably call him a boor for saying "we was." It drove her crazy when he mispronounced words, so just to vex her he'd walk around the house repeating them over and over: "Chick-*kago*! Chick-*kago*!"

The snow came down faster and heavier as we drove across the bridge and onto the Harlem River Drive, south. Dad's knuckles were white, and his hands gripped the wheel hard. He pushed his fedora back and continued: "Later on, when they finally built the airstrip, we were called radar operators. Then we had real jobs to do. But it was the time before that, the time when we first got there, before supplies came and the barracks was built, before we even had a chance to fight the war, when the weather was against us, that's when real trouble happened.

"The captain gave me the name 'Armenian.' Guys from the South, they never seen a Jew, a Turk, or an Armenian. It was all the same to them; they thought Jews were devils. Also, they never seen snow, and they was scared of all those things. One guy named Mickey from Alabama, he asked me: What's an Armenian? So I take out my pocketknife and pretend I'm gonna slit my own throat. '*That's an Armenian!*' I tell him." First he smiled at the memory, and then he laughed. "*That's an Armenian!* What a hick!

"It was cold. None of us, even us guys from the North, was used to that kind of freezing cold. We had guys there from Michigan, from Wisconsin, from North Dakota, where temperatures went to twenty below; they thought they could take it. After a while they could of been from Florida. This was different cold, you know what I mean? Not what any of them was used to. It got into you, and it never left you. You couldn't warm up from it.

"Minute we landed, we couldn't breathe. It cut right through, and, if you spit, it froze straight up out of your mouth." He spit a little to show me. "Icicles grew on our beards. We danced with each other like we was in Roseland, just to keep warm and keep moving. You had to keep active. Still, some of us were going to lose fingers or toes. Chopped off from frostbite." He pulled off a glove with his teeth and tickled my cheek with the two stumps on his right hand until I cried from laughing. I guess I had thought his fingertips had been shot off with a rifle.

As we pulled onto the East River Drive, my father continued: "Eskimos helped us build temporary huts for shelter; something like igloos. Some boys were shocked when they got there and saw that the Army had no barracks waiting for us. 'You're in the army, boy,' the captain says. 'Get used to whatever happens. This is the war!'

"We wore six layers of clothing plus gear: our boots, our fur earmuffs, our sweaters, our parkas, another jacket on top of that, two or three scarves, hats, and hoods. And we still shook all over trying to keep warm. I shivered all the time. Inside the shelter or outside, don't matter. Same wind, same cold.

"The wind. It was so loud you had to shout over it. Howling, screaming wind. We'd open the hatch, try to go out, and be pushed back inside by the wind. Knocked you off your feet. Took two or three of us at a time just to get the hell outside. And there was nothing out there anyway except the lights. The lights. That's what happened. It was those lights."

I listened, entranced. This was one tale he'd never told.

"They're called the 'northern lights,' aurora borealis—and don't ask

Northern Lights   161

me to spell it. You've never seen nothing like the northern lights. So beautiful, so strange. They call to you. Sometimes they take shapes, like green ghosts in the distance. Picture it: green, white, sometimes purple, blue, swirling colors in a black, star-filled sky. Gorgeous! Like a genie coming out of a bottle."

I knew better than to interrupt, but I wondered if the lights were like Mother's crystal necklaces. They had all the colors of the rainbow when you held them up to the light. She called them "aurora borealis." My father had bought her several, long ones and short ones, some with matching earrings.

"When the winds died down and you could see, it got kind of pretty out there, white and peaceful, you know? And always the beautiful northern lights in the distance. Well, that was the problem. The lights. City boys like me never seen stars as big as those or lights like that, so we'd just stare and stare until we near froze. But the country boys, they gave us the bad problems; they wanted to go *after* the northern lights, to find them and touch them.

"Trouble was, they did call to you: violets, blues, greens, streaks of white; bigger, better than a rainbow. Pink bursts and orange fire seemed to come up over the mountainside beyond, and they wanted to go find it, see where it was coming from. You thought maybe you dreamed the aurora borealis—until the next time you saw them appear in the distance.

"We'd stand outside on that snow as long as we could take it, looking yonder, and out of nowhere the natives came on sleds with dogs, straight out of the whiteness. We bought beaded necklaces, fur gloves, other knickknacks they made. They wanted the chocolate we had; they didn't care about the money. Then they drove right back into the white from where they came. I thought maybe I dreamed the Eskimos, too, you know, like I dreamed the lights. That's how your mind starts going off, you know?

"This was the world's end, kiddo. Indescribable. Jamjík, desolate. Though some poor slobs believed they could find the lights, I can tell you, wasn't anything on the other side of that snow, really. Nothing. That's why they didn't make it. They couldn't *wait*."

The story lasted the whole trip, but it wasn't finished. It was the first Sunday I spent with my father in Goose Bay, Labrador. There would be many. I was so completely wrapped up in the story I didn't realize that we had stopped and were parked in front of the Rusk Institute.

"What happened to the guys?"

Dad turned to me. "I'm gonna finish it," he said, "when I take you home for the wedding. It's just two weeks, kiddo. Wait'll you hear what happened to the ones who went looking for the northern lights!" He got out of the car and came around to my side.

"Listen. You're gonna walk good after this, you'll see. They come from all over the world to be here."

I wouldn't budge. I begged him to finish the story, anything, just not to get out. "Why do I have to stay here? Why?"

"Because Y is a crooked letter."

After I was admitted, they allowed my father to come up to my room for a few minutes. He looked around and then put my things on the bed right by the window, facing the East River.

"Look at that! Nice, huh?"

I grabbed him and dug my nails into his suit lapels—it's a wonder my dad had any suits or shirts left whole—and I cried inconsolable, loud, gulping sobs. There was only one other girl in the room, and she quickly wheeled herself out. I didn't care if I was a baby—I wouldn't let him go. He stood me on top of the bed and showed me how pretty the lights were, reflected on the water. In the daytime, he said, I would see boats pass by.

"Remember the guys in Goose Bay. Some did what they had to do; others, they didn't stay put, they couldn't wait. You'll see what happens to them!"

I cried harder. I didn't care, and I was out of patience.

Dad sighed. "You know I'll be back. As early as I can." He pointed to the completely black sky. "Look there. After I go, you'll find the North Star. That's our star. And I'll be watching it, too." Then he sat me down gently on the bed, kissed me, and left. He was so fast. By the time I grabbed my crutches, got off the bed and hobbled to the doorway, his hat had disappeared into the elevator.

Again, the anchor of my life had lifted and the boat rolled away. There is a feeling of being lost, forsaken, and totally alone in the world after hospital visitors leave that is like no other lonely feeling. They go; you stay. No bars, chains, or locked doors hold you, yet you're in jail. For me it was like the bottom of my belly had slipped down and left a burning ache. This sensation would return to me year after year, at the oddest times and in inappropriate places. At house parties, in department stores, in the theater before the curtain goes up. Those times I'd feel suddenly adrift, panicky, like that moment at Rusk when Dad left.

I refused to talk to anyone the first night, although the other girls in my room seemed okay. I fell asleep sobbing and was in the middle of a dream of parachutes and snow when a loud thwomp! on my bed awakened me. I sat up. Something looking like a boy was sitting at the foot of my bed rocking back and forth. The boy had a face and a body but no arms or legs. As I stared, eyes wide open and now fully alert, he wiggled his little stumps that were like fingers at me. They seemed to be attached to the area where his shoulders should have been. Fascinated, I noticed he had normal-looking feet connected to the bottom of his torso. I was inside of a nightmare.

Anticipating my scream, the boy begged me not to: "It's only me, Juan!" he said, jumping up and down on the bed. Then somehow he catapulted onto the next bed, waking that girl up.

"Get lost, Juan!" she said, yawning, and rolled over.

Juan was born without limbs in Bolivia, where, after his mother took a look at him, she threw him away. He was found in a trash barrel by a visiting doctor, who saved his life by bringing him back to the institute for treatment and to live, permanently, as he had nowhere else to go. Howard Rusk, the charismatic founder and head of the institute "adopted" him. He would live there for two decades.

Juan was a familiar figure around the halls, barreling down them like a torpedo with feet. How he got around was amazing to watch; how he leapt from bed to bed to bed without arms or legs was even more amazing. But the most extraordinary thing about Juan was his personality. He was happy. At sixteen he had no other family but the staff of the Rusk Institute, yet he was genuinely cheerful. He spread joy wherever he happened to be. Juan was the official "greeter" for new people like me.

At the Rusk Institute I saw, just like Dad said, a whole other segment of the world's population: kids and adults from different countries speaking foreign languages as well as New Yorkers and folks from the Midwest. There were polios, of course, but not exclusively, as in

Warm Springs, Georgia, Roosevelt's rehabilitation facility that he built especially for polio survivors like himself. Many celebrities came to Rusk, too. Some I recognized, even when I didn't know their names. They walked the halls and did physical therapy like the rest of us, joking with the other patients as if they were ordinary folks.

Baseball great Roy Campanella was one of those rehabilitated at Rusk after his near-fatal car accident that left him a paraplegic. For a brief moment in 1958 our paths crossed, when I had to go to the institute again, and Campanella and I were there at the same time. Although he was too sick for me to see him, I remember the place being mobbed by reporters and photographers.

Whoever came to Rusk came for rehabilitation by the top physical therapists in the field, maybe in the world. They came minus one leg or both, with deformed or missing arms, as quadriplegics, and as victims of accidents or disease. Maimed and often desperate, these were the worst cases, and many were reborn. And then there was Juan, in a class by himself.

All deformities welcome, all languages spoken: Russian, French, Arabic, Hebrew, and Greek. It took me only about a week to feel at home there, to know that I was among extraordinary individuals. Though I hadn't yet seen much of the world, I would learn much in my time there. An atmosphere of determination and fortitude was established, like nothing I'd seen so far. People walked with fake legs, and they ate with fake hands. There was work to be done at the institute, and catastrophic loss was made to seem as if it were par for the course. I felt a part of the place.

Juan became a familiar figure to me and, soon, a friend. He was nocturnal, like me, so I often saw him hurtling his compact torso from bed to bed to "visit" with his friends. During the day, when he wasn't tumbling around by himself, he walked on specially fitted prostheses and had what looked like arms attached to his stumps. He often looked comical, as if he were walking on stilts, and anyone could tell he was much happier without the fake limbs. He enjoyed spinning around on his own stumps and often picked up more velocity than most wheelchairs. Juan was content to be who he was.

Mother was right. The institute wasn't at all like the other hospitals.

I had hard work ahead of me. There was OT (Occupational Therapy), PT (Physical Therapy), and HS (Hospital School). I shared a big, bright room with seven girls of varying ages, and, because I was the best off as far as getting around, I was appointed "morning aide" to help the other girls, most of whom were in wheelchairs, get ready for the day. There was a bureau in our room with a stack of donated clothing, such as shorts and loose pants that were suitable for exercising, to choose from. Every day I went to the bureau and shamelessly picked first the nicest blouse and pants in the batch. Then I distributed the rest. Each day that passed, I got around faster on crutches, and my fervent hope was to ditch each brace.

The institute was a big camp for the crippled. We ate our meals in a common room, and after that we went down the hall to "school," where I finally got to be in third grade. After a couple of days, however, the teacher declared me smart enough to be in fourth, and, to my delight, she gave me harder things to read. We had school until lunch; afterwards, everyone went to the physical therapy room for individual help.

Every afternoon, Monday to Friday, I was worked: I practiced walking between the parallel bars in the massive gym, back and forth, and then taught how to go up and down a flight of four steps with my braces on. When they came off, I'd have to practice doing that all over again. They stretched my legs and made me do knee bends lying down on the mats, and then I had to practice my gait, walking, walking, and more walking. After a few days three therapists conferred and decided that I was able to stand sufficiently straight enough to do okay without the Milwaukee Brace. I was thrilled to have it removed. By week two they had also determined that a half-brace on my right leg—now called my "good" leg—was enough. With half of a leg brace on the right, one long one on the left, and that oppressive body brace removed, I felt lighter, free, almost as if I could dance.

My physical therapist, a pretty blonde named Jackie, worked me hard all day. The good news was that rehabilitation wasn't a long-drawn-out affair; I made progress fast and every day. Unlike in the hospital, the mood at Rusk was always upbeat. There was a fighting spirit instilled, but there was camaraderie also among the patients and their therapists. Jackie told me she had little doubt that I'd soon be walking on my own without any braces whatsoever, and I loved hearing it.

This was my constant goal, and I was never allowed to forget it or become lazy. I loved my therapist, so it was easy to listen and do all that I was told. Although I went to bed at night sore and exhausted, I forgot that because I had a real purpose; there was something concrete I could do. And no more crying. If I even *looked* like I might cry, everyone picked on me, especially Juan, who'd jump on my bed and ridicule me.

"What a baby, what a little *baby*," he'd say, shaking his head from side to side and wiggling his stumps.

Jackie taught me how to fall down so that I wouldn't get hurt. This skill was the most important one polios could learn. We were taught that there was an art to falling, so we fell, on purpose, time after time. If we balked, they'd push us back down again, harder. Some of us fell again at night, in the hallway or in our rooms, mainly because we were so tired from those workouts.

I learned how to spread my fingers out in a fan before I went down — palms flat, hands first — without hurting my hands at all, avoiding impact to my knees. I was luckier than some because I had two strong arms to make this possible, although they ached, and so did my hands, even though I fell on rubber mats.

Mercilessly, Jackie made me fall again and again. "You'll have no pity from the pavement," she said. At first she or another therapist helped me up, until we got to the stage where I had to learn how to rise up by myself from the ground. If I stayed down too long or complained of being tired, she'd nudge me with the tip of her sneaker until I moved. Fight! fight! fight! was, would always be, the polio theme song. There was no such thing as feeling sorry for yourself, crying, or saying "it hurts." Unless you wanted to be a "helpless cripple," synonymous with "hateful devil," you fought, you fell, you climbed, you stretched, you kept working.

It was up to me, Jackie said, to design a way for myself to get up from the floor. I had done it at Lenox Hill the first time I walked when I got into the chair backwards. Some kids were able to get up only like that, by holding onto a chair and then sitting in it. That was fine, they said, I could do that, too — sometimes. But it was obvious that I could also do more. I could learn how to get up without holding onto *anything*, and without having anyone boost me.

After falling a million times and practicing endlessly, I figured out a technique: I could arch my back like a cat, stick my rear end high, balance like that on all fours, then spring into an upright position by the strength of my arms alone. If I did it right, smoothly, I stayed upright; if not, I fell right back down. And sometimes I pushed up so hard and so fast that I fell over backwards and landed on my head. That hurt, but even then they made me do it all over again.

They pushed the polios harder than any other group. It was believed that we could accomplish more than others, accident victims or those born with birth defects, could. I was indoctrinated with the idea that I could do *anything*, miraculous things, but that I'd never ever achieve the physical mobility I wanted unless I pushed harder than anyone else — in the *world*. And if I did not reach my goal, it meant that I didn't work hard enough, try my best. Our supercharged therapists were our gods; they alternated between brutal taskmaster and loving coach, while we were expected to be nothing less than tough athletes-in-training. They never let up on us, not even to the point of exhaustion, and the psychology of this kind of punishing regimen would eventually be examined. No doubt, it left some of us, who failed to scale Mount Everest, furious with ourselves and depressed.

At the start of the week of Lorraine's wedding, the brace on my right leg came off. That left only one.

"Walk!" Jackie commanded. I grabbed for my crutches, but she took them away.

"Go without them! Come on! Unless you'd rather walk with crutches your whole life — "

Scared, I stood completely still. My left knee felt rubbery, as if it would buckle; often it did buckle, when I least expected. They had shown me how to thrust my left leg out and then snap it back really fast so that the knee wouldn't give. This compensated for the inactive quadriceps disabled by surrounding nerves. But it required a hairsbreadth of thinking first, and I couldn't think. So I became rooted to the spot. I looked around the room for help.

Steel-voiced Jackie said: "No! You don't need the parallel bars. Walk on your own. Now."

I took two steps, unassisted. I felt like I was walking on top of a shaky bed. Unsteadily, I took two more steps, then three, then four. I had become twice as strong as I was that night at Lenox Hill, when I first tried it. In almost four months I had lost completely not only the ability to automatically move my legs but also the memory of what real walking felt like. I yearned for it. We all did, and we'd all strive for just that, to walk like we used to, as if polio had never occurred.

Jackie stood behind me and monitored my gait. She showed me how to swing my arms and legs naturally and how to pace myself after stepping down. No matter how I faltered, it was still better than not walking. I eyed the wheelchair in the corner and vowed never to sit in it again. Of course, by the time that session was through I gratefully sank into the chair, exhausted, barely able to wheel it to my room.

I was sleeping, eating and exercising well, and socializing. At night I stayed in the recreation room after supper and watched TV or sang along to show tunes that played on the record player they had set up. During the day, though, there was no time for relaxing or becoming lackadaisical; always there was a therapist around to treat me rough and remind me of the work yet to be done: "You think you're finished? Get on those mats and bring your knees to your chest! What a lazy one this is!"

A couple of days before I went home for the wedding, Mother paid a visit. She hadn't met him yet but was determined to talk to the supreme god, Dr. Howard Rusk, and ask him about me. Dr. Rusk often walked the halls looking in on his "family" of survivors. Rusk was a towering figure: distinguished, remarkably handsome, tall, and of elegant speech. Some thought of him as an evangelist because of his inspiring speeches to patients and their families. It was Dr. Rusk who gave us the impetus to go on when we became discouraged. He'd find you wherever you were, at dinner or resting in your room, pull up a chair, and sit down to chat with you, like a friend. He was well known for his comments to patients.

"Remarkable! What an accomplishment you are! Did you ever think you'd be so far along in recovery by now? I pick you as a model for others in your situation. What an example of courage you are!"

He'd even forget he was chief and took the time to explain to polios the workings of certain muscle groups and how remaining nerves over-compensated for ruined, useless ones. No matter what he talked about, everything out of Dr. Rusk's mouth mesmerized.

Mother was determined to meet this angel. She'd seen him strid-ing through the lobby with his entourage but wasn't able to get close. Then Serendipity had it that he was visiting my floor one day as Mother stepped off the elevator. He wasn't getting away this time! Mother man-aged to penetrate the throng of visitors he was lecturing, who hung on his every word. The great doctor liked to talk, and the moment he stopped for a breath Mother picked up where he left off, engaging him in conversation, which she did quite well herself. When she got her chance, she zoomed in and asked the big question: "How far will she go, Doctor?"

Mother wanted specifically to know if my progress was spectacular or just average. She wanted impossible answers: Would I get better and better? Would I walk normally? In other words, would I again be *exactly the same as before*? The same as *others*?

Dr. Rusk bent over me as I sat in my wheelchair. The crowd of admir-ers looked on. He lifted my face in both hands and smiled directly into my eyes. This was so unlike most of the doctors I'd known so far, who avoided eye contact totally. As he looked at me, he addressed Mother, speaking deliberately, slow, as if she, he, and I were the only people in that hallway, the only ones who mattered. His voice was velvet.

"Mother, this child is already normal. She's perfect. She not only has outer beauty, but she exudes an *inner* light. Certainly, I see it. Truly, she is blessed. Hope for her future? I have nothing *but* hope that this lovely girl will go very far indeed." With that he and the group walked on.

For once even Mother was stunned speechless.

My big job was to learn how to redirect my thinking in order to achieve balance on a body that was off-kilter. My left leg—the "bad" leg—was a tiny bit shorter than my right, but it was possible to learn to walk nearly as well as I had, they said, as long as I made the effort. I had to go through an un-training, forgetting everything I used to know, used to do automatically, and concentrate on *thinking* before I performed any physical move. To think *before* I thrust out my right leg, to think *before* I sat down and again *before* I was about to stand up. Unconsciously, all these things once happened on their own. If I didn't plan every move, I'd fall fast and hard, maybe get hurt. Jackie assured me I'd get used to it and that with practice it would one day feel natural. She was so cheerfully positive I had to believe her.

My days were full. In Occupational Therapy I made a picture frame and painted it blue and also a jewelry box that was once an old cigar box, decorated with dried macaroni, for Mother. I sprayed it gold. Each kid had a file. They took our pictures for the file, kept one, and gave us the other one to paste underneath the lid of our jewelry boxes. After the therapist clipped my picture to her file folder I saw that she wrote something down, and when she turned her back I took a look at what she wrote. Only two words: "Well adjusted." I didn't know exactly what she meant, but I knew that the word well was good, in any case. My mother never used the box I made her for jewelry, but she kept it on her dresser, empty, for the rest of her life.

Most nights I stayed up until blackness covered the East River and I could find our North Star. Sometimes Juan came and sat with me. I knew he had neither family nor home, so I didn't verbalize my home-sickness. He was perceptive, though. He knew I looked forward to the day when my dad would come to take me home for my cousin's wedding.

"Is it Friday yet?" he'd ask, jumping on my bed. His bubbly, sunny nature lifted my spirits always, and he loved making me laugh. With Juan around you couldn't feel a tiny bit sorry for yourself. If a new arrival tried to cry herself to sleep, he'd hurl himself onto her bed and jump up and down on his stumps. That usually stopped the sobbing! There were a few pitiful ones who came and went and, every now and then, an angry girl or boy who didn't mind telling everyone how much they hated being there. But most were usually turned around by Juan's comical presence: the gap-toothed smile, the wiggling stumps, and the nightly announcement: "It's only me, Juan!"

I stayed put like the guys in Goose Bay, Labrador, as my father so slyly instructed, and Jackie said I made extraordinary progress. I walked unassisted most of the time and was ready to ditch the crutches now, too. When I got tired, though, I fell.

"You'll always fall," one of the therapists told me. "That's polio. You fall."

So I practiced doing it right so that I wouldn't get hurt. Polios were falling all over the place at Rusk—accidentally and on purpose. Falling was a project we had to master, or they wouldn't let us out. I got an A+. Even when I would later fall on the Grand Concourse, on the hard concrete, I rarely scraped my knees. If there can be such a thing, I was prepared to fall and also was able to leap up, albeit awkwardly, within seconds. I remembered to be careful about the heels of my palms so they wouldn't get bruised, which is amazing, because I fell on them 99 percent of the time.

In Hospital School there weren't many my age, and I got special attention. I learned to read one of the Nancy Drew mystery novels I had brought, *The Quest of the Missing Map*, in its entirety. I hated math, but the teacher liked me, so she gave me very few exercises to do. The Rusk Institute was a good place for me all around; my parents were happy and relieved when they saw me. The physical therapy room was open all the time, and when Dad came I often took him there and showed him how I could climb the four steps, one at a time but quickly.

"Soon you won't have even the braces," he said.

If that pressured me, I didn't recognize it. I agreed with him, pushing, pushing, doing whatever they said I should do, no matter how tiring or painful. Only hindsight could have foretold the weight of that self-competition. At the time I was a model for other children.

I got an education in many ways at Rusk. We had three teenagers in our room; one girl was thirteen. One night the thirteen-year-old, Esther, woke up screaming that she was bleeding. Everyone came running, and my heart stopped. I had never actually *seen* anyone die before my eyes. Because it wasn't a hospital, it took a while to locate a doctor, but when the floor nurse came running in she sighed, relieved, and beamed at Esther.

"Congratulations!"

Still worried, I watched as Esther's bedding became soaked with blood, and the nurse made me turn away. "You're a woman now," I heard her whisper. The next day our therapist explained what had happened, and I listened intently as Esther received instructions on how to care for herself monthly. She was in a wheelchair, unable to walk, but had use of her arms. The therapist told her that because she wasn't active she'd naturally bleed more than other women. I was no longer scared, but I was still confused. I made a vow then to become as active as humanly possible before I "became a woman," although I had no idea why, and when the therapist left the room, I did twenty leg raises with my good leg.

As promised, Dad arrived promptly at six on the Friday of the wedding weekend. I was so excited to go home that I barely ate lunch that day. Each week I had mastered a new physical feat and was anxious to show him everything I could do. Jackie tried an experiment; she took the half-brace off my right leg and had me walk around a while, telling me that, if I felt okay, I could probably leave it at the institute for the weekend. I had no problem deciding.

Jackie stayed late that day to wait for my father, happy to share news of my progress. She reiterated, looking at me but talking to him, that, if I worked hard when I returned, I could count on one day having no brace on either leg. Then she put her arm around me and told my dad that she was very proud of me and how much I had accomplished. It was basically her first compliment, other than "Good girl! Try again!"

Dad was predictably thrilled, so much so that he gave Jackie a big kiss on the cheek for being such a good therapist. Her face turned red, and mine, for some reason, felt hot. Jackie was all dressed up that night; she had told me earlier that she had a date. I had never seen her in anything but therapist clothes: loose blue pants and matching shirts, a white coat, and sneakers. Like nurses, therapists were there to help us; they didn't have other lives outside the PT room.

I took a good look at her outfit. She had on a shiny, tight black dress, decorated with a long string of pearls, and high black heels, like Cousin Dottie's. Her blonde hair was fixed up in a French twist. As she talked with my father, I became uncomfortable, aware of something bother-some that I couldn't put a name to. They both suddenly forgot I was there. I thought of the word, *hermoza*, beautiful, a word that had often been applied to me by relatives. Jackie was *hermoza*, for sure. But she was also something else. It was the way she stood as she talked, with her shapely legs fitting neatly into nice shoes—a perfect fit—that I found disquieting.

My father leaned against the wall tapping a cigarette into his palm, which he knew he couldn't smoke in the institute, smiling all the time, as if Jackie were saying the funniest things. I knew what Mother would say if she saw it: "Your father's a magnet for women." She would not have been happy with the way they were talking to each other, engrossed, and for so long. The way Dad looked at Jackie made me afraid. As usual, I knew the feeling before the word: Desirability. A new challenge no one had mentioned that I'd one day have to meet. It was different than being "pretty."

Jackie was also a magnet. As they spoke, my dad stared so intently at her that, had the wall he was leaning on wobbled, he would not have noticed. They talked about dancing the lindy hop, and Dad mentioned how he had won many lindy contests, including one for the Harvest Moon Ball. They talked about families and what her boyfriend did for a living and where she liked to go at night. All this while I sat, bored to death, in my wheelchair.

Finally, she leaned down and kissed me—another thing she had never done—and wished me a good time at the wedding.

"Remember all you've learned so far," she said. "I'll see you when you get back."

My father stared after her, watching her legs as she walked up the hall. For too long, I thought. I watched her also. How rapidly she click-clacked on those high heels! A thought came, and I pushed it back, but it came again. For the first time I doubted some things Jackie told me. I wondered if she could have lied to me about practicing walking, about getting better, about *really* walking. The feeling hit my stomach. I wondered if, no matter how many times I fell, got up, walked stairs, and did the parallel bars, I'd ever walk that fast or that well.

El kazar es un regalo, el parir es un mal passo,

el kriar mal todo el anyo. Marriage is a gift,

birth a passing pain, the rearing of

children, an ache for the whole year.

LADINO PROVERB

7 ❊ Quiche Lorraine

The first chords of the wedding march struck. In unison two hundred heads turned toward the back of the chapel, where, on a revolving pedestal, the silhouette of a bride stood in profile, bouquet in hand. We gasped before breathing, *ohhh* . . . My jaw dropped when I saw Cousin Lorraine standing there looking exactly like a paper doll cutout—ten times the size.

A soft spotlight illumined her smiling, beautiful face framed by dark curly hair. We were the only two with that kind of hair mass, although mine that night hung limp, having lost its curl from my illness. Then the spotlight spread gradually down her bodice and past her waist, until it reached the folds of her gown, gathered in satin swirls at her feet. When the bride was all lit up, the pedestal began to turn again. Finally, she faced the audience, posing for a minute with her bouquet, a broad smile visible from underneath her veil.

The photographer, who had been waiting to get this shot, ran up from the front of the chapel, kneeled, and took her picture. Flashcubes popped. The music, which had paused for effect, then resumed, and a gauze curtain parted as my cousin stepped off the pedestal. Now the organ *pounded* out Mendelssohn's "Wedding March"; I held my breath.

On cue, and as if by magic, Tante Sultana and Uncle Ovadiah appeared on either side of their daughter. Taking measured, sure steps, her back straight and her head high, and flanked by her much shorter parents, Lorraine marched down the aisle to meet her groom.

Behind me two old Turkish women broke the mood by laughing out loud. One of them poked me in the shoulder, teasing me about drooling. They were hysterical with my being so awestruck. But seeing my cousin Lorraine on that revolving pedestal was like seeing Cinderella jump out of my Golden Book. It was the best part of the ceremony; the rest was long and boring, and I fell into a stupor until the groom's heel smashed the glass and everyone clapped, shouting, *Mazal Tov!*

The wedding was held at Parkside Caterers on River Avenue and 161st Street, across from Yankee Stadium. It was my first wedding and also the first time I'd seen a bride close up. December 19, 1954, was to be a night of profound entrances. The wild Turkish party that came after I was used to. But I was not prepared for a heavenly apparition on a revolving pedestal or for some relatives' reactions to my own entrance.

Lorraine's wedding marked my reentry into family life, and it also began a new phase in my emotional recovery. When I limped in, everyone who was standing around enjoying the cocktail-smorgasbord hour put down their drinks and plates and clapped. Those who were seeing me for the first time since I went to the hospital broke down and cried. Others turned away, unable to look at me. That night I learned how my status had changed. Although they were all thrilled that I survived and made it to *azer kyef*, participate in a family celebration, some were still deathly afraid of the disease that almost killed me. Those who were kept their distance. They were only a few, but they were relatives who had always hugged and kissed me, often more than I could stand. Now they stayed back.

If I thought anyone would try to drag me onto the dance floor for a belly dance, it was a figment of my childish imagination. It became apparent to me that my former self, the active little girl I used to be, was what people missed. Merely walking wasn't miracle enough. Also, I was surprised at myself that I felt like hiding my imperfections from some of them. I wondered if they still loved me as much as before. Right then, while I couldn't very well hide my brace—although later they tried that, too—I learned to hide my inner feelings and pretended not to care what anyone thought. I knew Mother dreaded being pitied, so I did, too. I reasoned that it was vital to give everyone the impression that I was happy and "well adjusted," just as my folder at the institute stated, and, if I did, then no one would be "upset" at how I looked.

Lorraine took me under her wing that night and for years afterwards. She perceived my discomfort with the subtle but very real demarcation in my family status and also with my increasing awareness of human nature. At the wedding there were people who exhibited bizarre behavior when they saw me. One aunt stood a good distance away when she talked to me, and another one, who'd never paid me much mind in the past, acted overly solicitous. And then there was that customary blessing said to young girls, especially at weddings: *Novia ke te vea!* I should see *you* a bride! Glaringly missing from nearly everyone's greeting. No one chucked my chin or pinched my cheek either, calling me beautiful. It was an early education in how some people perceive beauty.

No doubt, my appearance shocked them. I felt fine but was still anemically pale and so thin that Mother couldn't find a proper dress for the wedding that fit me. My fingers were straw sticks; no ring stayed on without slipping, not even the ruby-and-diamond pinkie ring Nona Behora gave me for my fifth birthday. It kept falling off my index finger until finally Mother put it in her purse. Robbed of its curl, my hair was a big problem, too. They didn't know how to fix it until someone found a flowered tiara headband to hold it in place, which looked pretty and gave me needed color. One of my aunts came up with a white lace blouse that actually fit pretty well, and, to go with it, Mother found a black taffeta skirt splashed with multicolored polka dots. Of course, they had to tighten the waist with safety pins.

My mother insisted I wear a sweater, a furry white one with half-sleeves called a "shrug," in case I got cold. She still had her fear of contagion, even though the worst had already happened. I loved the whole outfit and felt pretty—except for my shoes. Although they promised that ugly shoes were only temporary, I hated them on a daily basis. That day I fought and lost the battle to wear my favorite black patent leather dress shoe on my right foot, which probably wouldn't have fit anyway, and the ugly oxford brown shoe on the left. I couldn't understand why I had to wear *two* ugly shoes.

"Impossible. You can't wear two different shoes; you'll be unbalanced. What if you fall?" Mother said.

"I promise I won't. I swear! And, even if I fall, I know how to get up fast! I practiced!"

That was the wrong thing to say. The very thought of me falling at the wedding horrified her, and the answer remained, of course, no.

For Sephardic girls the debut cotillion was the family wedding. That is where you "came out" as a good dancer, especially if you belly danced; then you were worthy of your sultan's harem. In this area, complete with blue-veiled costume, I formerly excelled. Young as I was, at the first strains of the double-strings dance, when the clarinet hit the high notes, I always got excited, and my arms would automatically go up in the traditional Turkish way. I'd rotate my hips alongside my fat-armed aunts. They said I was a natural who couldn't wait to bounce onto center stage in someone's living room. This was my first affair, and it felt strange not to be dancing at Lorraine's wedding.

When everyone jumped from their seats, held hands, and danced around in a circle, which got bigger and bigger as the music got faster and faster, I stood in the background holding onto a chair, watching and stamping my good foot as hard as I could in time to the frantic beat. *Opa! Opa!* the room shouted, as the band switched from the *horá* to the Greek *miserlou*. The circle got bigger and bigger as more people got up to join in. Several men took out white handkerchiefs, à la the Greek way, to make a chain for the circle to hold onto and expand. Round and round, faster and faster, kicking the right leg then switching direction and kicking the left. *Opa!* Everyone, even my father, forgot about me standing alone in the background outside the circle. It was as if I weren't there.

Not participating came as a shock. I felt my chin tremble and my eyes well up, but I knew how to hold back from crying. I suddenly wanted to go home. The dancers kicked and laughed, having a great time pounding the floor with their good, strong legs. The circle passed two, three, four, times in front of me until the band finally got tired and it was time for the second course. The turquoise blues and reds and golds, all the individual colors of the women's bright cocktail dresses, shimmered before me as one blend through my veil of tears. That was the *only* veil; the long one of ignorance I wore until then had lifted as I watched everyone dance back to their tables.

Later, when I went into the bathroom, I sat in the stall and found myself studying the kinds of shoes the women wore; most were dyed-to-match-the-gown high heels, and some were spike heels. I marveled at how even the fat ladies were able to dance in those shoes. I had never paid much attention to shoes, but they fascinated me now. I did not count one, not one, orthopedic shoe, not even on the old *viejas* who customarily wore ugly, chunky-heeled black shoes. This, too, I swore would be temporary. Just as I'd learned to walk, I'd learn to walk in beautiful shoes.

Before they cut the cake, Lorraine came and took me by the hand into a private room to take a fateful picture. The photographer sat us close together on a red velvet bench and "fixed" us. First, he folded my hands neatly in my lap and straightened my shrug and headband. He spread out my taffeta skirt. Then he posed the bride, whose veil and train had been removed, arranging yards of satin and lace into neat folds. I felt so small sitting next to my cousin in her big gown; as a bride, she seemed larger than life to me. The photographer fussed over us until he was satisfied, and then he stepped back. But just when I thought he was ready to snap the picture, he ran up to us again, fixed our hair, bent Lorraine's arm at a different angle, and then ran back to his tripod. My cousin held me close, her arm snug around my waist throughout the whole setup.

Finally, he was ready: "A *big* smile now, for the bride and her little maid of—"

He never finished the sentence. A split second before he took the shot, my aunt Allegre, who had been standing in the background look-ing on, hurried over, gathered up a large part of Lorraine's gown and flung it over my legs so that my metal brace and the orthopedic shoe were totally covered. Then she backed up, and he took the picture.

It all happened so fast, I didn't have a chance to think about what she did at the time. That picture haunted me for years. I'd study it closely in our album at home and also look at it when I visited Lorraine, won-dering what bothered me about it. But no matter how many times I scrutinized that photo of the two of us, I couldn't figure out what was missing. It was only when Mother told me, many years later, that I knew:

My aunt hid my brace in order to save me from "un rekuedro mal," experiencing a "bad memory" of my suffering, when I looked at the picture.

It worked. My brace was so buried under the bridal gown that I even forgot I wore it. I'm sitting next to my bright-eyed cousin; she's staring straight ahead at the camera; I'm smiling tentatively, hands folded peacefully on top of her dress. Nothing at all to indicate a subterfuge. I thought for a long time that, because Lorraine's gown was so beautiful, they just wanted to show more of it than my taffeta skirt.

By the time I was thirteen I had done a really good job of forgetting that I ever wore leg braces, period. And, of course, my family helped in that regard. I could not conjure up the memory of what they felt like on me. The idea that if you don't see something it's not truly there worked. Between my aunt, the photographer, and my own deep desire to be like everyone else, the appliance on my left leg disappeared without a trace—not just in the photo but also in life. There were no pictures of me taken, at any time, wearing braces, standing with crutches, or, God forbid, sitting in a wheelchair. They did not exist in anyone's album anywhere.

Thus began the mental and emotional, if not yet physical, eradication of polio in our family, and it lasted as long as I lived in their house. Polio as an idea evaporated; it just never happened. No one spoke the name of hospitals I went to or children I'd known there; there were no such things as iron lungs, hot packs, leg braces, or, especially, the polio vaccine. If I brought something up, they'd change the subject fast. Mother talked around it, substituting the word *sick* for *polio* if she had to talk about it at all.

"After she got sick—" she'd say, or "When she used the chair—" leaving out the word *wheel*. What happened to me and the fear that surrounded it, that awful autumn of 1954, was efficiently extracted from our collective memory, simply by omission. Polio, the P word, was a dirty word nice girls didn't mention and adults had the discretion to avoid. I was the opposite of a polio poster child: They were plastered everywhere with their appliances and sweet, sad faces in order to get sympathy; my mother's goal, and later mine, was to always repel sympathy and concentrate on being "normal."

Lorraine recognized this from as early as the night of her wedding, that my life had taken a different turn from everyone else's because of a virus and it would be harder for me in seen and unseen ways because of that. Inherently honest, she never flinched from saying the P word, and hated that some members of my family, on both sides, were ashamed of it, which translated to being ashamed of how I walked. No one wanted to face the residuals of polio, what they meant to a child who once loved to sing and dance and perform pantomimes for company.

If it weren't for my cousin, the only one brave enough to bring it up casually, as if it were a natural thing, it would have been my secret in the closet for who knows how long. As a teenager, I had convinced myself that I was just "clumsy"; the truth was, I didn't even know if I had actually had polio. "It might not have been that . . . disease," Mother once cryptically stated. But Lorraine refused to deny it or use euphemisms for the word, even though I winced the first time I heard it said out loud.

All this took years to figure out. Whenever I looked at the photo, all I saw was a small girl with a sad-eyed smile, a child who resembled me, sitting close to a very happy bride. But if you looked really hard at the bottom, where my covered-up legs were, you could definitely make out a tiny piece of silver metal peeking through the lace.

I already knew that I was going back to the institute after the wedding, and I wanted to be there in time to attend their Christmas party and get a stocking from Santa. Because of the weather, I got my wish. There had already been two snowfalls that December, and Mother was worried I'd be snowed in if I stayed another week. Also, it was nearly impossible for her to take me downstairs the way I had to be bundled up for winter, and with the crutches, all by herself. Then there was little Charlie to worry about. Although he was the kind of kid who did exactly as he was told 99 percent of the time, he would still have had to stay alone until she got back upstairs.

Practicing in Rusk's gym with portable steps was nothing like walking up and down the stairs in my building. Going down by myself was not yet feasible, and even with somebody by my side it took forever to navigate the flights using only one crutch and the banister then cross the lobby on both crutches and then tackle the inner and outer stoop. I was getting better and better at stairs, but in certain spots the banister stopped, and there was only the brick wall to hold onto. Mother got so tense I'd fall that she made me nervous. And when I finally did get downstairs there wasn't much I could do anyway, except stand still in one place.

The Monday after Lorraine's wedding Dad was home, so he carried me down to "take air and sun." This was an absolutely necessary habit for apartment dwellers. Every day, no matter what the weather, in bitter cold of sixteen degrees or during a light snow, they'd "take air." You only stayed in the house if you were sick with fever. Although the weather was bleak and blustery on that particular day, it was decided I should take air, anyway.

As usual, I was overdressed; I wore two sweaters, a red woolen hat I hated that covered my ears, furry mittens I was too old for, a woolen scarf around my neck, a long winter coat handed down from some relative, snug even though I was thin, and one red rubber boot on my right leg, big enough to fit over the orthopedic shoe. It wasn't snowing out, and the boot was horrible to look at, especially since I wore only one. Mother insisted, in case it did snow. I had never been so uncomfortable, and, to top it off, my crutches had to be wedged under my armpits.

Dad stationed me below the DENTIST sign on the first floor, so that I leaned—was actually frozen in place—against the brick wall. Then he said he had to run across the street to Jaffee's; he was out of cigarettes and needed to get the paper. So I stood there propped up under the sign, which was the first bad omen. The following year Dr. Meyers, the dentist, committed suicide by throwing himself off the roof.

"I'll be right back, kiddo, okay? You okay? You're good there?"

I nodded but wished he wouldn't go. I felt as "good" as I imagined a stuffed turkey felt, puffed up and rocking gently back and forth as the wind picked up. The moment he walked away I regretted being outside. If they thought I'd be happier in the street watching the rest of the world come and go, especially the girls my age, they were wrong. I stood there for what seemed like a whole day, while the wind grew stronger and whipped my face raw. It's an awful feeling to want to move and not be able to, to be trapped in place.

Two old ladies passed by and stopped to ask if I needed help. They must have seen my unhappy face. Even so, they did not take one step toward me, and the minute I shook my head no they hurried away. Next came the roller skaters. Three older girls whom I recognized from the Astor Court zoomed past me to the corner, coats flying behind them. Then they zoomed back, their skates grating, making quite a racket rolling on the cement. Then they raced to the corner once more. Finally, they skated down the hill toward Sheridan Avenue, and the street got quiet again.

Apparently, it was Skating Day, because my friend Ellen and her cousin Carol, who was visiting, came down to roller-skate, too. They looked over at me, said "Hi," I said "Hi" back, and then they sat on the stoop to put on their skates and do something magical with skate keys. When they got up they sang out: "Ready, set, *go!*" and took off.

One thing I had always wanted, for some reason, was not so much roller skates but a skate key. I had no idea what you did with it, but I wanted one. Standing there, I wanted one very badly, as Ellen and Carol found it necessary to continually skate back and forth in front of me. They'd look in my direction, giggle, whisper something secret to each other, and then skate off again. This happened five or six times, as if there were nowhere else, no other piece of sidewalk on the block or around the corner, or in the entire Bronx, to skate on.

My father was taking forever to come back, and I was really ready to go upstairs. I figured he had to be placing a bet in Jaffee's back room, but for so long? How could he have forgotten me? Just to keep busy, I started counting cars that passed on the Concourse; at first only the green cars, then I switched to counting only black ones. When I least expected, caught completely off guard, the worst happened: A fierce wind picked me up and knocked me right off my feet to the sidewalk. There was no time to put my arms out and spread my hands like I had been taught. I landed face down; because I wore so many layers of clothing, my nose didn't hit the pavement, but my chin did, and I scraped the bottom of it pretty hard.

There I lay, on my belly, floundering like a fish. I knew for sure there was absolutely no way I would be able to get up by myself; I was too padded, and it was too windy. Everything I had practiced in the institute's gym was useless. When I fell and got up there, it was in light clothing and optimum conditions, very well supervised by therapists.

They hadn't prepared me for the winter winds on the open plains of the Grand Concourse.

Ellen and Carol skated to a stop in front of me and stared, while I made eye contact with the roller balls on the bottom of their skates.

"Can you get my father?" I whispered, looking up.

"Where is he?"

"Jaffee's."

"But I'm not allowed to leave this block."

"Please."

"I *can't*! I'll get in trouble. And here he comes, anyway."

I lifted my head higher, and, relieved, I saw his shape, back facing me, about halfway down the block. He had stopped to light his Lucky against the wind, both hands cupped around his cigarette lighter, and had not yet seen me. Then two things happened: He looked up and saw me lying face down on the ground, and his hat blew off at the same time. Ellen and her cousin laughed spontaneously. Under other circumstances I probably would have thought it funny, too. I prayed that he'd go after his hat instead of running to me; I didn't want to be the cause of him losing one of his precious fedoras.

But he let the hat go, and, with only a backward glance at it as it danced away across the avenue, he ran to my rescue. As fast as that, the girls skated off, too. Once he righted me and I was propped up again, he took off after his hat, running for two blocks. The wind would stop, the hat would stop, he would stop, he'd reach for it, and again the hat would blow away.

He never caught his hat, but he caught it good from Mother when she saw my bloody chin: "You left her alone, didn't you? *Para fumar!* You just *had to buy smokes!* Then placed a couple of losing bets at Jaffee's, too, right?"

Not only did my father lose a fairly new fedora, but he also had a huge fight with my mother over "responsibility." That was the end of my "taking air" for the rest of the week. I felt so stupid, allowing myself to get blown down, like a hat, by wind. More important, I hated that I couldn't roller-skate, that I had never roller-skated. The rest of the day I sulked because I worried that I'd never skate. I was jealous of all those girls who skated past me that day and mad at Ellen and her cousin for taunting me. I don't know what I did with that rage, where I put it, but I suspect I drew it inside of me and then closed up the zipper.

I couldn't wait to go back to the institute. I felt happy there, like my old self; life was easier with Juan and the others who were like me. I even liked hospital school because the teacher gave very little math. I missed working out with Jackie, too, and I wanted to try harder to get better—maybe good enough to roller-skate. It didn't occur to me that I might never; I was filled with an abundance of false hope that, at the time, I needed in order to fight on. I would not have believed them, anyway, if they told me I wouldn't.

I had figured out ways of protecting myself, making myself feel better in certain situations. I could effectively block the embarrassment I felt when I fell in front of people, if I immediately switched my thinking to other areas. I'd concentrate on an image of a hospital friend, like Juan or my old chum Alice Cook, and it worked. That day the girls skated back and forth in front of me I did that, even before I fell; I remembered Alice's mother walking in, day after day, with Alice's skates slung over her shoulder. From time to time I'd wonder about my friend. Had she even left the bed? It naturally followed that I pacified myself by deciding I didn't have it so bad. At least I was walking.

If polio delineated a chunk of my childhood lost, that loss I realized when I hit the streets. It drew a line through my life and gave me a Before and an After, and it was the end of all pretense: At Rusk I could work hard and aspire to athletic heights, but on the Grand Concourse I was different from the other kids, and that was here to stay. Even if I refused to believe that that difference was permanent, it was fact at the time, not because my family ate Middle Eastern foods and belly danced and spoke Spanish but because my body was different. I couldn't run in hide-and-seek or hop the chalk-marked potsy squares on one leg, or jump rope, or bounce a Spalding ball and raise my leg high up over it. I might not ever roller-skate, ice-skate, or leap off the stoop again, four at a time. And I had to do something called *rest*, which no other kid had to do. Even if I got much better at walking and my one last brace came off, I wasn't so positive, deep inside, that I'd walk exactly like the other kids.

I knew it—and I didn't know it. I would do my best to blend in and forget about what I couldn't do because, if I believed that I'd never get any better than I already was, I would have stopped trying. The new girl

I had become confounded me; I didn't know her yet. Who would have thought that I'd long for a bloody knee? Or to hear my mother scream: "Stop running, you'll fall!" I promised myself that the wind wouldn't get me again, although of course it did. Many times. I just wanted to walk better. I *had* to walk better. I hated being out of step and wanted back into the parade.

"Morale was low. The guys felt trapped and wanted out. Supplies were getting short, and as a sergeant it was my responsibility to keep things together. 'Let's get outa here, Armenian,' this guy named Levine kept begging me. 'We could make it over the snow.' Not only was he talking AWOL, but also we could definitely not make it over the snow. Twenty feet deep? You kidding?

"More guys started disappearing. We'd wake up in the morning, and they'd be gone, drawn to the northern lights. They took off to find the rainbow bands and disappeared. We figured out they must have walked and walked then lost track of how far and for how long. Never saw 'em again."

It was Christmas Eve. Dad and I were driving back to the institute when he started telling the Goose Bay, Labrador, story again, picking up where he left off the Friday before, as if he had never stopped. I had to ask:

"Weren't you scared?"

"Sure, I was scared, kiddo. Of a lot of things. We all were. Those were dark days, guys lost in the blizzards. Stuff like that makes you scared unless you're crazy. I'm no big-shot. My buddies went missing night and day. But that still wasn't the worst of it. Wait.

"We'd organize search parties when it got light and go out looking for them, with ropes tied around our waists so we'd stay connected. A guy could fall into the deepest part of the snow, go down, maybe fifteen feet, who knows? We near froze to death looking for this one guy who went missing, an Italian guy. Either we found them sitting up, frozen to death in a snowbank, or we wouldn't find them at all. Sometimes we were looking for guys who were already ghosts." He made a monster face.

"Like that, that's how a frozen face looks. We found the Italian; he was one we came upon, sitting with his back to us, just sitting there, like he was waiting for us. 'Hey Jack!' We called him, hoping maybe he'd turn around, you know? But he was stiff as a board. Probably sat there two, three, days.

"Or we wouldn't find them at all. Whole planeloads of soldiers dropped out of the sky. My job as radio operator was to guide them in, and I did, but the planes just disappeared. Then, when the blizzards stopped for a while, we'd trek out in a group again, tied with ropes, to try to find the plane. Sometimes we got lucky and found the fuselage or parts of it—filled with frozen corpses.

"Fifteen miserable, long months in that place. A guy could be joking and talking with you one day, and the next you don't see him; you never lay eyes on him again. Some guys, they felt like they were choking, and they said 'I have to go out,' and they did. You couldn't stop them. We'd try to distract them, we'd say, 'Listen, Jack, you'll dance with that beauty of yours in Roseland again, come next Thursday. You'll see. It's almost over!' We talked about back home like that and about eating a bagel at Siegel's, takin' a dive off the West Side pier. A Lindy's cheesecake. The woman you loved. I had your mother's letters and pictures, but some of the guys had no one. That was hard.

"Finally, supplies arrived. No planes could land until the bad storms stopped. It was better after that for a short time, then it got bad again, and, same thing, some guys got the cabin fever bad, 'I'm chokin'! I gotta get out, let me out!' And they'd run out into the snow. Terrible. If we distracted them, we saved them—sometimes. Other times they got lost.

"There was this big colored guy named Jack, a chaplain, friend of mine. Nicest guy. He'd pray with them, try to give the guys hope, you know? Sometimes he did, sometimes not. Guys disappeared in front of our eyes.

"Then we had the hangings, and this, this, was the worst. A new thing—guys hanging themselves with their belts. Lost about four of our men that way. You'd look up, and there they were, dangling from the beams." He slowed down then turned to show me how a hanged man looks: He grabbed the collar of his shirt, bulged out his eyes, and let his tongue loll from the side of his mouth. When he saw my expression, before I covered my eyes with my hands, he threw back his head and laughed.

"This one particular guy who hanged himself was a guy you'd think would never give up hope. He was a joker, made us laugh, told stories about fillies—girls he went out with—played poker, everything. Nice guy. Regular guy. One morning there he was, hanging from the rafters. That was the last one, though; everyone, including me, had to give up their belts after that. Confiscated all of 'em. It was hard keepin' your pants up, too. We weren't exactly getting fatter in Goose Bay, you know, that's for damn sure!

"What you gotta do in that kinda situation is you try to remember the reason you're there. You gotta remember the job you're supposed to do. We were gonna win a war—for everyone. You gotta think it's important, you know? That it would show to be important at some time, one day. There were weaklings, and there were tough guys, and sometimes the weakest guy, the guy you *thought* was the weakest, anyway, wound up giving strength to a guy twice his size who looked like a wrestler or one who talked big. Those are the situations where you never know who's gonna come out good, you know?

"Some things, they seem like they'll never end. Goose Bay, Labrador, was a place like that. The aurora borealis, those northern lights, they were the problem because they called to you. Hell, I myself wanted to go out and find 'em! The lights—they seemed so close.

"I still dream of them, always will. But even when we lost some of our best guys in the snow, following the northern lights, or when they hanged themselves, even then, I knew. You know what I knew?"

"What?"

"Ah, you don't wanna hear it!" He'd always tease me like that when he finished a story. He wanted me to beg.

"Yes, I do! Please, tell me!"

Then a long pause while my father thought about it, turning serious again.

"I knew, *chika*, that I would be one of the guys who made it out of there. Much as I was homesick and disgusted like everybody else, and much as those gorgeous lights called to me, and they sure did, I knew I wasn't gonna follow them. I was stayin' put in that cold, miserable place the army sent me to until it was over, or 'til they sent me someplace else. I knew I'd get home, eventually.

"You gotta be tough at the very time you think you can't be. It comes from inside here," he said, pointing to his stomach. "Not from la cabeza, your head, and not even from la corazon, your heart. It comes from here, from your gut. That's where you get your strength to be tough."

We spent every Sunday, Dad and I, during that bitter winter of 1955, in Goose Bay, Labrador. I got to know his buddies' names, the guys he talked about and loved, the brave ones who made it, and those who gave up. My father never called them "cowards"; he felt sorry for them. I knew that even when he kidded around and tried to scare me with some of the grisly details of what took place, he was still shook up about it himself. Ten years had passed, and he wasn't over it.

These were our car stories, the tales he told to make my trip back to the institute exciting. They were never repeated at home, and, when I got discharged from Rusk, he never mentioned those soldiers, the aurora borealis, or Goose Bay, Labrador, again.

By spring of 1955 I lived at the institute from Monday to Friday and went home on weekends. It was a disruptive arrangement for Mother, but I got used to it. Fridays I loved because my father came to pick me up. I couldn't wait to see him or to spend the ride home inside Storyland. He always had a good kuenta to tell me, and when he ran out of war stories he told about his courtship with Mother, how they met and married in one day, up in Presque Isle, Maine. I had heard all these stories before, yet they always sounded new, as each time he'd add an extra piece of information or embellish an old story with vivid details.

My father's tales were peppered with daring acts and risk-taking adventures. There was the time when he was stationed in Wales—he said it was before he married Mother—when he got attracted to the lord mayor's daughter and wanted to take her out. The lord mayor of the town said an emphatic no, but he took her out anyway and was threatened with military jail. Then there was the time he "borrowed" a colonel's car on a buddy's dare, so he could take my mother for a ride in the Maine countryside. Even when things made no sense, I never asked questions I knew he wouldn't answer. For instance, I wondered how, if he wasn't married to Mother at the time, she acquired the wrapped package stored in her closet of Scotch plaid woolen skirts and jackets marked "Wales." Whether or not he stretched the truth or totally fabricated it, I knew for a fact that my father loved getting away with murder.

Sundays were another matter. The mood was opposite that of Fridays. Sad, even gloomy, affairs, the entire day centered around my leaving. No matter what we did or who visited, we knew that by four-thirty, rain or shine, I'd be going back to the institute. It was accepted, but it wasn't a natural life. Also, my parents still fought like crazy every Sunday, worse than ever and more and more over money.

Mainly, they fought about my father's family—why his brothers were getting rich in business while he still worked like un perro, a dog, in a factory. Every other week he'd stop speaking to either Kelly or Albert, or both, and then the sisters-in-law would act cold to one another also. Then they'd reconcile. Soon someone would prick someone else's honor again, and they'd all be mad. This went on with the three brothers for the rest of their lives. Why, exactly, they were always so furious with each other was never clearly defined.

In general weekends home were chaotic. If Charlie and I got lucky, and if my parents were flush enough, they'd go dancing at the Egyptian Gardens on Saturday nights and come home very late, so they'd be tired and more subdued in the morning. I'd get scared to be alone after my brother fell asleep—I kept him awake as long as possible—and often had to call down the dumbwaiter for Millie, Ellen's mother, to come up and stay with me. Since the Dark Room incident I could never be alone for long without panicking, nor could I sleep without a night-light.

The Black Sundays never really ended. My illness had drained the household financially for years with added expenses, such as continued physical rehabilitation, orthopedic shoes and appliances, and special transportation. We got some help from state agencies and from the March of Dimes, but in essence we were poor. My mother wanted me to walk well, not just "okay." She arranged for a visiting physical therapist every other week, to come exercise and massage my legs. After I was discharged, although I don't know how they paid for it, the therapist came to our house once a week.

Her name was Gail, and she was British. She stayed in the country several months, just to help out during our polio epidemic. Mother met her at the institute one day, and they became friendly. Before Gail went back to England, we visited her and her husband and two little girls in their West Side apartment, where a butler actually served us lunch. Mother adored Gail. She said she was "a cut above us," and the two of them had good conversations. I knew Mother would be morose when

Gail left, and that would make my life harder. I begged her to take me with her to England.

As predicted, after Gail went home, Mother was unhappy. She needed a project and found one: taking me to visit doctors. These weren't ordinary doctors; they were what she called "big doctors," orthopedists and neurologists with fancy addresses on Park and Fifth avenues. We never had an appointment, and we never paid a fee. We sat, often for hours, in a waiting room until all the doctor's other patients had gone, and then Mother managed to worm us into his examining room. I don't know how she did it. Once inside, she'd go into her routine.

"Look at this child's face, doctor. Can you tell me there is nothing you can do for a beautiful girl, no way to restore her left leg? Make it straighter? Have her walk a bit faster? They conquered polio, but they can't fix this?"

The big doctors were often so shocked that they examined me, and I must have endured at least ten on-the-spot physical examinations like that. They knew we were poor, and many were too ashamed to charge, but some sent a bill later, which either my mother or my father tore up, whomever saw it first. Bill collectors called for years.

Finally, one particular doctor in a beautiful Park Avenue building took pity on me. What I always had to do was walk back and forth in front of them, usually in my underwear, so they could watch my gait before they shook their heads and said nothing could be done. But this one doctor refused to have me undress. After I walked back and forth for him a few times, he pulled Mother aside, sat her down, and told her: "Madam, you are doing a great disservice to this child, dragging her from pillar to post. She is fine as she is; she may even walk better one day. But *there are no miracles!* Accept it!"

Naturally, she was furious. As soon as we got outside, she lit a cigarette then angrily stamped it out before she took one puff.

"Anti-Semite!"

That was the last big doctor we went to.

I knew I was the cause of much of their fighting. When they talked about "before," they usually meant "before she had polio," the time when our lives were easier all around. I tried keeping out of their way as much as possible, losing myself in any book, comic book, or magazine I could find. I read everything: the Cherry Ames nursing series, Nancy

Drew mysteries, *Glenda of Oz*, discarded paperback novels, O. Henry stories, everything. And if I wasn't reading I was writing, mostly rhyming poetry, that I thought of as songs.

It bothered Mother that I didn't want to socialize with anyone or go downstairs anymore. Little kids stared at my legs, and even my "friends" called me names, like "peg leg" and "slow-Flo." I still needed crutches for support, especially when climbing stairs, but after I got to the street I'd chuck them in the side garden behind the bushes until it was time to go up. Even though I couldn't walk far, I wanted to look as if I could. The crutches, like the braces, would be gone soon as well, but until they went I preferred staying home. I'd even get sick when it was time to "take air" or when Mother asked, didn't I want to "see if the other girls were out?" No, I didn't. I hated most of the girls I used to be friends with. They excluded me from games, even those where you didn't need to run, and behind my back they made fun of the way I walked, so, naturally, when it came time to go out, my heartbeat picked up, and my stomach burned. I even convinced myself that I felt dizzy.

"I think I'll fall down the stairs," I'd lie. "Everything is going 'round and 'round—I can't go out today."

Mother knew I was lying, but what could she do about it? I tried to keep the heartache inside because if I complained to her about certain girls, she'd attack their mothers verbally so hard she'd bore holes into them. I'd seen her do it, and that made it worse for me. So I neglected to share the taunts and the hurts I endured with her, and, wisely, she rarely forced me to go out.

How sharp a difference from the way I felt in November, when I first got home from Lenox Hill. Then, even in a wheelchair, I had felt like the same person I'd always been, just skinnier, and couldn't understand why everybody didn't think so. Paradoxically, after my health and stamina improved, after I'd gained some weight, looked better, and walked nearly unaided, with barely a limp, I began to recognize how much I had changed. Indeed, I *was* different from the others; I knew it, but I hadn't yet devised a method where I could live with that difference. That took a long time, but eventually I coped by being happy to *not* be "just like everybody else." Enjoying a singular uniqueness worked, but it took a few years until I found it.

The worst day came in late 1955, when my father brought home the

Daily News with its blaring black headline in huge print: VICTORY OVER POLIO! It was the single most important news since the end of World War II. Jonas Salk's vaccine *worked*. The end of the plague of our time, the dreaded contagious disease, the summer pestilence that stalked helpless children, had come at last.

There were celebrations and jubilation across the country and around the world—just not in our house. It meant thousands, millions, would be saved from being killed, maimed, or crippled by polio. By the end of 1955 there were 75 percent fewer cases, and within a couple of years only a few hundred cases existed in the United States. Polio was disappearing, becoming a thing of the past. But not in apartment 3A. The mood in our house, after seeing that headline, was as somber as if there were a death in the family.

On Sundays at seven o'clock the institute showed a movie for all the kids. My dad usually dropped me off at six so I could have dinner and make it to the show. The first thing I did was find an empty wheelchair and race to the hall window, where I'd search for my father as he crossed the street to where he parked. I don't think I ever made it in time to see our car pulling away, but I'd watch the red taillights of some car I thought *might* be ours until it faded from sight.

I cried every Sunday after my father left. There wasn't one that I didn't. You'd think I'd get used to the routine, but I never did. He left as fast as he could, so he wouldn't witness it. Every single week I thought: This time, for sure, I won't be a baby, I won't cry. And then, automatically, I did. I wouldn't eat or go to the movie either. After I wheeled myself back to my room, I'd lie on my bed thinking about the stories he'd just told me. It was hard to believe that a man like my father, who did not make conversation easily, had such an exciting repertoire of tales to delve into and that he told them so well.

I'd think about the guys in his stories who made it through all that snow, and I'd wonder how they were doing. When the war ended, Dad said they all went their separate ways. I also thought about the guys who died, and I'd put my hands around my neck, trying to imagine what hanging felt like. Sometimes I'd draw pictures of the northern lights, coloring it as I thought the lovely aurora borealis should look.

Before falling asleep, I'd always make a wish on the biggest, brightest star I could pick out hanging above the East River—our North Star. This wish I would write down in my diary for the future and put it in a secret place.

My cousin Lorraine became increasingly involved in my recovery. She encouraged me and promised me that when I finally got discharged from Rusk I could visit her in her Brooklyn flat any time I wanted, even stay for a weekend. I definitely looked forward to it—for one, so I could escape the many arguments at home and also because Lorraine's husband was an English teacher who had a lot of books. She was as good as her word, and it came to pass that I spent a lot of holidays at their first tiny apartment in Brooklyn, then at the bigger one in Far Rockaway, and finally at their house on Longacre Avenue, in Woodmere, Long Island.

Hopalong Cassidy may have been my first hero, but he wasn't my only one. I worshipped my cousin Lorraine as one does an older sister. She seemed to do everything right. I don't remember exactly when, but, shortly after I spent a few weekends with them, I began calling her "Lois," after Lois Lane, Superman's reporter-girlfriend. I was the only one in the family to call her that. She reminded me of the Lois Lane character, who also had short dark hair and a knack for "investigation."

There was no bargain she couldn't find and no information about a person she couldn't learn. It wasn't that she gossiped; she simply liked people—she had a way of talking and listening to others that was as facile to her as caring for the perpetual litter of kittens in her garage was. So, people volunteered their confidences. I always had the feeling that Lorraine wanted to fix things for the people she cared about—all of them—but I'm not sure if any of us ever knew what *she* needed fixed, if anything, or even what she was truly feeling inside.

As a second-generation Sephardi, my cousin lived the dichotomy of having one leg in America and one in Istanbul. She was a good old-fashioned Turkish housewife, married to an Ashkenazi, as well as a completely modern American woman. A great cook, she mastered *fasulya* and *fijónes*, Turkish string beans and black-eyed peas, in addition to the Eastern European dishes her husband favored, like stuffed cabbage, which few Sephardi wives knew how to make.

Lorraine hid her cultural dislocation well. She matured in married life and grew up along with her two children in the community of Woodmere, Long Island, considered one of the elite "Five Towns" on the southern shore. These hamlets were known for housing the wealthy and status-conscious, folks primarily involved with "keeping up," and somehow Lorraine managed to fit in, even on an English teacher's salary. She was the best "antiquer" around and could find a treasure at every garage sale she visited. How they thrived in that competitive community is a mystery; my cousin was thrifty, like Sultana, her mother, but I never got the impression that she thought of herself as anything less than her neighbors. She may or may not have—I was much too self-involved at the time to really notice.

It's hard to believe that this sparkling, gregarious woman came from the likes of Ovadiah and Sultana. At least my uncle was quiet, but my aunt was nothing short of an ordinary peasant who did backward, crazy things. Once, when Lorraine was a teen, Sultana went to a rival fortune teller—personally, I think she was afraid of Nona Behora—taking along Lorraine's bra, so that the psychic could "read" it to get a "feel" for when and what type of guy her daughter would marry. This may have been common practice in Turkey among the old Sephardim, but few did it in America. Mother termed it "crude." Tante also would spit all over her children's fingers when she cut their nails, believing this would ward off their *enimigos*, enemies. And the worst was the vulgar folk song she liked to sing as she cleaned her house, about a woman called Basara la Preta, a black mammy who "misplaces" her breast just at feeding time and can't find it anywhere. We all realized that Lorraine had quite a backwards legacy to overcome.

It was at the house on Longacre Avenue where I took refuge many a Christmas, Passover, and Memorial Day holiday. I fled not only my mother but also my parents' incessant arguing as well as all the neighborhood girl-bullies whose sole job was to torment other girls who weren't exactly like them. The older I got, the more I ran from the routine of Bronx life in general. Everything seemed better, fresher, in the suburbs.

Even simple things, like buying home appliances, were exciting. My cousin was the first in the family who bought a refrigerator with the freezer on the bottom instead of on top. Believe it or not, this was a gigantic step for a housewife in the late 1950s. According to both of my aunts, buying an "untested" appliance, or one that nobody they knew owned, was daring and bold. I remember the Sunday afternoon that all of us, the entire family, even in-laws, crowded into Lorraine's kitchen to watch her load steaks and chops and pot roasts into the bottom freezer and then stack the milk, juice, and eggs on top.

As you'd expect, she was a superb cook and baker. She didn't take after Sultana in that way either; my aunt's cooking was haphazard. Sometimes good, sometimes not so good. According to Mother, Ashkenazi men loved eating huge meals, and this proved true: The English teacher ate big. Lorraine cooked him stuffed peppers, stuffed cabbage, and our stuffed *yaprakes*, grape leaves, too, as well as pot roasts, rump roasts, and eye-round roasts, all hefty portions. She made lots of different pies and an Orange Kiss-Me Cake so delicious I couldn't keep my hands off it. She made spinach quiche, zucchini quiche, and, of course, quiche lorraine.

She copied elaborate recipes from cookbooks and made simple ones as well from the files of friends and neighbors. Give her a can of Campbell's Mushroom Soup, and she'd make a meatloaf as good as any restaurant and in much less time. The only rule for me, after my appetite returned, was that she forbade me from noshing after dinner or getting up in the middle of the night to stand in front of the fridge and cram my face.

Until 1959 I attended PS 88's handicapped class, where I was bored to death much of the time. A school bus picked me up in front of the building every morning, which I hated, because I was the only one who went to school by bus. After I cried and carried on about it, refusing to get on the bus, Mother arranged for the driver to pick me up last, so the girls walking to school wouldn't see me boarding the handicapped bus. I hated that I couldn't walk to school with the others and had to get on a bus for only a few blocks.

I was put into a class that consisted of a mishmash of younger and older kids; some were severely handicapped and could not leave their wheelchairs, not even to do the simplest things for themselves. Some were better off than that but were still pretty disabled, either from cerebral palsy, polio, or spinal deformities. And there were those, like me, who were more able-bodied and got around on their own. The result was you had some very smart children mixed in with illiterate ones; fourth-graders were in a class with teenagers, and there were even some who had previously been institutionalized and were attending school for the first time.

Our teacher was a middle-aged woman named Mrs. Kelly whose daily occupation was making bouillon soup for herself, all day long. She used this strange-looking device that plugged into the wall outlet on one end and got dunked into her soup cup on the other. She'd drop the little cubed chicken or beef bouillon into the water when it boiled then stir and stir, dreamily looking out the window and beyond. Mrs. Kelly was nice, but she taught us nothing. Anything I learned in her class came from the others who were older and wiser and from the shelf of books in her closet that she referred to as her "private collection."

I was considered an "advanced" reader, but at home they were already beginning to nag at me for reading too much. Girls who read all the time wound up "spinsters, *solteras*, who'd never marry, be happy, and have children." That, of course, was the ultimate goal, but at the very least reading "would ruin their eyes forever." I already wore glasses from the age of eight—did I want to be blind, too? I had to read in a library, I had no choice, so I practiced walking, first with my crutches and then without them, to the Mt. Eden Library six blocks away. I read everything I could find there—stories, poetry, biographies, even *National Geographics*—in order not to have to walk back home right away. Also, Lorraine's English teacher husband often gave me or recommended books that were beyond my age, and I happily read them all.

One novel in particular, Brian Moore's *The Lonely Passion of Judith Hearne*, affected me so much that I dreamt about the main character. The life of Judith Hearne, an Irish Catholic spinster, was a strange new world to me, and it was a good read as well. I had about as much in common with spinster Judy Hearne as I had with small-town Angie, the protagonist of *Seventeenth Summer*, another book I adored, who picked "bachelor's buttons" for her hair from her own garden.

The loneliness of passionate-but-repressed Judy Hearne frightened me. The only ones ever there for her, her only company, were the little buttons on her shoes "winking up at her . . . friendly little shoe-eyes" were all she had. What if that were all I ever had in life? This scared me, as I didn't have many friends either. I put two and two together and saw why my family stressed getting married: Married people weren't lonely. That had to be it.

So I hung on Lorraine's words and tried to copy her habits. Not so much to insure that I'd one day get married—by the time I was ten I knew that, because of polio, this was the family's big fear—but because she was popular. She had so many friends and such an easy time of making new ones. And they all loved her. Her telephone never stopped ringing. I believed that if I copied what she did, acted as she acted, learned to make quiche lorraine, that I'd be popular, too.

I pored over my cousin's high school yearbook, wondering what element gave her the edge over the other girls. She wasn't the prettiest or the smartest, but she was voted "Most Popular." How does one get to be that? While it was possible to learn the secrets of making a good quiche, other recipes were much harder to decipher. The magical gift of having everyone like you, as they loved Lorraine, eluded definition.

"How did I get to be 'Most Popular'? I don't know! Well, let's see . . ."

But even she, of course, didn't know the formula; that's why it worked. She would tick off the things she did: "I don't lie to my friends, I listen to their problems, and I'm always available to go shopping. That's all I can think of." But we both knew it was more; she was not only unselfish but also modest.

After I got to be ten, I became moody and was sad a lot of the time, also still bewildered about why some girls who used to like me had turned unfriendly, even cruel. When Arlene Schacter didn't invite me to her tenth birthday party, I called up and tried to find out why. In the background I heard her mother whisper, "*Arlene, you have to ask her now!*" Still she refused, and I hung up. When Lorraine found out about it, she was quick to offer: "I'm *sure* you'll have a lot of friends one day. These aren't the right ones for you, I just know it!" She said it with such conviction, I had to believe she was right.

"Having polio," she said, "has nothing to do with getting married or making friends, you'll see." She was the only one in our family courageous enough to mention the P word in a sentence, so how could she be wrong?

At about the same time that my weekly trips to the institute ended, the fighting in our house escalated. My brother went into kindergarten, and, without Charlie around, whose presence calmed Mother down, she was unleashed. She found almost everything I or my father said and did irritating. I had a home teacher who came twice a week after I complained bitterly about my boring school classes and Mrs. Kelly. At least Mother stopped raging when the teacher came. But the following September I was forced to return to PS 88, as New York State deemed me "able enough" to do so.

I was going on eleven, getting closer to graduating from PS 88. I could not wait. All I wanted was to attend regular junior high school with the other kids, even though I knew that for me it would be harder. That weighed heavily on Mother's moods, too. She didn't know where to put me if I couldn't go to the nearby junior high; therefore, everything I did angered her. Were it not for Lorraine, I surely would have run away from home.

"We're cursed! *Desmazalados!*" It was Mother's repeated theme song, and, like Nona Behora's eight ball would have agreed, *It seems so . . .*

I didn't know what, specifically, their problems were, but they had a lot to do with money. The verbal viciousness at home got worse by the day instead of better, and I was able to judge by the words themselves how bad a fight would get. For instance, when Mother called Dad an "avanak," a donkey, he'd get mad but not crazy. On the other hand, if she dared to call him an "hijo de un azno," the son-of-a-jackass, this inferred an insult to his beloved mother, Behora, and he'd pop like a firecracker.

"What did you say, Rose?"

"I said, your mother *kito ranas y kulevras de la boka!*"

It was the worst insult to a fortune teller, to accuse her of "spitting frogs and snakes from her mouth."

"Lonso!" Jerk!

"Edepsís!" Ill-bred!

"Budák!" Hard-head!

"Budalá!" More stupid!

"Miskín!" Ugly slob!

Finally, the Turkish curse words would get dirtier until they called each other all the vilest, lowest names they could think of or until one of them, usually my father, had had enough.

"Chok chujuk var!" Be careful what you say; there are children here!

Too late for that now. I listened and copied these exotic-sounding adjectives into my diary as: *eedip-sees, boo-dock, boo-da-la, mees-kin,* and *choke-chuck-jar.* I had no idea what I'd do with them, but I just loved their sounds.

They had a lot to be tense about. Bookies were demanding payment, and new business ventures my dad had begun were going sour. No scheme he tried worked out. It was obvious that he disappointed Mother. She used to comment about what a dashing soldier and good talker he'd once been, then, under her breath, she'd add: "And I thought he'd burn up the *world!*"

It got worse than that. One day in the factory a piece of metal my father was polishing flew into his right eye and blinded him. He had to have surgery and get fitted for a contact lens. He got so frustrated trying to put it in that he finally flushed it down the toilet, and then they fought about that rash act, too. He couldn't afford a replacement, so he went around blind in one eye. Still, my dad believed his luck would turn, that Heaven would eventually "adjust" his star.

They were both hotheaded, and I was used to that, but I wasn't pre-pared, nor would I have believed, that a word my father said one day, in heated anger, could have such power over me. That's why they say, *La boka haze, la boka deshaze:* The mouth creates, and the mouth destroys.

During a particularly vitriolic Sunday fight, while I was trying to read a book of love poems by Shelley that I had yanked from someone's bag of garbage as it passed by our open dumbwaiter door, my father slammed a cabinet door hard enough to send the book in my hands flying. I was suddenly furious.

"Shut up! Both of you!" I screamed.

Next thing I knew, my father's head appeared in my bedroom door-way.

"What did you say?"

"I said *shut up!* I can't stand it anymore!"

"Kósha!"

We were both stunned. Had he just called me a *kósha? Cripple?* Maybe I hadn't heard right. *Kósha.* That horrible word—used on *me.* Just as fast as he uttered it, the fight was over, and the house became deadly silent. He quickly jammed his hat on and flew out. I knew Mother had heard it, too, because she instantly appeared in my room and stood looking at me for a long time. She smoked but said nothing. I, meanwhile, kept blinking, refusing to meet her gaze and vowing not to cry in front of her. She had no rejoinder for this knife that had been thrown into my heart. At that awful moment I grew up about ten years. No longer was my father perfect. No longer was I his darling, his *hanúm*. He was one of them now, and I'd never trust him the same way again.

We were all fighting battles: My parents fought to keep their heads above water and get ahead of "the eight ball"; I fought to walk "normal," like the other girls; and my brother fought just to remain sane and calm in a household that did everything possible to prevent that. As early as age seven, he began to study the Torah and Talmud and talked about becoming a rabbi.

If Cousin Lorraine fought any battles herself, I was blind to them; we all were. I thought her life was better than the TV version of Ozzie and Harriet's, and, if it wasn't, I wouldn't have known; on the surface all seemed calm and happy. She was definitely an iconoclast, a personality trait not easily tolerated in the Five Towns, whose job it was to mold women into carbon copies of each other.

Lorraine's random and intentional acts of kindness are even more precious because she died young. Each holiday weekend, when I might have suffered loneliness or worse, I was rescued instead. I knew I'd be welcome at her house and could read all the books I wanted and also have a big sister to talk to and guide me. I was almost thirteen years old before I discovered Lorraine was the Hopalong Cassidy who sent all the loving birthday and Valentine's Day "Love, Hoppy" cards. She was my "cowboy hero," the person who gave me hope, during the dark times, that miracles can happen.

She was forty-seven the day she died, an overcast Sunday in February, the kind of day one looks out the window and feels the portent of trouble. A coronary embolism traveled to her heart in the space of a few hours, and, though she was rushed to the hospital, it was too late. It was the second time our family had been shattered by sudden illness. My mother made it through mine and lived, despite wanting to die, but my aunt Sultana's fate was doubtful. Whether she would be able to go on without her vibrant Lorraine remained to be seen. As expected, my aunt died a short time after her daughter, and, though they said it wasn't from a broken heart, nobody believed that.

There's a small alcove with a ledge in my memory where Lorraine sits. There she's always twenty-five and dressed as a bride, never older or younger, never sad, disappointed, or sick. Sometimes I step into that memory niche and sit close to her again, and we're both in the wedding photo. I see her happy bride smile, feel her supportive arm around my waist, smell her perfumed hair. The yards of white lace from her gown brush against my leg. And sometimes, within that memory, she draws her skirts back, away from my leg, so that my brace is exposed for all to see. That's what she would have wanted in the first place.

It's good to be alive! Man, it's the mostest

thing there is, and any time you feel different,

don't be afraid to get down on your

knees and talk things over with the Lord.

ROY CAMPANELLA

8 ❧ Celebrity

One day, I must have been about six, Mother allowed me to stay home from school so I could go with her to visit her friend, a Turk named Mrs. Gormezano. I got rather dressed up for this visit, although she insisted it wasn't a party, and I was also allowed to wear my Mary Janes. This was before my long hair had been cut, and I remember she braided my hair twice, nice and tight.

We crossed the Grand Concourse, walked a few blocks past the synagogue on 169th Street, and wound up on Grant Avenue, in front of an ordinary prewar building, like the kind we all lived in. The Gormezanos lived a few flights up, and, as we got closer to their apartment I heard singing, which became louder and louder as we climbed.

"Hear that?" Mother said, excited. How could I not? "That's her daughter, Eydie; have you ever heard a stronger voice?" She leaned down to tell me, confidentially, "This one's already a star—on her way to The Coast!"

We rang the bell, but it took a while until they heard it over the singing. Finally, Mrs. Gormezano opened the door.

"*Bienvenu!* Welcome! *Komo 'stas?*"

"Fine, Fortunéh, *bien!* And you?"

Fortuna was a common enough name among Sephardi women, but I'd never heard it pronounced the way Mother said it, so that it rhymed with *day*.

The woman took my face in her hands, kissed me, and then we went into her kitchen, where she had prepared the usual tray of *dulces* and Turkish coffee for Mother, plus some Turkish Delights for me. A man I guessed to be Mr. Gormezano was sitting in a corner sewing a glittering, beaded gown.

I soon learned that their daughter, Eydie, was not just any talented singer; she had big talent, the kind the Sephardis had a phrase for: *En kada dedo tiene un marafet!* She's got a talent on every finger! Mother got caught up in the excitement of her success, her upward climb. It seemed like Eydie had quickly skipped the ingenue part and had gone straight into contract signing and TV appearances. That meant she'd bring honor—and also money—to her family. She was about to tour the country with the Tex Benecke band, which made her a True Performer.

Eydie was also very attractive. Her tailor father, who worried about his daughter going on tour *sola*, unchaperoned, sewed the beautiful gowns she wore by hand. In that regard Mother always believed that she had played a small part in helping further Eydie's career because she pacified Mr. Gormezano by telling him, in Spanish, that he shouldn't worry, that "God would watch over her." Both mothers then bit their curled forefingers to ward off any Evil Eye.

A Performer was the best thing alive to be. This, I knew, was what Mother wanted for me. My father was content to have me belly dance when we had company or sing my version of a lusty Sophie Tucker song, but Mother felt I could do more. If it meant singing like Eydie, I knew that would never happen; she definitely had the strongest, loudest voice I'd ever heard. With pride Mrs. Gormezano said that when Eydie practiced you could hear her all over the neighborhood. Again, the women uttered some words for protection, plus another Ladino blessing. At that point I, too, prayed—that she'd stop singing. It gave me a headache. I was disappointed to have been kept home from school just to hear someone practice.

I don't remember much else about that visit nor what Eydie and I talked about, if anything. But I do recall sitting down next to her on the piano bench, and I think she humored me by letting me pretend we were playing a duet. Of course, Mother bragged about it for years, me playing piano with "Our cousin, Eydie Gormé." She got plenty of mileage out of that "duet" and also from telling people what the singer's name had originally been.

"She's Sephardic, you know. Powerful voice, powerful."

I'm pretty sure we weren't related, but my mother always referred to her as "Cousin Eydie." Then again, all Turks were somehow related, especially if they happened to be famous. When the singer Neil Sedaka became well known, Mother claimed that he was our kin also.

"He may have changed the spelling of Sedacca, but I know he's part of my father's family!" Actually, he did bear a striking resemblance to my cousin Harold.

"So why don't we ever visit him?" I asked.

She gave me that special sneer, which basically meant, "dummy." "Because he lives on The Coast."

And when the time came that I asked for piano lessons, like my famous "cousins," we couldn't afford it, anyway. I reminded Mother of my duet with Eydie Gormé, but she countered that if my voice had been anything like Eydie's, then it would be different. Although I carried a pretty good tune, singing, according to Mother, was not my forte; it would definitely not get me to The Coast.

Physical beauty and talent were at the center of every family situation. A True Performer was the best thing in the world you could be, and if you did it right you'd definitely wind up on The Coast—also known as Hollywood. But if you were, God help you, fea, ugly, every talent was canceled out. You not only had to perform, but you had to look gorgeous doing it. Being a top model, like a cousin of ours who modeled in magazines for Ship 'n Shore blouses, wasn't bad either. Not much had changed in the way of family values since the days our people mingled with sultans, when the hanúms, or harem stars, were the breathtakingly beautiful ones and were treated like gold, while the homelier wives were equivalent to servants. In any event being an early reader didn't count.

Before the age of seven, when my world turned around and went in the opposite direction, I had mastered popular songs and jingles, could belly dance like a miniature version of Little Egypt and my cousin Bellina, complete with veils and zills, and was, according to everyone in the family, hermoza. At least they said I was beautiful. So, naturally, Mother figured I had a good chance of becoming a celebrity on The Coast. Not that I wanted to belly dance my way across the country—secretly, I wasn't all that enthralled with it. I got so sweaty and so tired turning, bending, and rolling my stomach. And when the equally sweaty uncles plastered their dollar bills on my forehead and then passed me hand to hand for some wet *besitos*, smooches, it got really annoying. I knew I could never do that for a lifetime.

But Fame, and its inevitable partner, Wealth, were vital. After polio I would learn just how critical they were. Nothing was more important to either of my parents. Dad was driven to make more money, an accomplishment that eluded him by degrees, while Mother continued to be obsessed by the celebrity status of most everyone. And there were other kinds of celebrity besides Performers. There were the Professionals, the doctors and dentists, attorneys and accountants; and the Manufacturers, those who made it in the dress-suit-and-coat business, who had *labels* inside the garments that they had designed.

Those who owned businesses were respected. One Sephardi operated a thriving fruits and vegetables franchise in the Bronx, where everyone referred to him as "the Tomato King." I would have hated to be called a king or queen of vegetables; nonetheless, among us he was a celebrity. Another Turk in the neighborhood owned a "schlock-shop" store on 36th Street, near Macy's, that sold only five-dollar dresses, nothing above. He got rich from it. My uncles owned a buttons-and-belts business and a lamp-and-fixture factory in New Jersey, respectively. As Manufacturers, they were included in the third class of celebrity.

Most of my Ashkenazi friends were marginally poor, like we were, with relatives who had become Professionals—or high school teachers, at least. If not prestige and high pay, then a good pension awaited them. But something much better happened to the Performers, and that was *fame*. If the Ashkenazim wanted their children to attend college, our family traditions were different. We put a high price on entertainment: music, parties, singing and dancing, and acting. Mother had respect for the proud Eastern Europeans, the "refs," as she called the refugees from Hitler's Germany, for being smart and literate survivors, but for the long haul she herself wanted celebrity.

Eydie Gormé notwithstanding, of all the Performer types, Mother loved dancers the most. The teenager who lived directly above us might have once been a nobody, until she became a Radio City Musical Hall Rockette. A long-legged, springy-haired brunette who never stopped practicing, her dancing routines were as regimented as an army's. Day and night she tapped, jumped, thrumped, and whomped above my bed. Whenever she was not at the Music Hall, she was practicing, and it seemed as if the entire line of Rockettes were upstairs with her. Undaunted and undisturbed—my parents' bedroom was on the other side of the apartment—Mother referred to the dancer as "the stunning Rockette."

"She lives to *dance*," I was reminded whenever I complained about the noise, as if I should know better. Her practicing may have been sacrosanct, but what did bother Mother were those times she ran into the stunning Rockette's mother at the market or mailbox. Like it or not, we'd get a detailed itinerary of the dancer's exciting schedule: She was going to be a *featured* Rockette in the Easter Extravaganza—not just another girl in the line; she was picked for the next Christmas pageant to lead one of the animals onstage; and so on. After reciting the list, the Rockette's mother would always finish with a reminder.

"Don't forget to count—she's number four, the fourth kick from the left!"

The Radio City Music Hall Christmas Spectacular, for Mother, was the pièce de resistance. When she learned that the stunning Rockette would actually be leading a *camel* onstage during the Nativity scene, she flipped. I was confused. For us the height of an insult was to call someone "un gameyo," a camel. Even joking, your relatives rarely called you that, although they might direct the insult toward strangers, as it inferred an ungainly, clumsy, stumbling slob. Who would want to be associated with such a slob of an animal?

We were lucky enough to see for ourselves because one day my dad came home with tickets for the pageant. He announced it at dinner, proudly, as his big surprise.

"Someone owed me."

"I'll bet," Mother said.

It would be an exciting, whole-day affair, as they always showed a full-length movie with the show, and afterwards I knew they'd take us to the Automat for lunch. Even though they'd go through their usual mashed-potatoes-or-home-fries fight at the Automat and embarrass us, it would be worth it. That season the movie starred an Italian actor named Rossano Brazzi. I'd never heard of him, but Mother said he was "divine." I had, certainly, heard a lot about the star of the Spectacular, the "fourth-kick-from-the-left" girl.

Earlier in the week her picture and the entire Rockette chorus line appeared in the local newspapers announcing the show. I was very tired of her by that time, not to mention hearing Mother talk about it. Now, finally, we'd all see her kick in person.

We went down by subway to catch the early show and the movie afterward. I liked it the other way around; I knew that by the time the movie was halfway through I'd be bored. I sat sandwiched between my brother and my mother on the right and my father on the left. When the lights dimmed and the curtain rose on the line of girls dressed in skimpy versions of Santa Claus suits, kicking their famous legs, there were cheers and thunderous applause but nowhere louder than from our section. Silently, we all counted, even my brother, four kicking Rockettes from the left, in order to focus on our upstairs neighbor. If her mother hadn't told us that, however, we'd never have known she was number four. They were all identically stunning Rockettes—all pretty, all the same height. That was the point.

When it came time for the Baby-Jesus-in-the-manger scene, "camel time," Mother drew a sharp breath. It wasn't a very loud gasp, but I sure heard it. I looked over and saw that she was gripping my brother's hand. She then turned to the complete stranger sitting next to her and said, "Watch for the girl who comes in leading the camel."

"Oh? Is she a relative of yours?"

Mother smiled one of her knowing, mysterious smiles. But what she didn't count on was there being more than one camel; in fact, there were three. It was easy to count fourth from the left in a lineup, but with everybody onstage dressed in Nativity costumes it was impossible to tell who was who. And we were so far back in the mezzanine they could have replaced one stunning Rockette with another and we'd never have known the difference. When I blurted out that they all looked the same to me, Mother threw me a look. She was counting on the camel procession to distinguish the stunning Rockette from the others.

Stars appeared in the night sky over Bethlehem. The entire theater became still and hushed. A spotlight fell on the first person to walk on, a shepherd, I guess, who was leading a donkey. Next came another shepherd, or maybe a shepherdess, leading two lambs. Finally, the three Wise Men and their attendants, leading one camel each, walked on-stage. Mother's head jerked left and right, as she tried to pick out our famous neighbor.

"She's the second one!" she said, in a stage whisper. "The one carrying the frankincense!"

My father disagreed: "Nah, too short to be her. It's the third one, carrying the gold."

"Maybe it's number one," I said, getting my two cents in. Everyone in our row leaned forward to shush us.

Of course we couldn't tell from so far back, but Mother swore it was number two. Not that it mattered. She was fourth kick from the left, period, and she had led a *gameyo* onstage during the fabulous Christmas pageant that people came from all over the world to see. The stunning Rockette upstairs was a True Performer.

My fate was sealed. No matter how many interesting compositions or clever poems I wrote and regardless of how many stars, commendations, and notes of praise the teachers sent home about my writing, one disappointing thing was certain: I would never become a Radio City Music Hall Rockette. I would never kick high enough.

By the time I was eleven-going-on-twelve we no longer went to Rockaway Beach for the summer. Since the year I got lost and wound up with gypsies, who may or may not have given me polio, Mother hated the beach. Instead, she found us a tiny shack in the Catskill Mountains, at a place called Blue Paradise Bungalow Colony. It was a very far drive, farther than Monticello or Ellenville, where some of the kids I knew stayed, way up in the hills of a tiny town called Wurtsboro.

It wasn't really a town at all, just a few paved streets, a general store, and a fruit market. The owner of Blue Paradise, a wizened, leathery old man named Louie, who smelled of liquor every day but probably wasn't as old as I thought he was, liked to visit town once a week and take his "family" of colony children with him. He drove an old black pickup truck—the same truck for the three summers we went there—which rattled and shook and made grinding noises as if it would die at any moment. But he let the kids in his bungalow colony climb into the back, and sometimes, if we begged, he even drove us around the area and showed us some local landmarks, like old firehouses and one-room schoolhouses.

The countryside smelled so good to me, as I guess it did to most of the city kids. I made friends in Blue Paradise just like Lorraine had predicted. Other girls thought I was funny; they liked me, and I certainly liked all of them, a lot better than the girls in my neighborhood. I had put the hospital loneliness behind me and was beginning to be myself. I felt warm and safe, unafraid, all the sensations that come with being well liked and accepted, feeling loved.

On our trips to town we'd sing songs and tell jokes in the back of the truck, pretending we were all part of one big family, Louie's, and that he was the father. Louie seemed to favor me. He liked it when I sat close to him, insisting I ride in the cab of the truck instead of in back. I did that for the first two rides to town then never again. I had a couple of incentives for getting into the back of the pickup, and one definitely was so that Louie's "fatherly" hand would not be stroking my bare shoulder.

In order to ride with my friends instead of sit next to Louie, I had to practice getting in and out of the back of the truck myself. I did it in my usual way, in the middle of the night, when no one was around to witness. Louie parked the truck near our shabby bungalow, so I didn't have to walk far on those pitch-black country roads. We didn't even own a flashlight, but we did have Shabbot candles to light the way, and many times the moon was bright enough. Still, it was a miracle I didn't fall and break my neck.

I'd steal out when I was sure Mother and everyone else but the rackety crickets were fast asleep.

It was a high climb for me to get into the back of that old pickup, but after several nights I managed it. I'd grab the bottom of my pajama pant on my good leg and then fling the leg as high as I could until it reached the truck's bumper. Using all my strength, I'd pull the rest of my body up until I was able to stand on the bumper, and, finally, I'd haul myself over the edge. There were usually a couple of blankets in the back of the truck to soften my fall into it, but I still flopped noisily and got banged up in the process. Getting out of the truck was even trickier: I had to balance on the bumper with my bad leg, careful not to fall, and then lift my right leg over and lower myself backwards to the ground. More than once I fell out and landed in the dirt.

I got the hang of it after a few tries, just like I had learned to fall and get up at the institute. And being out in the dead of night had other benefits as well. I saw all kinds of strange things, like the crazy woman who walked around the colony talking to herself; around and around she went, until she got tired and stopped. Then one night I saw my friend Rosalind's father kissing Paula's mother. Rosalind's father was a lawyer who was often at the colony during the week, unlike most of the other fathers. I guess the moon was particularly bright that night, and I'm glad they didn't spot me. I couldn't believe my eyes when I saw how Rosalind's father was touching Paula's mother all over, especially her chest, squeezing her and slurping her neck. They made such strange noises that at first I thought it was a fox. We had been warned about red foxes in the area. I hid in the back of Louie's truck, watching, for what seemed to me like hours and caught a bad cold for being so nosy.

Because I loved having friends to do things with every day, I didn't read as much and was getting lots of fresh air, which made my mother happy. No matter what it took, I made sure to keep up physically as best I could. I walked everywhere my friends walked, up down and around the grounds, even when my legs ached. When they went swimming, I went swimming, up the two winding hills to the ice-cold chlorinated pool, swallowing my fear of the water. Some afternoons I had it easy; we played mah-jongg, just like our mothers did. And when they ran relay races I was sure to hold the watch as the timekeeper, so I wouldn't be excluded. We even spent afternoons gossiping like our mothers, but, though I was tempted, I never told Rosalind about her father nor Paula about her mother. I had a feeling that telling them would make them mad and that would not help my popularity. I so wanted to have friends that I couldn't take the chance.

My dad came upstate most every weekend, but toward the end of the summer he stopped and came only once in a while. The old car he bought at the beginning of the summer usually needed big repairs by August. I missed him but not as much as I used to because Mother generally left me alone; she had her love—my brother, Charlie—they were a happy couple, and I had my friends. What my father did in the city alone I'd wonder about, but I don't think any of us really wanted to know. Mother was happy—at least for her—in Blue Paradise, she didn't rage often, and she had her wish of performing. Before we were two weeks into the summer Louie appointed her "recreation director."

Mother took to this job as if she'd done it for pay forever. She had lists and schedules and ideas for the end-of-summer show, and she signed people up early to do skits and performances. The show took place every year in a crappy, dilapidated room that needed painting and that reached degrees of 100-plus on the cooler days. It was down the road from the farthest bungalow, practically on the highway. They called it the "Rumpus Room," but Mother soon changed its title to the "Blue Paradise Theater Company Playhouse." Louie was considered very lazy, so how she got the old man to paint her a blue wooden sign and hang it over the door, I don't know, but she was persuasive.

From the middle of August until Labor Day weekend the "company" practiced in the cleaned-out Rumpus Room. Mother was good at directing other people to haul out the garbage and get some decent chairs for the future audience. The production occupied my mother so totally that she had no time for mah-jongg or sitting by the pool, socializing with idle women. Her job was to prepare and arrange the show. There were singers—too many, she said—dancers, two stand-up comics, and even a retired ballerina who had danced to *Swan Lake* with the New York City Ballet. My father ridiculed the woman, labeled her titarέk, which in Turkish meant "a teeter-tottering, aged wreck." Because she was someone's grandmother, Mother took pity and let her dance in the show.

My mother had many responsibilities for the operation of this show: she was the master of ceremonies, so she introduced every act and literally ran the whole show; she was one of the stand-up comedy acts, and she had a part as one of the lovers in the play *Lunatics and Lovers*, a two-year-old Broadway farce that had starred Buddy Hackett, whom Mother loved. Her one-woman comedy routine was, by all standards, hilarious; she had a knack for memorizing comedians' routines and jokes. The other comic on the bill was a man whom Mother claimed was "dead before he laid down." He was in because she said she needed "fillers."

Mother was finally able to perform her favorite role, one she became locally famous for: playing a groom to a man who played a bride in the final skit of the evening, the mock marriage. This "wedding" was an annual rite of summer; they couldn't end the season without having a mock marriage, and my mother excelled at being a bridegroom. As one of her mah-jongg cronies remarked, "God should have made her a man to begin with."

It scared me seeing her like that, dressed as a man, because she so completely looked the part. Being a groom was written for her. If there happened to be another woman interested in the role, Mother wouldn't allow it. She was to be the man, the bridegroom, period. The audience waited all night for this end skit, which got more laughs than anything else they put on, and even those who wouldn't think of going to the old Rumpus Room performance showed up at the end to see the wedding. Maybe my father got scared to see Mother like a man as well because he never seemed to be able to make it up on the weekend of the show. He was always "tied up" in the city or "laid up" with his back.

Mother's height came in handy for this part. When she put on a black tuxedo and somehow flattened her breasts, you swore it was a man's body. One year she even had a top hat and tails that someone had donated. She'd gather all her hair under a black wig, color her eyebrows darker, and paste on an authentic black mustache. With her glasses on she was then unrecognizable as my mother—or as a woman.

The bride was carefully handpicked from the fattest, baldest, most awkward-looking men in the bungalow colony. Mother would scout him out the first week, from men sitting around the pool to those who pulled up in their cars on Friday nights. This was serious business to her. "There's my little bride," she'd say, when she found the right one. And there was no such thing as a man refusing either. Then he would be taught how to act, walk, and talk like a woman—how to tone it down, not clown around too much, and especially how to be her straight man. When my mother got done, they seemed like a real couple.

Every detail was planned. There were four "bridesmaids" in unbecoming dresses and four "ushers" in suits. If one did not take the mock marriage skit seriously, he or she was fired immediately. The guy playing my mother's bride was always hilarious, and you could hear them laughing a mile away. Even the kids in the colony laughed, although I never really understood the whole thing or why they all loved it so. I just knew that Mother was never happier than during that skit, never funnier or more electrified than in August at Blue Paradise, when she got married in drag.

Sometimes she put kids in the show, but I always refused. Mother tried to bill me as the belly dancer, but I was already past that. Then, in the summer of 1958, she got the idea to have a Miss Rheingold beauty contest. The model Jinx Falkenburg was the first Miss Rheingold, and the brewery's promotion of her representing the beer had been so successful that it was made into an official beauty contest. Each year people voted for the next gorgeous Miss Rheingold, in restaurants, stores, and bars throughout New York, and Mother was always one of those who filled out a ballot.

The contest in Blue Paradise wasn't for anyone under eighteen either, but on the night of the big show my friends and I thought we'd dress up as beauty queens anyway, just for fun. While everyone was at the show, we raided our mothers' closets and put on their most revealing blouses, plus piles of their makeup. I painted a Marilyn Monroe dot with black eyebrow pencil, somewhere near my chin, and freely used all the purple eye shadow and blood-red lipstick I could find. Then, toward the end of the performance and right before the mock marriage finale, the six of us walked into the Rumpus Room dressed as we approximated the next Miss Rheingold would look. That the others didn't trip in high heels was amazing; I, at least, wore flats. We made quite an entrance, and it gave Mother the idea.

"Okay, Miss Americas, you think you're contestants? Then come up on the stage and compete for real!"

Two of the girls chickened out and ran. I could not run, so I had no choice but to walk forward. The small stage had quite a huge step, but my mother seemed to know what would happen: A man from the audience jumped out of his seat, picked me up, and planted me in the middle of the stage. At Mother's command, to thunderous applause and cheers, the four of us turned, curtsied, and bowed. They whistled and stomped; it was fun—for a minute. We'd all had enough by then and were starting to file off, but the crowd protested loudly, insisting we stay. So it happened that four eleven- and twelve-year-olds joined the twenty-year-old hopefuls in the Miss Rheingold beauty contest.

There were about ten girls in the competition, standing in the shadows, waiting to walk onstage and parade around in their bathing suits. One by one they did, and one by one they were eliminated by fierce applause or a lack of it, until only four remained. Mother's "assistant," a retired English teacher from Queens, placed us how Mother wanted us: Every other girl was in a bathing suit.

I snuck a look at Paula and Rosalind, farther down the line. They looked ridiculous; Paula had put on magenta lipstick and then smeared her lips with Vaseline because she said that that was what models did "for the wet look." Her lips looked like a bruised purple blob. Rosalind was no better; she had misjudged the application of rouge, and on either cheek were two deep red circles. They looked like clowns! That's when I realized that I must look like one, too, because I had put on piles of face powder, which was feeling heavier on my face by the moment, and there was that silly black "beauty mark," plus red lipstick and a fair share of bright green eye shadow. My face began to itch.

The comedy of it was too much. I felt like doubling over, but I knew that, if I laughed like I wanted to, Mother would kill me. So I kept smiling and smiling, holding it in, turning, pretend-posing, and prayed the thing would end so we could leave and laugh ourselves silly outside.

And I think the smiling is why I won. I was *really* smiling, while the other, older girls were deadly serious. Mother kept hissing at them to "relax" and "smile," but you could see that each one wanted to win so badly that their usually pretty faces were contorted in trying to appear natural.

Mother stepped away as the three judges, one of whom was Rosalind's father, walked back and forth in front of us, looking at the line of girls up and down. When he stopped at me, I felt my face go hot, remembering how he squeezed Paula's mother that night. I made myself not look at his hands, but I know I turned beet red; my face felt like it was on fire. I didn't know the other two men who were judges, but they too stared intently at me, at all of us, smiled, and winked as they passed. One of them stared at me for so long that my mother stepped forward and made a wisecrack about "robbing the cradle," and she yanked him away. The audience screamed with laughter.

The judges went backstage to make their decision; there was a drumroll; one by one they filed out, and the last man handed Mother a scrap of paper. She made a few more jokes, and then there was another drumroll. When she finally opened the paper and read who won, her face registered true surprise; I could tell she was really stunned by the decision. She signaled for one more drumroll.

"Ladies and Gentlemen! The new beauty queen for the Blue Paradise Bungalow Colony in Wurtsboro, New York! The 1958 MISS RHEINGOLD BEER! I give you—"

I turned and saw that all the girls in the line were staring at me, clapping, although not every one of them smiled.

"NUMBER FOUR!"

Mother had put that number on my card, for luck, because I was born on the fourth of November. Apparently, I appeared dazed; she pulled me forward, and as I reluctantly edged toward the front of the stage, still not comprehending that I'd won the contest, I heard Rosalind say, "It's not *fair*! It's only because her mother runs the show!" Then one of the judges handed me a ten-dollar bill for first prize. The two runners up, both older girls, got five dollars apiece.

"That wasn't true at all," Mother said later, regarding Rosalind's comment. "She isn't the most attractive kid in the world, is she? Sour grapes. You won for one reason only: You were the prettiest girl up there, period. The judges knew it, I knew it, and the audience knew it."

"So why did you look so surprised?"

"Because I thought for sure they'd lie and pick someone else; nobody wants to be accused of favoritism. I give them credit for not being weak. They did the right thing!"

"Really?"

"You heard me."

And that was it; I was the new Miss Rheingold Beer, 1958. I posed for a picture that night and again the next day, on the lawn, holding a can of Rheingold and wearing a red cape made out of crepe paper and a makeshift banner that some idiot had painted: "Miss Rheinghold, 1957." I didn't care. I was happy to have won ten dollars. Unfortunately, my friends weren't that happy for me, and they acted a bit colder through Labor Day, even telling secrets behind my back. "Sore losers," Mother called them. She was happy to be the celebrity emcee, married to a man with celebrity good looks whom all the women flirted with when he came up. And now she had a daughter voted "beauty contest winner." Finally, I, too, had achieved celebrity.

"Beauty can be a curse," Aunt Kadún used to say. I guess she knew; at the end of her life she was still beautiful, even when wracked with osteoporosis of the legs and hips and even with deep sorrow etched into her features.

"The Greek women, they have the white-white skin; they are more beautiful than Turkish women, by far. Shhh!" She would put her finger to her mouth, as if the sultans were eavesdropping. She had that kind of white, translucent skin herself.

"Who knows? You think there was no intermarriage in five hundred years, with Greeks? With Arabs? Ha!"

Aunt Kadún was learned and well read. She also had the distinction of being the very first woman in our family of the generation from Turkey to drive a car. We'd sit on her spacious porch in Long Beach on Saturday afternoons and talk about family, about personalities, and about women's expectations.

"We do expect, *chika*," she'd say. "Oh, yes, we expect."

But no matter how often I brought it up or how cleverly I approached it, she never spoke about her son, the pianist, killed in Europe during the war or about her early life in the Dardanelles. I asked what I thought were sly questions concerning the town she came from and the old order of sultans, but she answered them only generally, sometimes describing the clock tower and the streets surrounding the docks where the ferry still runs today.

Kadún was an aunt once removed, yet I, and Lorraine before me, both felt close to her and admired her. I knew we shared an individual suffering that was old, one that would never go away; we didn't have to verbalize it. And we had our rituals, too. Even if I wasn't hungry, I was obliged to eat something before I left her home, a Turkish dish she had prepared, like lamb with rice or stuffed eggplant. Afterward we'd have Turkish coffee. I knew how to make it, but she never allowed that. The woman of the house brewed the *kave Turko*, always. She did allow me to read her cup, though, paying homage to Grandma Behora.

"Your Nona was a famous fortune teller, you know. She knew things."

One day I read her fortune and tried to lie about what I saw. All the coffee had glumped together into one black splotch on the side of the cup. There were no more patterns to decipher, no more life to figure out.

"It's not good, right, my future?" She knew and let out a laugh.

"What do you mean, Tante? I see a handsome gentleman in your cup! Maybe you already met him!"

She laughed again. "En otra vida, hija." In my next life.

She didn't last long after that day. Right before I left, sorry that I had even looked at her cup, she held my face and said, "Put a light in your window." It made no sense, but she was far from crazy. In her eyes I saw the world she had come from, an old world, nearly extinct, where she had suffered and buried a secret that I would never fully learn in detail. Maybe, like a lot of old people, she remembered things so far back they were part of her genes, things inherited from other centuries. That day I think she was already in another place.

"Helen had beautiful hair, too, like you," she said. "Put a light; don't forget."

The current that runs through the Dardanelles strait connecting the Aegean and the Sea of Marmara is swift and strong, made more intense because of the fierce winds that blow in one direction. Poets and writers have loved the Dardanelles for centuries. Lord Byron, in 1810, swam the strait and lived, and who knows how many more romantics? There are the famous legends, of course, like the one of Helle, who drowned in the strait when she fell off the back of a ram; and Helen of the beautiful hair, who started the Trojan War. Then there was Hero, high priestess of Aphrodite, goddess of love, who lived in the region when it was called Sestos.

Hero's vow of chastity forbid marriage, but she fell in love anyway. Leander, her love, swam to her every night across the Dardanelles, guided by a lamp Hero placed in her tower. One night she forgot to light the lamp, and Leander lost his way and drowned in the strong current. Hero was so grief-stricken that she threw herself into the sea and perished.

Not that they were any more tragic than the local legends, like the one about my Aunt Kadún, kidnapped when she was a young, beautiful girl by a sultan and taken to his harem, in Çanakkele in the Dardanelles, the region once known as Troy.

Discussion Questions

Was Brenda's recovery from polio "magic," something like her grandmother's gifts of clairvoyance and healing? Or was it just faith and a fluke that got her walking?

Why was it so important for girls to be married? Was Brenda's family more hung up on her being "marriage material" than the average family?

Was there any upside for the hospital kids who had their toys and dolls taken away because of contamination? Was that really necessary?

What were the parents' and communities' attitudes toward polio then? Would an epidemic today bring the same attitudes—or worse?

Readers have expressed sorrow that this particular sick child did not have her mother with her to provide comfort. Was her mother a selfish person? Could she have been mentally disturbed to begin with, or did she become that way when Brenda fell ill? Who stepped in?

Could it have been a noble act on the part of Brenda's mother to stay away, protecting the other child, her younger brother?

Going by the narrative, do you think the author ever resolved certain issues with her mother?

As far as treatment, what has changed today when a child is hospitalized?

Some reviewers have said that The Fortune Teller's Kiss reads more like a novel than a memoir. Why do you think that is? What are elements contained in some of the novels we love? Do they compare to this story in any way?

What is the true "main event" in this memoir?

Why not call the book an autobiographical novel rather than a memoir? What's the difference?

The main character is age seven to thirteen in this book. Do we want to read about the character's life afterward, know a continuation of her story? Or is this tale sufficiently complete?

IN THE AMERICAN LIVES SERIES

Fault Line
by Laurie Alberts

Pieces from Life's Crazy Quilt
by Marvin V. Arnett

Songs from the Black Chair
A Memoir of Mental Illness
by Charles Barber

This Is Not the Ivy League
A Memoir
by Mary Clearman Blew

Driving with Dvořák
Essays on Memory and Identity
by Fleda Brown

Searching for Tamsen Donner
by Gabrielle Burton

American Lives
A Reader
edited by Alicia Christensen
introduced by Tobias Wolff

Out of Joint
A Private & Public
Story of Arthritis
by Mary Felstiner

Falling Room
by Eli Hastings

Opa Nobody
by Sonya Huber

Hannah and the Mountain
Notes toward a Wilderness
Fatherhood
by Jonathan Johnson

Local Wonders
Seasons in the Bohemian Alps
by Ted Kooser

Bigger than Life
A Murder, a Memoir
by Dinah Lenney

What Becomes You
by Aaron Raz Link
and Hilda Raz

Turning Bones
by Lee Martin

In Rooms of Memory
Essays
by Hilary Masters

Between Panic and Desire
by Dinty W. Moore

Sleep in Me
by Jon Pineda

Thoughts from a Queen-Sized Bed
by Mimi Schwartz

My Ruby Slippers
Finding Place on the
Road Back to Kansas
by Tracy Seeley

The Fortune Teller's Kiss
by Brenda Serotte

Gang of One
Memoirs of a Red Guard
by Fan Shen

Just Breathe Normally
by Peggy Shumaker

Scraping By in
the Big Eighties
by Natalia Rachel Singer

In the Shadow of Memory
by Floyd Skloot

Secret Frequencies
A New York Education
by John Skoyles

Phantom Limb
by Janet Sternburg

Yellowstone Autumn
A Season of Discovery in
a Wondrous Land
by W. D. Wetherell

To order or obtain more information on these or other University
of Nebraska Press titles, visit www.nebraskapress.unl.edu.

CPSIA information can be obtained
at www.ICGtesting.com
Printed in the USA
LVOW08s0920090217
523553LV00001B/1/P